A WIDE SPOT IN THE ROAD

A WIDE SPOT IN THE ROAD

By
Bob Budd

Illustrated by
Jerry Palen

LAFFING COW PRESS

Library of Congress Cataloging-in-Publication Data

Budd, Bob
A wide spot in the road / by Bob Budd; illustrated by Jerry Palen
p. 296 cm.
ISBN 0-943255-28-7 (hardcover)
ISBN 0-943255-29-5 (paperback)
I.Title.
PS3552.U3465W5 1990
813'.54--dc20
90-7826
CIP

ISBN 0-943255-28-7 (Hardcover)
ISBN 0-943255-29-5 (Paperback)

—For Lynn

Everywhere I've gone, people have asked me why the heck I was writing a book about Friendly Creek and Buzzard Butte, a pair of little towns in the heart of western Wyoming. Experts tell me that if I'm going to be "taken seriously, " I should write about bigger towns—places like New York and L.A., cities where there are bright lights, pretty women, men who dress like women—stuff like that.

Well, I guess I have about as much business writing about stuff like that as I do challenging a badger to a hole-digging contest.

I don't know the first thing about big cities, and while I wouldn't mind seeing some of those bright lights and pretty girls, my only experience with men who dress up like women is when the 4-H fathers put on a skit at the county fair. Even in dresses and floppy hats, you could still tell they were men.

I figure that's a good thing.

The *real* reason I started to write this book is because the gooseberry-picking Sisters of the Survivors of the Friendly Creek Flood of '49 wanted to mark the fiftieth anniversary of the flood. They claimed that because I was fifth-generation and had won the high school essay contest in 1978, I was the "logical choice" to write a history of the valley.

I saw right through that one.

For one thing, every family only remembers favorable events from the past, so a really true accounting of historical fact is pretty much impossible. In the Barnes family, our heritage has always been entrusted to an elderly aunt for safekeeping, and a certain amount of sorting. My Aunt Bess is such a woman. Whenever an event which reflects poorly upon the family is mentioned, she flies into a rage of waving and shrieking that would drown out a flock of nervous guinea hens.

Of all people, Grandma Wilsz should have known better than to question history according to Aunt Bess, but the Barnes and Wilszs have been on the creek since day one, and they have been known to disagree about most everything. Anyway, out on some gooseberry picking trip in 1985, Grandma Wilsz popped off about something Aunt Bess said, and Aunt Bess threw a hissy fit. She quit belonging to the Sisters of the Survivors, the Cowbelles *and* the Eastern Star, and that was serious. You see, Aunt Bess has the Barnes diary, and somehow or other, she got ahold of the Wilsz diary as well. Most of the history of that portion of the free world is locked up in Aunt Bess's attic, and she isn't about to let a single one of the Sisters of the Survivors see it.

So, the way the old girls had it angled, they could appeal to my vanity and bribe me with a jar of gooseberry jelly, and I would get the goods out of the diaries and write the history. My choice was to incur the wrath of the Sisters of the Survivors of the Friendly Creek Flood of '49 or to serve as an informant and betray Aunt Bess.

The last person who questioned the Bess Barnes version of historical fact was a bright young humanist by the name of Miller. Mr. Miller went so far as to declare Aunt Bess's version of history as "folklore" and Aunt Bess responded to that by whopping Mr. Miller on the skull with a lead-crystal bowl which had traversed the Atlantic on a sailing ship, crossed the Appalachians in an oxcart, floated the Missouri on a raft and plodded over the Great Plains in a covered wagon.

My worst option was to write nothing. If I did that, I would be regarded as a shiftless, unmotivated clod who didn't appreciate his own heritage *or* gooseberry jelly. The Sisters of the Survivors would be hacked off, and Aunt Bess would be mad that I didn't ask about her version of history, so that she could tell it for about the thousandth time.

After all that, all I can tell is that real history lies somewhere between fact and fiction, depending on who is telling the story. And, as far as Mr. Miller and I are concerned, as long as Aunt Bess can raise a lead crystal bowl, her version of the "good old days" is totally acceptable.

The Friendly Creek valley was sort of settled by my great-great grandfather, a man named Luke Barnes. He was just a boring dry-land farmer back in Kansas until he left to claim a herd of cattle his brother left him

in Carson City, Nevada. The only reason the cattle were left to Grandpa Luke was because his brother got shot eleven times by some woman the sheriff called an "acquaintance." [According to the report, the Sheriff accounted for the eleven shots by guessing that the woman had missed her first shot, emptied the gun, reloaded and emptied it again.]

Anyway, Grandpa Luke claimed the cattle in the fall of 1879 and headed back for Kansas. Two months later, he posted a letter from Ft. Bridger, Wyoming Territory, noting that he was certain he was getting closer to Kansas and would be home soon.

Aunt Bess says that Grandpa Luke appreciated the character of the land and let the cattle wander up the river and graze to their heart's content, thinking more of the cattle than himself.

I figure he was lost.

Face it. Ft. Bridger isn't on the way to Kansas from anywhere, least of all, Carson City, Nevada.

Whatever.

Grandpa Luke was snowed in a full hundred miles north of Ft. Bridger, holed up in a lean-to hut, and he was still six hundred miles from Kansas. For companionship, he had four hundred head of Texas steers, a milk cow named Bess, and five horses. Beyond that, his wealth amounted to fifty-four dollars in gold coins, a Winchester .45-.70 rifle, two Colt pistols that didn't match, and three bottles of cheap whiskey.

Seven months later when the sun came out, Grandpa Luke poked his head out to have a look around. Incredible as it must have seemed, his cattle hadn't died or scattered. In fact, they had wintered well in the shelter of the red willow bottom, and as luck would have it, a fat steer was staring right at him. Grandpa Luke hefted his rifle and shot the critter between the eyes, then fried up the liver and ate it with his knife, because he didn't have a fork.

As it turned out, he wasn't eating his own steer's liver.

A ragged individual climbed out of the creek bottom and accused Grandpa Luke of rustling, an offense the other fellow claimed was a "hangin' crime." Fortunately, the two men had cut down every tree on the hillside and there was no place to have a hanging. The scruffy neighbor considered other forms of punishment, and determined the only fair solution was a gunfight. Luckily, before any shooting could begin a dozen Indians rode up to see what was going on. Upon finding a pair of white men eating the guts of a perfectly good steer, the Indians shook their heads in amazement, helped themselves to a decent slab of meat, and rode off.

"Whew," Grandpa Luke whistled, "yesterday, I hadn't seen a human being in half a year, and now the country's so crowded I might hafta' move!"

"Well," his neighbor suggested, "if you're figuring to eat any more of my steers, that ain't such a bad idea."

The scruffy neighbor was a man named Oscar Wilsz, and like Grandpa Luke, he had been following a herd of steers when winter caught up with him and left him in a lean-to along the creek. Aunt Bess says that neither man was too keen on staying, but neither of them was too anxious to leave the whole valley to the other, so they spent most of the spring sizing each other up and jockeying their cattle onto green grass.

Finally, they decided that they would just split the valley evenly; Luke would have the south side of the winding creek, and Oscar Wilsz would have the north. The two of them shook on the deal, which made it binding as all get out, and to celebrate, they wandered around the bluff for a sip of Oscar Wilsz's Missouri sippin' whiskey.

The celebration cooled considerably when Luke noticed the front quarters of Bess, the Barnes milk cow, hanging in a willow bush next to Oscar's lean-to.

According to Aunt Bess (no relation to the cow), Grandpa

Luke was appalled by the vile nature of a beast who would murder and eat a milk cow. Had it not been for the fact that Oscar Wilsz hadn't hanged him for rustling, Luke would have killed him on the spot.

Instead, Luke delivered the first of many blistering lectures from a Barnes to a Wilsz, winding up with the admonition that this so-called western justice might peg an innocent steer shooter as some kind of criminal, but in a land as civilized as Kansas, by God, a man who would murder a milk cow was a thief and a dirty, rotten, no-good coward.

Like I said earlier, the Barnes and the Wilsz families have had a few disagreements along the way.

Luke moved every critter he could find onto the south side of the creek, while Oscar gathered cattle and pushed them into the hills on the north.

Neither man spoke a word to the other. But every night when the cattle were settled and the chores were done, the two men sat outside their lean-to huts and stared across the creek at each other. In that last light of day, when the nighthawks dove for mosquitoes, one man would raise his arm and wave across the creek, and the other would wave back.

In retrospect, I suppose if they were going to have any friends, it about had to be each other, whether they were enemies or not.

On the morning he thought was the 4th of July in 1880,

Grandpa Luke saddled his horse and crossed the creek below his hut. He let his horse pick its own way through the red willows until he was in the meadow below Oscar's hut.

"You're on *my* side of the creek," a voice called out behind him, and Oscar Wilsz levered a round into his Winchester.

Luke spun his horse around and cocked his Colt.

"You're trespassing," Oscar spat.

"So, are you gonna shoot me?" Luke asked

"Thinkin' about it," Oscar admitted, and he stared at the pistol in Luke's hand. "Are you gonna shoot *me*?"

"I reckon I might," Luke nodded.

Both men stared at each other for awhile, spat a lot and gawked around the country some. Finally, Oscar cleared his throat and spit again.

"What are you doing over here?" he asked

"Come to see if you wanted to name this creek?" Luke spat.

"I already named it," Oscar spat again, and his eyes narrowed.

"What did you name it?" Luke wondered.

"Named it Wilsz Creek," Oscar smiled.

"That's dumb." Luke scoffed, "That will never do for a name."

"It will if you're dead!" Oscar suggested, and he raised the barrel of the Winchester.

"Well, I ain't dead!" Luke reminded him, and he waved the barrel of his Colt.

"So?" Oscar asked. "You got a name?"

"How about 'Friendly Creek'?" Luke suggested.

"I like that," Oscar nodded, and he slid his rifle into the scabbard. Luke eased the hammer on his pistol down, and shoved it into his holster. The two men eyed each other, and finally, Luke turned to go.

"Stay on your side of the creek," Oscar warned.

Both men set to the task of converting their lean-to huts into houses, crude structures fashioned of mud, logs, sticks, and rocks (not unlike beaver houses on dry ground). Apparently, they spent some time sizing up each other's construction; by Fall two of the biggest houses west of the Mississippi were no less than a quarter mile apart on Friendly Creek. Unfortunately, the only people able to appreciate the structural majesty were Oscar Wilsz and Luke Barnes. So both men high-tailed it back to the flatlands to fetch their families.

By the time they returned, people were wandering around the West like aimless buffalo. Grandpa Luke figured there was money to be made selling dried beef, smoked trout, flour, pickles, gingham, gunpowder, nails and other junk. By the time wagons full of families came across the trail in 1881, the Barnes house was doubling as a trading post.

The trading post did not fare well, despite the fact that it was the only stop in nearly three hundred miles of trail. The only people who stopped by at all were a little gang of outlaws who ranged out of Brown's Park and robbed the store once a month. The outlaws were young, and they were pretty predictable, so Luke only left a little bit of cash in the kitty when he was going to be robbed, but it seemed enough to satisfy the outlaws. Luckily, the outlaws liked Luke, and after every robbing spree, they came back through without masks and bought supplies, so Grandpa Luke kept a little ahead. When the law finally caught up with the outlaws the trading post went to hell.

With Luke's entire clientele in jail, Oscar Wilsz convinced Grandpa Luke that it was time to make a *real* town, and the two men rode off to lay out the site. The only possibilities were the boggy lowlands on the south side of the creek or a mile north on top of Buzzard Butte. Grandpa Luke favored the lower site, arguing that the swamp could be drained, water would be plentiful, and the winter winds would be tempered by Buzzard Butte.

Oscar wanted to locate on top of Buzzard Butte. He said that a town on top of the hill would never be flooded when the spring runoff hit, and it would be considerably cheaper and easier to dig a well and charge for water than it would be to drain the entire black bog. The breeze would keep mosquitoes, deerflies and horseflies from sucking the blood out of living things, and as Aunt Bess always points out, it was on the Wilsz side of the creek.

The two men argued back and forth for awhile, and then they just went to punching each other in the face. At last, Grandpa Luke decreed that *his* town would be named "Friendly Creek," and he located a mercantile and blacksmith on the creekbank. Not to be outdone, Oscar Wilsz founded Buzzard Butte on the top of the hill. He erected a building and called it the "Buzzard Butte Dance Hall." The Buzzard Butte Dance Hall did not feature music or dancing, but Oscar imported a half a dozen women who became quite popular in the region despite the fact that none of them could dance a lick.

Over time, people stopped and some of them stayed. They came to cut ties for the railroad, spending their winters in the timber, cutting logs, shaping them by hand and floating the ties down Friendly Creek when the runoff came. The singsong voices of the Swedes and Norwegians were friendly, and the tiehacks were good for business, especially at the dance hall.

Others came to dig a living out of the earth. Some of them found spot gold and a pair named Wilkerson and Sherman found a deposit of silver and copper. They left their names on a pair of creeks, but the metal played out and they moved on. Another handful of miners dug coal out of the red hills, and they made a living stoking stoves in the valley.

A little Frenchman named Louis Filiatreau bought the Barnes Mercantile in Friendly Creek, and a freighting outfit established a station in Buzzard Butte. A tiehack named Swenson quit the timber and hired out his team and slip to dig irrigation ditches. A doctor came through and set up a practice. A pair of churches grew out of the sagebrush.

But above all, from the rock uplands to the boggy mouth of Friendly Creek, at the head of every little draw and spring, men and women scratched so hard in the dirt that their big hands turned black and hard. Just as Oscar and Luke had been determined to have a place of their own, so too were others who homesteaded there; teams of gaunt horses pulled rusty plows through the soil—wispy dreams following worn-out teams. Blizzards froze some of them out, but they weren't gone long enough for the pack rats to get a meal before another family moved in. The sun dried them out, the soil starved them, and hard work killed them, but there was no end to the line of people, and there was no end to their dreams.

Grandpa Luke and Oscar Wilsz died. They were planted on the hill above the valley. Life went on. Young men won the

conference eight-man football championship, then went off to fight the war and didn't come home, and life went on. Friendly Creek and Buzzard

Butte became "town," and people forgot why there were two towns in the first place.

In 1949, there was a flood. Nobody died or anything, but there was a flood. About the only thing that came out of the flood was the founding of the Sisters of the Survivors of the Friendly Creek Flood of '49, and like I said before, they asked me to write a history of Friendly Creek.

I wasn't there before the flood, and I wasn't there when the flood came, and Aunt Bess wouldn't let me read the diaries. About the only contribution I can make to history is to tell people about the creek like I know it.

Bud's Sinclair station is an anchor on the creekbank; Bud sells worms to the fishermen who come through town, but he gives the fattest ones to the little kids who fish in the creek next to the station. Old Bud can change a tire in a blizzard, and he sells the best jerky in the world. He keeps it in a big pickle jar on the counter, despite the fact that it's illegal in the eyes of the Department of Agriculture, Food and Drug Administration, and if the truth were known, the Game and Fish Department. When one of those people comes in though, he puts the jar on the floor.

At the Friendly Creek Mercantile, Fingers Filiatreau cuts fresh meat every day, exactly the way people like it. Dick Wilson has a hardware store on main street, between Barnes Avenue and Wilsz Street, across from the high school. There's a new post office, and a library in an old bar that used to be called Rosie's. On the edge of town, the cafe has a tall, neon light to slow up truckers. The only office buildings are the Forest Service and the Bureau of Land Management and the Soil Conservation Service, and all of those are full.

Up in Buzzard Butte, there's a construction company, an implement dealership and a feed store. Other than that, there's the Hoosegow Bar and the Mountain View Motel, where you can get a room for less than twenty bucks. If you check in early enough, old Earl, the owner, will usually invite you in for a cold one. Best of all, up at the Mountain View, there won't be any maids beating on the door first thing in the morning to wake you up, unless you stay for a few days and don't pay. In that case, Earl knocks on the door with the butt end of a twelve gauge.

The main reason for the existence of the towns is cows and cowboys. Friendly Creek is ranch country, and it's the grass that pays the bills. The people who harvest the grass buy groceries at the Merc, and gas from Bud. They drink beer in the Hoosegow Bar, and they put their dollars in the collection plate so the churches will stay. They serve on the school board and the library board, and they fight like hell with one another.

If you want to know more than what I've told you, you can read the book. Or else, stop by the Hoosegow and ask Bobby Baker, or buy a little gas at Bud's Sinclair.

Actually, unless you can get into a meeting of the Sisters of the Survivors or the Eastern Star, the best place to find out what is going on is the barber shop. There's only one barber, and with all the information he takes in over the course of a year, he must be the smartest man in the whole world. He sure acts like it when you're sitting in the chair.

Then again, he is the only guy on Friendly Creek who gets paid to hold a razor to people's necks and when a man has a razor on your neck, it's best to massage his ego and tell him what you know.

Common sense is valued most on Friendly Creek.

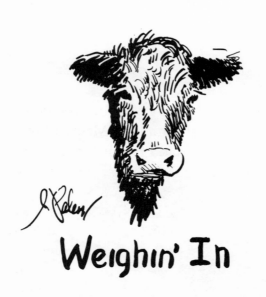

Weighin' In

"Cut out that heifer with the crooked nose!" the cattle buyer yelled from the scales, and I eyeballed the heifers, trying to figure out which of them was afflicted with a crooked nose.

I was standing in a sea of cattle, and they all looked pretty much the same to me, which made it somewhat remarkable that the buyer could see a crooked nose from the scale house, but he had also pointed out a crooked leg and a bad ear, so I just assumed he had better eyes than mine.

"Try not to take all damned day!" he yelled.

I poked a heifer with my stick and turned her back. The buyer frowned and nodded, then looked back at the scales, and I looked at the heifer I had cut back. Her nose was straighter than the cattle buyer's, if you asked me.

"These cattle are weighin' up heavy," the buyer growled, and he tapped the slide on the scale to the right.

Joe Barnes read the weight over his shoulder and smiled, then walked over to the pen where I was sorting the heifers.

"Run that heifer back through," Joe said, and I grinned and worked her in with the next bunch.

"You said these heifers would weigh seven," the buyer frowned, obviously perturbed to see the heifers weighing a good bit heavier than that. "My bid was based on seven weights."

"I said they've *been* weighing seven," Joe corrected, and he wrote the weights in his little spiral notebook. "But, then again, you've been weighin' 'em for a long time."

The buyer, a man now known as "Magnet" Martin, had previously been regarded as one of the most upstanding cattle buyers in the country, despite the fact that everyone seemed to have weights far lighter than their best estimates. Magnet Martin had always been a very busy man, and it was his habit to place his thick notebook on the end of the scales when he was weighing cattle, so that it would be close at hand. But when we were shipping old cows in the Spring, Joe accidentally knocked the notebook off the scales, and when he bent down to retrieve it, he discovered a very large and powerful magnet stuck to the bottom of the scales. With the magnet pulling down on the beam, it was necessary to tap the bar to the left until a lighter weight would balance the scales. When Joe grabbed the magnet, the beam slammed up, and a pen of cows that had averaged 900 pounds suddenly weighed in at nearly 1100 pounds apiece.

I didn't hear everything that was said at the time, but I heard enough to know that Joe's heifers would be weighing heavier than usual in the Fall, in exchange for Joe's not blabbing all over the valley about the magnet. To my knowledge, Joe never said a word about the magnet, but within a matter of hours Richard Martin became "Magnet" Martin, and he made some *fast* offers on cattle in the valley.

Since nobody wanted to stir things up by going through a bunch of legal hoops, the ranchers accepted his generous offers, and since Magnet Martin didn't especially want to go through the legal system, he paid through *his* crooked nose.

"Tell your hired man to move 'em along a little faster," Magnet growled at Joe, and I crowded another bunch of heifers onto the scales. Down the narrow alley in front of them, the rear end of a truck waited to haul the cattle to Iowa.

"I taught my hired man not to stir 'em up," Joe smiled. "I'd sure hate to shrink 'em."

I ran another bunch of heifers onto the scales, and Magnet Martin cussed the weights. Joe stood next to him and smiled, and the truckers worked the heifers up the ramp, onto the trucks.

Joe and Magnet bantered back and forth, and Joe, true to his word, never once brought up the subject of the magnet. I suppose that was a bridge already crossed, as Joe liked to say, and it really didn't deserve the time and energy it would require to constantly revisit the moment. Magnet Martin had been found out, and he would probably pay for it for a long time to come. That was enough said.

Joe Barnes was a pretty good judge of people, I figured, and that's what made him successful. He could've raised hell about the magnet, maybe even hauled Magnet Martin into court and sued him for a lot of money, but Joe sized up the situation and handled it his own way. As a result, Magnet Martin was still buying cattle, and he was paying top dollar for all of them, despite the fact that they were weighing up a little heavier than they used to.

When the last load of cattle was on the truck, Joe shook Magnet's hand and led him up to the big house to pour him a drink. I fed the sick pen and the horses and finished up my chores, and by the time I was done, the cattle buyer was smiling. Joe poured him a drink for the road and let him keep the glass, and Magnet Martin pulled out of the yard and headed off to weigh another bunch of cattle.

"Crooked nose, my eye," Joe laughed, and I followed him into the house.

The big house had been built in 1915, the year after Joe was born, by a man I never knew, despite the fact that he was some sort of uncle of mine. It was a huge log cabin really, with a kitchen as big as the living room and a stove on the porch, put there specially to warm calves outside of the kitchen. It was one heck of a house at the time, with a huge rock fireplace in the living room, a fancy wood stove in the kitchen, and a pot-bellied stove upstairs to warm the bedrooms. Now, there was gas heat and electric lighting, but the house was as tight as a tick, just as it had been when it was built.

"How about a beer?" Joe asked, and I nodded.

He tossed me a cold can.

"You aren't quite old enough to be drinking beer yet," he frowned, "but you do a pretty good job weighin' cattle, so I'll let you slide."

"Well," I took a sip, "at least I don't have a crooked nose."

"Good genes." Joe winked.

Joe Barnes was some sort of cousin of mine, technically a first cousin twice removed, or something like that. His father was my father's uncle, or maybe his father and my grandfather were first cousins, not removed. Whichever it was, Joe and I were *cousins*, despite our age difference. Joe was the oldest of the Barnes family in the third generation, and I was the oldest in the fifth. Somewhere back there, we had a common ancestor whose greatest claim to fame was the fact that he had been one of the two men who settled the towns of Friendly Creek and Buzzard Butte, a couple of wide spots in the road.

I was born 80 years after my great-great grandfather came to the country, but I was all Barnes, or so the old-timers tell me. Anyway, my being the first boy born in the fifth generation on Friendly Creek made the event truly memorable for most folks in the area. Darned near everybody on the creek dropped by to have a look at me, just like the time when Shorty McGregor's cow had a calf with two heads.

My dad was raised on Friendly Creek, and so was Mom,

but by the time I was born, things were tough in the country. The place where Dad was raised was too small to support more than one family, and Mom's folks sold out when she was in college at Laramie.

"People were like badgers in a hole, then," Dad tried to explain to me later. "Everybody was backed into a corner but there was nowhere to go. About all folks had left was the sense to know they were in a fight, so they hunkered down, just like an old badger, and waited for times to get better."

It wasn't any different in town. Without any money in the rancher's pockets, there wasn't any money to spend on parts, labor or other stuff. The bank didn't have any money to loan, and nobody had any desire or inclination left to borrow it anyway. The people who wanted to buy couldn't afford to buy, and those who wanted to sell couldn't afford to sell. I suppose in times like that, a new baby really is about as exciting as a two-headed calf.

Dad got a job teaching English at a junior college in Sheridan, and it worked out pretty well. We could all go home to Friendly Creek in the summer, when Grandpa Barnes really needed the help, and Mom and Dad could still make a living. In fact, it is those days I remember best: walking through the hay meadows with my dad, catching frogs, and feeling under the creek banks for fish. Joe Barnes used to stop by to visit, and he took the time to talk with me, not like big people talk to little people, like big people talk to big people.

"When you get big enough," he always said, "I want you to come and work for me. You'll make a good hand someday."

The little place Dad grew up on had never seemed quite big enough to provide a living for even one family, yet it was too big for Grandpa and Grandma to handle, so they sold it to Joe in the summer of 1969. I don't know how much Joe paid for the place, but there were two conditions to the sale. The first was that my grandparents could live there until they died, which was in 1973, and the second was that Joe would teach me to be a cowboy.

I went to work for Joe the next summer, not long after my sixteenth birthday. His daughter Maggie was out of college, and between a fifty-five year old man and a twenty-two year old girl, they figured they could keep an eye on me. Even if we were only cousins, however many times removed, we were still *family*, and on Friendly Creek, that still counts for something.

"Those heifers looked pretty good, huh?" Joe interrupted my thoughts, and I nodded, not that I knew all that much about heifers. I guess I figured that if Joe thought they were good, then they looked plenty good to me.

Maggie walked in and shook her hair out of her hat, then washed her hands and poured herself a scotch and water. Maggie was Joe's only child, a daughter filled with fire and ice, loyalty to her father beyond question. Maggie was a better hand than most men, but like every wife, mother and daughter on a ranch, Maggie was a lady, and if you happened to forget that and act improperly, she just might beat your eyes shut.

"I see you got the heifers shipped," she said, and she let an ice cube settle in her cheek like it was a wad of tobacco. "How'd they weigh?"

"Over eight," Joe said, "paid just under eight."

"And I suppose Magnet whined about it the whole time?" Maggie grinned as she ran a brush through her hair.

"There ain't a lot of room to whine when your name is *Magnet* Martin," Joe shrugged. He wandered out of the kitchen and turned on the television, a squarish box that received static and other noises. When the wind came from the right direction a picture which rarely matched the sound would appear, but it was cause enough to call the neighbors to see if they too were receiving a picture.

"I'd better go," I suggested, and Maggie handed me another beer.

Outside, the ranch yard was coated in a thin layer of fog that suggested snow, and my breath rose into the humidity and disappeared. There was just enough wind to rattle the willows, and not far off, I could hear Friendly Creek gurgling and sighing, making its way to the river. A cow bawled at her calf, and the calves set up a chorus of bawling, until they were all raising hell in the meadow. In the bog, a pair of sandhill cranes made sandhill crane noises, and overhead, a flock of Canadian Geese announced their travel plans.

The night air smelled like sagebrush.

In the distance, through the thin layer of fog, I could make out the lights of town; Friendly Creek along the creek and Buzzard Butte on top of the hill. My family had settled this valley, and standing in front of the bunkhouse, I felt as much a part of it as the leaves on the trees. My own roots were trying to sink into the rocky soil, but as I stood and listened, I knew that my roots would have to earn their place in the ground. Maybe when they did that, the hard earth and rocks would hold them there and keep them from being torn away.

I sat in the back corner of the Hoosegow Bar and sipped on a cold beer, despite the fact that I wasn't exactly old enough to sip on a beer in the Hoosegow, or anywhere else.

There wasn't anybody in the Hoosegow to worry about it, and that seemed rather odd. Usually the place was full of opinionated individuals who were concerned about everything. Tonight, if it hadn't been for me and Bobby Baker, the owner, the Hoosegow would have been deserted.

I'd been walking in and out of the bars in Friendly Creek and Buzzard Butte since I was old enough to walk, but back then, there were three or four "joints." There was Thar's Bar, a crowded little counter where about ten people could get a beer and a sandwich; Rosie's, where you could get a beer and a broken nose; and there was the old Buzzard Butte Dance Hall. I suppose a guy could sit in the little bar at the Lion's Den Supper Club and drink a beer or two, but if there were any people on Friendly Creek who were that high-and-mighty, I hadn't met them. Then again, when I was little, I kept quiet and played shuffleboard and the bowling pin game. As long I did that, the old-timers took turns buying me "Shirley Temples" and "Roy Rogers," so I didn't pay too much attention to social stations.

Everything changed in 1974. All of a sudden, every corner of Wyoming was awash in oil, coal, uranium, and other minerals. The Arabs had oil dried up to the point where it was more valuable than gold. Heck, anything that came out of a rock was determined to be either "strategic" or "scarce."

The State of Wyoming quickly determined that if all these valuable things were out there in the dirt, the state was obligated to tax them, since they would only be there once. Besides that, if the mineral companies were going to be filthy rich, then the state deserved to be filthy rich as well. But, there were so much money that even politicians couldn't spend it all. The elected officials put most of the dollars in the bank for a "rainy day," and handed the rest of them out to anyone who would take them, which was everyone. Even little towns like Friendly Creek and Buzzard Butte became incredibly wealthy.

The city fathers in Friendly Creek and Buzzard Butte, being safely described as "fiscally conservative," accepted the free money, but all they did was stash it in the State Bank of Friendly

Creek, until some of the locals began to grumble about the size of the bank account. Not wishing to offend even one voter, the elected officials got together and bought a new police car, a string of Christmas lights that would reach the top of the pine tree in the middle of Friendly Creek, an old cannon to serve as an historic attraction, and a new jail.

Well, right off the bat, the two towns got into a ruckus over where the police car would be parked. In order to settle the dispute, they either had to buy another police car or sell the new one. Most of the people who attended the town council meeting agreed that buying *two* police cars would be a burden on the taxpayers, and it was really just "empire building" by the government. There was only one policeman, afterall, and there was no reason for him to drive one car in Friendly Creek and another one in Buzzard Butte. Furthermore, if there should happen to be some sudden outbreak of crime, surely Buck Martin, the Deputy Sheriff, could handle it.

By the time the meeting was over, the lone policeman had been fired, the new police car was sold to the town of Kemmerer, and while Friendly Creek and Buzzard Butte each had a police station, neither of them had a policeman.

The Christmas lights made it all the way to the top of the tree, but they only worked for one night. The Mayor explained that they were "those blinky kind that all go out if one of them goes out," and while she was sorry that they weren't blinking, there was no way that she and the town council were going to take a bath on the police car and the lights at the same time.

The cannon turned out to be a poor investment too. Not only did visitors find it strange that a little town in western Wyoming should have a Civil War cannon, but the sixth grade history class also discovered that the cannon was a fake, a fabrication made from oil field drill stem and a dump rake. It was pretty embarrassing, and the Mayor offered to resign over the whole thing, but was finally convinced to stay on, since it was the first error of any magnitude in her thirty-two years of service.

In all fairness, the only capital expenditure which really worked out was the new jail, and that was only because it paved the way for the old jail to be converted into something of a civic center, the Hoosegow Bar.

Bobby Baker was the proud owner of this fine establishment, and he didn't do a whole lot of remodeling before opening the Hoosegow, but it didn't need much. He took out the cells and put an old slab of Douglas Fir in front of the sinks, hung his moose head on the wall and plugged a juke box into the socket. Bobby tended bar, took messages, and passed along information that might have been called gossip had it not been true. Usually the place would be full by now. Instead, it was just me, Bobby, and the moose.

"Busy place," I smiled, and Bobby looked at the clock.

"Damn near seven o' clock," he shrugged. "I thought sure Fingers would be here by now. Must've had a lot of pigs today."

Fingers Filiatreau was Bobby's best friend, a little Frenchman whose grandfather had bought out the old Barnes Trading Post years before and passed it along through the family. Usually, Fingers closed the Mercantile promptly at six, and was sitting on his stool at the end of the bar at six o' five, but this was a Thursday, and on Thursdays, Fingers butchered pigs, if there were any pigs hanging around to be butchered.

"I'm going to dinner," Bobby hollered from behind the bar. "If you want another one, go ahead and get it."

"What if somebody else wants one?" I hollered back.

He stopped at the screen door and looked at me like I was an idiot, "You know how much a beer costs."

The door banged shut, and I sat there for a minute or two, then slid behind the bar and pulled out the key to the juke box.

I punched A7, a song by Tanya Tucker that rattled through my head day and night, then I wandered back behind the bar and grabbed a cold beer, twisted the cap off and stuck my dollar on the back bar. That much accomplished, I perched myself on Bobby's stool and wondered what to do with the rest of the evening.

"Wow," I said to the empty room, "I finally get to drink a beer in the Hoosegow, and everybody leaves, including the owner."

"Are you workin' here or do you just come here to whine?" a voice called out from the other side of the bar.

Shorty McGregor climbed on a stool, his little brown hands clasped together in anticipation of a scotch and water.

I poured the drink, Johnny Walker Red and a splash of creek water. Shorty handed over two bucks.

"I don't know how to run the cash box," I apologized. "The bar owes you four bits."

"Gimme another drink then," Shorty frowned, and he slipped another dollar on the bar. "I don't like the idea of the bar owin' me one. I may never collect it."

I threw together another scotch and set it on the bar. The way Shorty had worked through the first one, I didn't think there was much chance of the bar ever cheating him.

"So," he said after his third scotch, "what's a snotnose like you doing behind the bar?"

"Pouring scotch for old coots," I handed him another one. "Bobby went to eat dinner."

"Old coots, eh?" Shorty eyed me. "There's only you and me in here, and I'm no old coot."

"And I'm no snotnose," I eyed him back.

"Are ya old enuff to be behind the bar, boy?" Shorty asked, and his blue eyes disappeared beneath his bushy eyebrows.

"I'm here," I said.

27

"Aye," he snorted. "And however old ye may be, yer not answerin' my question."

If I wasn't totally educated, I was darn sure smart enough to know that when Shorty started saying things like "aye," he was on the fight, and I had no intention of stirring him up any more. Most people seemed to think the worst thing about the Scots was their noisy bagpipes, but it's a safe bet that none of them ever met Shorty McGregor on the fight.

I mixed up another drink, and stuck it on the bar.

"Who paid for the drink?" Shorty growled, and he looked around the empty room.

"On the house," I said, and I wiped the bar with a white rag, just like Bobby Baker always did.

"Ah," he pushed his hat back, "so, now we gotta *snotnose boy* behind the bar and a house that buys drinks! Isn't this the damndest day ya ever seen?"

"I'll have one of them drinks on the house," Red Barnes walked through the door and winked.

Red was some relation of mine, but it got even further into "cousins removed," so I didn't pay a lot of attention. I liked Red a lot, despite the fact that we were related. Red didn't get too worked up about things. He always seemed to be in good humor. Red always owed somebody money or favors, but he could always pay them off because Red Barnes was, without debate, the best horseman in the valley. When the heat was on, Red could break a good colt and trade his way out of debt. If a guy wasn't riding a Red Barnes' horse, he wasn't mounted. Either that, or he was pretty new around town and Red hadn't gotten around to borrowing from him.

"Well?" he grinned when he sat down. "Do I get a free drink or not?" I poured him a bourbon on the rocks and dug the money out of my pocket.

"Where's Bobby?" Red asked, but before I could answer, Buck Martin swaggered through the door and stepped to the side, then stared into the darkest corner to let his eyes adjust to the dim light. From behind the bar, it looked like Buck was trying to stare down the moose on the wall.

While his eyes were adjusting, Buck rested his hand on his trusty sidearm in case some bad hombre jumped out of a beer can and challenged him to some sort of quick-draw contest. As far as I knew, in the twenty years Buck had been Deputy Sheriff, no one had ever jumped out of a beer can or challenged him. The only time Buck ever used his quick draw was in practice and after he got pretty good without bullets, he tried quick-draw target shooting and blew two toes off his right foot.

"Thank God he has a poor aim," Joe said at the time, "or he would've blown off his whole driving foot."

That would have been a disaster, because about all Buck ever did was ride around in his Deputy Sheriff's Blazer and stop speeders.

"Where's Baker?" Buck asked as he slid the leather thong off his pistol.

"He's eating dinner," I said. "Would you like a drink?"

Buck looked around the little barroom and satisfied himself that there were no crimes being committed, then eased up to the corner of the bar and stood where he could see all of the doors.

"Seven-Up," he winked, and I poured a gin and tonic, known locally as a "Buck Martini."

"Are you old enough to be in here?" Buck looked me over when I delivered the concoction.

"Are you?" I asked, and Red spit a piece of ice across the bar. Shorty laughed, and Buck put his hand on his gun in case their humor might turn into some sort of dangerous situation.

"Howdy, Buck," Carl Loper walked in, and he jabbed a finger into the Deputy's ribs. "Shot anybody lately?"

"Careful, Loper," Buck snarled, "I'm a powder keg."

"I'd say you were a powder *head*," Loper laughed, then he looked at me.

"Are you old enough to be in here?" he asked.

"Bourbon and seven?" I poured a stiff one.

"I thought you were gettin' to be that old," Loper raised the glass. He walked over and sat at a table with Shorty and Red, using his thumb and finger to take imaginary shots at the Deputy Sheriff, who was not amused.

Fingers Filiatreau stepped through the door and I checked my watch. It was seven-thirty. Fingers was still wearing his white apron, pig guts and all.

Fingers looked around, then walked right through the hail of Loper's imaginary bullets and sat on his stool at the far end of the bar. I had a cold beer waiting.

Fingers was a capitalist. He owned and operated the Mercantile, but he was also a licensed realtor, a bonded cattle buyer, stock broker, certified public accountant, and an emergency medical technician.

Most people figured he got the name "Fingers" after he sawed the last three fingers of his right hand off in the meat saw at the mercantile. Fingers said he would have cut all of them off, but after the third finger, it got to hurting pretty bad, so he decided to stop. Just as soon as he got out of the hospital, he ran an ad in the *Friendly Creek Sentinel* and advertised "finger steaks" at a big discount. Like I said, Fingers was a capitalist.

In reality, Fingers got his name in the first grade when his teacher suggested to his parents that he seemed to have his fingers into everything, a premonition of sorts. If there was a deal on Friendly Creek, Fingers wanted to be a part of it, and whether or not he really was, Fingers claimed to be the catalyst for everything that happened on the Creek, as long as it involved money and the chance of a commission. It was always rumored that Fingers put any given deal on the creek together. I had come to believe that the source of the rumors was none other than Fingers Filiatreau himself. After all, a rumor didn't have to be true; the wilder the rumor, the faster it travelled. If it ever occurred to Fingers that the information he passed along so freely might be confidential, he never let it bother him much.

Come to think of it, nobody on Friendly Creek gave a damn about anything that might have been confidential. It once occurred to me that the best way to get word around Friendly Creek was to tell one person and then to swear them to secrecy. By morning, everyone in the county would have some version of the story.

"Are you old enough to be in here?" Fingers poked his finger in his ear and dug out a piece of hog fat, which he deposited in the ashtray.

"How old do you have to be?" I asked, and Fingers looked across the room, where Carl Loper was still shooting Buck Martin with his fingers.

"I used to be able to shoot like that," Fingers shook his head sadly, but then he brightened. "It looks like I'm the only one in the room who killed anything today."

"Day ain't over," Buck growled from the other end of the bar, and he raised his glass and winked, all the time keeping an eye on Carl Loper.

Bobby came back at nine, and most of the crowd had cleared out and headed home. Fingers was still sitting at one corner of the bar, and Buck Martin was working on his fourth or fifth "Seven-Up," still watching the moose carefully, in case it might attack.

"How'd it go?" Bobby asked when he came back.

"Loper shot Buck with his finger," I said, "but Buck must be wearing a finger-proof vest. Fingers smells like pig guts and Shorty is on the fight. If that moose head moves a muscle, Buck's gonna blow it to smithereens and I couldn't get the cash register to work."

"How much booze did you give away?" Bobby held up the bottle of scotch and tipped it against the light.

"I don't know," I said. "I tried to put some money in whenever I could."

"Thanks," Bobby shook my hand, and when he took his away, there was a twenty dollar bill in my palm. "I needed the break."

I slid out from behind the bar and headed for the door.

"Hey!" Bobby yelled, and he waved me back to the bar.

"Are you old enough to be in here?" he whispered.

"I'll only be a day older tomorrow," I shrugged. "Does it make a big difference?"

Bobby smiled and walked back to the other end of the bar, and I walked outside, not quite sure whether I was "old enough" or not.

But then again, I'm not sure any of us were.

Most of the mirror in the white Chevy pickup was long gone, shattered in a variety of crashes with trees, rocks, and hay bales gone astray, but the pieces that were left gave me a fairly good idea how bad I was cut. A jagged gash ran from my left ear to my forehead, and blood dripped over my ear to be sopped up by my shirt. On top of that, I was soaking wet, so that the blood got plenty of mileage when it mixed with the water. It was a little early to be coming in for lunch, but bleeding like I was, I didn't figure Joe would mind too much.

Joe walked out of the shop when I pulled up. He was wiping his greasy hands on an old flannel nightgown of Maggie's, or maybe it was one his wife wore before she died. It was a shop rag now.

"What are you doing back here?" he growled.

"I'm bleeding like a stuck hog," I said.

"I see that," Joe looked my gashes and bruises over. "I suppose this means that you didn't finish the fence up at the Keller Place."

"Not quite," I wiped some blood out of my eye. "I ran into a little snag."

"What kind of snag?" Joe asked, and he pulled my hand away so that he could look at the cut on my head.

"Victor Wilsz hit me over the head with a fence stretcher," I said, and he looked at the outline of the metal handle stamped into the side of my head.

"You're all wet," he observed. "How come you're all wet?"

"I'm wet because as soon as Victor was done hitting me over the head with the fence stretcher, he threw me in the creek," I explained.

"That's what I figured," Joe shook his head, and he led me across the yard and into the big house. "I guess you're about the only person in the valley Victor hadn't beat up, so it was about your turn."

Victor Wilsz was the sole heir to the Wilsz Ranch, a massive man who controlled his domain like a herd bull watches over his cows. Just like a herd bull, Victor spent most of his time at the watering hole, and the rest of his time bugling over the fence at other bulls and their heifers. He was a smart man, and he was a wealthy man; his ancestors had seen to that. Victor was loud, territorial and bold, and he had it in his head that the whole valley was rightfully his and his alone. He ranged up and down the creek in his regulation baby blue Wilsz Ranch pickup, yelling at his help, shoving people who got in his way, and, as I now understood, beating up guys like me.

"Why did you let him do this?" Joe mauled at my head with the expert touch of a butcher.

"I didn't *let* him do anything," I winced as the cold water ran over the cut. "I turned around and he coldcocked me."

"Never turn your back on Victor!" Joe scolded, and he washed the side of my head with some soap from a five gallon can. I noticed that the soap washed a little bit of the grease off his own hands, but Joe didn't seem to see a need for cleaning up before performing the operation.

"Did he say anything?" Joe threaded a suture needle that had most recently been used to sew up the prolapsed uterus of an old cow.

"Yeah," I remembered. "He allowed as how he didn't think too much of this 'good neighbor' fence policy."

The "good neighbor fence policy" was a brainstorm cooked up in the Hoosegow, late at night, after the whiskey had softened emotions and intelligence, and like most schemes designed to lure Victor Wilsz into rational behavior, this one didn't seem to be working out very well.

Part of the problem was that the "solution" to the ranch problem wasn't a rancher's solution. Every time the ranchers got to squabbling, Bobby Baker and Fingers Filiatreau came up with some great plan. Bobby sold it and Fingers took credit for it.

"You guys all share common fences," Bobby said as he twisted a straw in his teeth. "Why don't you all just agree on a friendly sort of good neighbor fencing policy and share the cost of fixing the fences?"

"Because," Red said, "any time you make a deal with Victor Wilsz, you get your throat cut."

"I'll talk to Victor," Fingers puffed out his chest. "Victor will listen to me."

"Not interested," Shorty McGregor said.

On the whole creek, no one could possibly dislike Victor Wilsz more than Shorty McGregor, and the feeling was mutual. Joe said it went back to a time when Shorty's grandfather beat Oscar Wilsz out of the place at the head of the creek in a card game, but whatever the reason, if Victor was involved, Shorty was against it.

"That's no surprise," Carl Loper snorted. "Your place is so grubbed out that even Victor's cows won't go there to eat."

Shorty and Loper didn't get along very well either.

"Look," Fingers bought a round of drinks, "those of us in town hate to see you ranchers fighting. All we want is for the town to be happy. Why not try my idea?"

"Fingers," Shorty squinted at the little Frenchman, "the only reason you give a tinker's damn about this is because you think we might not spend any money in your store."

"Shorty," Fingers opened his arms, "I'm hurt. I only want to help. This is our home."

"Why not try it?" Dick Wilson asked.

Dick ran the hardware store, and generally, Dick was pretty reliable. Being raised on a starvation outfit that Victor Wilsz had bought in the 1950s, Dick at least understood the ranching business, and since Victor Wilsz had beat him up and bit off half his ear when they were both nine years old, Dick understood Victor Wilsz pretty well, too.

"I can live with the plan," Joe decided, "but Victor Wilsz

hasn't stretched a fence wire in his life. I'm not sure Victor even knows how to fix fence."

"If I can get Victor to agree," Bobby smiled, "will the rest of you go along?"

"Not interested," Shorty said. "The last time I got into a 'deal' with Victor, he beat me up and threw me in the creek."

An uneasy silence filled the air, and everyone spent a lot of time twirling their beer bottles in the water on the bar. That incident certainly hadn't helped things much, and it was still fresh in everyone's mind. Victor had caught Shorty stealing water, and he was holding him upside-down in the creek when Joe rode up and talked Victor out of killing the little Scot.

"I'm willing to give it a try," Joe broke the ice, "but, I'm betting we'll all be fixing Victor's fence, just like always."

"How about you, Fred?" Bobby asked Fred Aspering.

Fred had one of the best ranches on the creek, but Fred wasn't even acknowledged most of the time because Fred raised sheep. Sheep were generally regarded as vermin, and the people who raised them were generally regarded as, well, vermin too.

"I don't really care," Fred shrugged. "I raise sheep. The law says I have to fence them in, and even *Victor's* cows can't get through a sheep fence."

"Red?" Bobby poured a bourbon.

"If Joe will try, I'll try," Red smiled.

"If Red'll try, I'll try," Shorty sighed, "but, I'll bet it won't work. Somebody's gonna get throwed in the creek."

When Victor agreed to the deal, all of the ranches on the creek devoted the days between calving and irrigating to fixing fence. All of a sudden, Fingers Filiatreau sold a lot of leather gloves, and Dick Wilson sold an awful lot of fencing supplies at the hardware store.

Loper started in on his fences around town, standing up the posts in the bog and sprucing up the pole fences around the ranch. Red Barnes decided to use a team and wagon to fix fence instead of a pickup, which slowed him down considerably, and Shorty McGregor went around all of the fences on his mountain pasture. Fred Aspering took a quick drive around the sheep fence between himself and Victor, then set about building corrals. Davey Boyd did his usual fencing job, adding posts and twisting wires with a stick until they were tight, and it seemed that if Davey kept up with his fencing plan long enough, he would have a wall built around his place within three or four years.

Even with all of the activity, it sure looked to me like everybody was doing their level best to fix every fence except the ones they shared with Victor Wilsz.

Victor, on the other hand, hooked a big auger on his tractor and drove up and down the road, and while everyone was quite pleased to see him actually doing something, they were still a little nervous. Finally, Joe decided that I should fix fence over at the Keller Place, if for no other reason than to scout out what Victor was up to.

Joe finished sewing up the biggest part of the gash on my head, then sprinkled some wonder dust on the cut and sprayed my head with iodine and purple oil. It hurt like the devil, and when he held up the mirror, I noticed that it didn't look a whole lot better.

"You call the vet if a horse gets into a piece of wire," I frowned. "I wish you would have called him for this."

"There are laws against veterinarians working on people," Joe scoffed, "and *you* didn't get into a piece of wire."

Joe looked over his handiwork and dabbed at the blood on my lip, then stepped back and smiled.

"Why do you figure Victor did this?" he asked.

"Because he's a jerk," I said. It was the best reason I could come up with.

"Other than that," Joe chuckled, and he stared into my eyes.

"I finished up the south side of the Keller Place and I was working up the west end," I remembered. "You told me to work up the west end to the creek until I met the Wilsz crew, right?"

"Yep," Joe agreed.

"Well, I fixed the south side and started up the west end, like you told me to, and I was about to the creek when I saw the Wilsz outfit coming down the fence line. Jimmy was walking along in front, stripping wire off the posts and rolling it in a ball, and Spudley was following Jimmy in a front end loader, wrapping a chain around perfectly good posts and pulling them out of the ground."

"Jimmy Wilsz was taking wire off and rolling it up?" Joe frowned.

"And throwing it in the back of a truck," I confirmed.

"Spudley was pulling posts out of the ground?" Joe asked.

"That's right."

"Where was Victor?"

"Victor was driving the post driver," I said. "Jimmy took the old wire off and Spudley pulled up the posts and Victor put the new posts in and the rest of the crew stretched wire behind them."

"Well, that's stupid," Joe said, and he shined a flashlight in my eyes. "Why would they do all that?"

"Their new fence is twenty yards inside of the old one," I rubbed my head. "They're moving the fence twenty yards onto the Keller Place."

Joe stared at me, then shined the flashlight in my eyes again.

"Are you sure?" he asked.

"Yes," I insisted, "I'm sure."

"Twenty yards of my land per mile is . . ."

"Twelve acres a mile," I said.

I told Joe how I had waited at the creek until the Wilsz crew pulled up at the water gap, and then Victor drove his tractor through the creek and pulled up next to the pickup.

39

"What did he say?" Joe asked, and he sprinkled a little more wonder dust and purple oil on my head.

"He said that I was a pinhead and a Barnes and that I was fixing the wrong fence," I recalled, "and I told him it looked to me like he was stealing land, not to mention posts, wire and staples."

"You shouldn't have said that," Joe sighed.

"No kidding!" I stood up. "He jumped off of the tractor and hit me over the head with the fence stretcher, and then he threw me in the creek!"

"Maybe this good neighbor fence policy *wasn't* such a good idea!" Joe frowned.

Joe put his hand to his head to help him think, and then he pulled a napkin off of the table and began to figure and draw. Finally, he sat back and ran his fingers through his hair.

"If we go out and tear down all of that fence that Victor built, it'll just get him all stirred up and he'll do something drastic," Joe sighed.

"More drastic than whacking me on the head with a fence stretcher?" I asked.

"You'll live, " Joe laughed. "Your head's a long way from your heart and there's not that much in there to hurt, but we've got to get this fencing thing figured out."

I played with the stitches Joe had sewn into my head, and Joe played with his white hair and scratched at the napkin on the table until his face brightened and he stood up.

"What *we* need to do is move *our* fence twenty yards inside of the old fence line and take back what he took from us!" Joe grinned.

"Joe," I stared at the floor, "to be perfectly honest, I'm not really very excited about doing any more fencing between us and Victor. I don't even like *fixing* fence and now you're telling me that you want to *build* a new fence around the whole ranch?"

"Not the whole damn ranch," Joe snorted, "just the border fences with the Wilsz outfit."

Joe sent me back to the Keller Place to move the south end of the fence twenty yards across Victor's property line, the result being a pair of brand new fences, each one twenty yards inside the property line of the neighbor, so that wherever Victor stole twelve acres on the north end of the fence line, Joe stole twelve acres back on the south end. The straight fences that once existed on Friendly Creek now darted and dashed across the landscape in a surveyor's nightmare, around the perimeter of the Wilsz Ranch. Nobody was willing to take Victor to task because they'd all seen my head, and nobody wanted to give up on the good neighbor fence policy, because they'd agreed to try.

The end result was a forty yard alley around the entire Wilsz Ranch . . . no man's land.

Down at the hardware store, Dick Wilson added on a whole new line of fencing supplies, and with local interest focused on the situation, Bobby Baker dished out a daily play-by-play and plenty of drinks to visitors at the Hoosegow. Fingers Filiatreau denied any connection with the original idea, and while nobody was very pleased with the runway around the Wilsz Ranch, even Shorty McGregor had to admit that the "good neighbor fence policy" was keeping Victor's cattle on Victor's land.

To be sure, there were a lot less complaints about Victor's fences, and whenever somebody tried to cook up a new solution to the problem, Shorty would call me over and lift up the hair over my left ear to show them what a fence stretcher could do in the hands of an untrained user. Most of the problem solvers decided that the fencing situation was better left to the ranchers.

As for me, I guess I'll always look back to Joe's advice on the whole mess.

"At least Victor Wilsz is fixing fence," he said, "and there's no sense screwing up a good thing."

41

A HANDSHAKE AND A PROMISE

The big buckskin was in one of his little moods again. In all the years I'd been riding him, he'd never once offered to buck me off, or even crow hop, and he was easily one of the best horses on the creek. When he set himself to walking, trotting or working cattle, there wasn't a horse on the creek that could stay with him. Red Barnes raised him and got him started, then sold him to me because Red thought I needed a horse that was better than average.

"He's smart, he's quick and he's stout," Red told me. "There's just one little thing about him you might not like."

Red didn't elaborate and I didn't ask. For the bargain, I didn't figure it would be appropriate to ask.

The "one little thing" turned out to be his wild moods, which didn't come all that often, but when he got into one of them, he would clamp the bit in his teeth and take off on a dead run, and when that happened, no amount of pulling, turning or jerking on the reins had any impact. I could yell, scream, beg or cry, to no avail. The horse was too big and too strong to argue with. But, like I said, when you got past that one little fault in his temperament, he was one hell of a horse.

At the moment, he was running all out, jumping ditches, dodging cactus and sagebrush, hell-bent-for-election to some place only he understood. Had it been any other horse, I might have just bailed off and accepted whatever cuts and bruises went with the territory. The buckskin was a big sucker, and he'd never stumbled or fallen, but I wasn't sure where he would stop, so I just hung on for dear life and waited for him to trap himself in the corner where the pastures came together. I knew that once he got there, he would stop, spin around on his hind legs and stand still to catch his breath. When he was done with that, he would shake his head, stamp his front feet and saunter back to wherever we left off, as if nothing had happened.

I could see the fence corner coming, so I took a deep breath and held tight with my knees to brace for the stop. He didn't stop. Some damn fool had left the gate open, and the buckskin sailed right on through and headed toward the Friendly Creek road like a rocket. He ran through the slough and splashed water twenty feet in the air, then charged up the hill past Red's house. I was hanging on and he was running right down the middle of the gravel road.

He finally decided to stop, and I was so happy to be through with running and jumping and dodging sagebrush that I never even noticed the car.

"Hey there!" someone yelled, and a short man stepped out of a white sedan.

The buckskin stepped backward, put his ears forward, and blew through his nose.

"That's sure a pretty horse!" the short man said. "I'll bet his name is `Buck.'"

"It rhymes with that," I growled.

"Stampede, huh?" the man asked, and he wandered over a little closer to the buckskin.

He was a funny looking little guy, about five feet six, with a sport coat that looked like it had been made for someone a foot taller. He had a pair of khaki pants that ended above his square-toed boots, and on his head was a rather hideous straw hat.

"Where you going in such a hurry?" he asked, and he jammed his hands in his coat pockets and rocked back on the heels of his new boots.

"I'm not sure," I smiled. "You'd have to ask my horse."

"Where you goin' in such a hurry?" he asked the horse.

The buckskin stared at the stranger, but didn't answer.

"Name is Sam Wilson!" The short man's hand shot out so fast that it spooked the buckskin, and I fully expected another wild charge through the brush, but apparently, the horse was as curious as I was about this strange person.

It was obvious that Sam Wilson wanted me to believe that he was some sort of cowboy, because he was all decked out like Howdy Doody. As a matter of fact, he smiled like Howdy Doody, and the way he waved his arms and moved his head, I half expected Buffalo Bob Smith to jump out of the car and get him under control.

"Yessir," he said, louder this time. "I'm Sam Wilson!"

"You said that," I nodded.

44

"What's your name?" he asked.

"Parker Barnes," I told him.

"Now, that's a real fine name," he decided. "Tell me, Parker Barnes, can you vote?"

"Not unless that's what this horse wants to do," I said. "He's more or less in control of my life right at the moment."

"That's where you're wrong!" Sam Wilson shouted, and he proceeded to explain to me that the reason people like myself were content to let horses and other things control our lives was because we allowed the Democrats to control the Congress and if everyone would just vote for him, he would by God clean up the mess in Washington and listen to the will of the people and change the world.

"Are you a registered voter?" he asked, and he jammed his hands into the pockets of his sport coat, and handed me some buttons, pens, fingernail rasps and a bumper sticker, apparently for my horse.

"Yep," I admitted that I could vote.

"Republican?" he asked, and he handed me some more junk, none of which seemed very valuable.

"Everybody here is a Republican," I advised. "I don't think they even let the donkey people vote."

"Great!" he stared into space. "Are you active in politics?"

"No sir," I shook my head. "I've been raised honest."

That night, when the buckskin was too tired to run and I was too tired to care, I ran into Sam Wilson again. This time he was on foot, limping down the Friendly Creek Road like Howdy Doody with a string broke.

"Hey Sam," I smiled when I rode up. "Where's your car?"

"Sam Wilson!" he yelled, and he jerked his hands out again. "I plan to be your Congressman. I'd give you a pen and a fingernail file, some balloons and a bumper sticker, but they're in the car."

"I've got some," I smiled.

"Hey!" he brightened. "You knew my name! Are you gonna' vote for me?"

"Sure." I laughed. "Where's your car?"

"Well," he limped alongside the big buckskin, "that's a heck of a story. My wife and I trade off driving, and after I got clear up to this creek, I was tired, so I told Mildred I'd get in the back and have a nap. Well, I got out and went around back to take a leak, and I slipped and fell into the car. I guess Mildred thought I slammed the door, because she took off."

"Where is she?" I laughed.

"That's the problem," he sighed. "I'm scheduled to talk again tomorrow morning in Worland, and when Mildred gets to driving down the road, she never looks back. Move ahead with Sam Wilson, that's our motto, and it was Mildred that thought it up!"

"Well," I smiled. "You can't walk to Worland in those new boots. It's four hundred miles, and you'll be late."

I pulled Sam Wilson up behind me, and after I'd turned my horse out, I gave Sam Wilson a ride to the Hoosegow.

"Who is this joker?" Bobby Baker whispered when Sam Wilson raced through the crowd, shaking hands.

"Sam Wilson," I said. "He says he a politician."

"I'd believe that alright," Bobby laughed. "He's the first guy I ever saw who could talk faster than Fingers."

Indeed, Sam Wilson was getting a full sentence in for every wag of Fingers Filiatreau's finger, and every time Fingers tried to get an opinion in, Sam Wilson was off on another subject.

"Seems to know quite a bit, don't he?" Bobby asked.

"Maybe," I held out my empty glass, "but his wife is headed over to Worland without him. He needs a ride."

"If he'll pay for the gas and the beer, I'll give him a ride," Davey Boyd offered.

"You're too drunk to drive," Buck Martin advised Davey.

"So, *he* can ride behind the wheel," Davey said, and he and

Sam Wilson headed over the hill in Davey's old Ford pickup with a cooler full of cold beer on the seat between them.

When Davey got back, he was sporting a chestful of ribbons and buttons, and he handed out pencils and finger rasps and all sorts of other junk.

"I'm a Sam Wilson man!" he said, acted like he'd got religion or something.

He explained they had passed Mildred going over South Pass, but she was so busy talking, they didn't catch up with her until she pulled in at Shoshoni to buy gas. Mildred seemed happy enough to see Sam, but she was mad as a wet hen to find out that she'd been giving him good ideas for two hundred miles and he hadn't even been there.

I voted for Sam Wilson that year, probably because he was the first politician who ever shook my hand, except for the time when Victor Wilsz ran for the State Senate. That hadn't worked out very well, because whenever somebody disagreed with one of Victor's opinions, Victor beat them up. By the time that election came around, Victor had beat up half the people in the country, and if he hadn't been so fat, he would have caught plenty more. Personally, I thought Victor would have gotten more than the nine votes he picked up. If he won, that would have meant he would have been out of the county for two whole months, but maybe people were more worried about having him out in public that they were about living with him. Politics can be pretty strange, I've found.

Sam Wilson was elected Congressman in a landslide. In fact, Sam Wilson was called the "most popular man in the history of Wyoming," and while it was often said that he could also have qualified as the goofiest man in the history of Wyoming, nobody ... and I mean *nobody* had ever shaken more hands than Sam Wilson.

Jeez, he shook both of mine.

It would be nice to say that there was only one time tempers got out of hand on Friendly Creek, but that would be too big a whopper for even a good liar to handle. It seems like there's some big drama played out on the ditchbanks every year, going back to the shovel fight between Fred Aspering and Joe Barnes, in which Joe finally got the better of Fred and blacked his eyes and broke his nose. Joe should have won the fight; he was only fifty-something and Fred was all of seventy, and besides, Joe was right in the first place.

Fred Aspering's sheep operation sat right in the middle of

the real ranches on the creek, and the sheep spent the winter on the desert, grubbing around for sagebrush and other stuff that sheep eat in the winter, so it wasn't like Fred needed the water in the first place. All he had to irrigate was a patch of desert-entry hay ground that he used to feed his horses and his milk cow, but every time Joe opened his headgate, Fred puttered out and diverted the whole head of water from Joe's ditch. After ten or twenty years of that, Joe finally decided to say something to Fred, and before it was all over, Fred bonked Joe over the head with the handle of a shovel, and Joe bonked Fred on the nose. And while all of that pretty well proved that Joe could whip Fred, it didn't deter Fred from stealing Joe's water. In fact, the only long-term effect of the shovel fight was that Daisy Aspering wouldn't speak to Joe Barnes, and she must have been pretty serious about it, because she wouldn't even wave at him when they passed each other on the road.

Like everywhere else in the West, the first people to arrive on Friendly Creek picked the best places to live, those patches of ground as close to the river as possible, but high enough to stay dry when the creeks flooded in the spring. Since they came along first, and since they were the first people to use the water on Friendly Creek, the law of the land gave them the "best" water rights, in terms of time. "First in time, first in right" sums up the legal hierarchy of irrigating, but all of that legal business, however well-substantiated in courts of law and records of justice, has never amounted to much more than a noble theory when water runs out of the mountains.

"Being right is fine and dandy," Red Barnes always said, "but being shot in the guts is worse."

"The best right on the creek is the oldest right on the creek," Victor Wilsz warned whenever anyone would listen. Obviously, Victor had the oldest right on the creek.

"Horse hockey," Shorty McGregor laughed. "The best right on the creek is the first guy with a shovel."

"Unless you get shot in the guts," Red Barnes added, but since nobody has been shot in the guts yet, the "oldest" versus "first" argument has raged on since the 1870s without much resolution. In fact, neither side has gained an advantage, but on Friendly Creek cleverness and treachery have generally been more highly respected than law books.

When the runoff comes, it is time to steal water, even if the only person to steal it from is yourself.

Every year, Shorty McGregor stole the whole creek just as soon as it came out of the mountains, which meant that Shorty stole water from everybody, since Shorty had the *worst* right on the creek in terms of time. As soon as Shorty was done with the water, he turned it loose and Ira Cusack took it over.

Ira Cusack, like most of the other people on the creek, was third or fourth generation. The Cusacks came to cut ties for the railroad, and when the timber run played out, the Cusacks were the only tiehacks who stayed. Ira still ran a little sawmill, cutting *really* rough lumber, but the commercial lumber yards were able to underprice Ira, and the boards at the lumber yards were straight. Still, Ira managed to make a living, selling fence posts, wood chips and sawdust for bedding, running a little herd of cows, and breeding draft horses.

Ira had no right to any water at all, but Ira took more than his share and used it to irrigate his horse pasture. Since Ira was six feet-nine inches tall, close to three hundred pounds, and as solid as the trees he hacked down with his axe, nobody seemed to question *his* right to use the water. It looked to me like when you got right down to it, the *biggest* guy on the creek had the best water right.

Davey Boyd got the water next, and he stole it from Red Barnes, who stole water from Carl Loper, who stole it from Joe Barnes. Whatever was left, Joe took, so that by the time the water made it to Victor Wilsz, who really *did* have the best right on the creek, there wasn't any water. As soon as that happened,

Victor blew out his chest, bugled a couple of times and called up the water police, and then there was hell to pay.

Out came the water police, and they led a caravan of pickups up the Friendly Creek Road. Every rancher brought his own truck, and every pickup was filled with loyal ranch people so that nobody would have to sit in a truck with a water thief from across the road. The water police went to the head of the creek and started to lock and chain all the headgates until the creek leveled off, and then they unlocked the headgates meticulously, Victor Wilsz first.

"This isn't fair!" Victor Wilsz and Joe Barnes yelled in unison, and then they both looked at the ground, amazed that they could have had the same thought at the same time.

"What do you mean it isn't fair?" the water police said. "Your headgate is open and all the others are closed! That's what you wanted, isn't it?"

"Well," Victor pouted, "according to *you*, my right is the best one on the creek, but I'll never get any water because Shorty McGregor will steal it all!"

"There is a chain and lock on Mr. McGregor's headgate," the water police put his hands on his hips.

"And there is a big hole in the ditchbank next to the chain and the lock," Joe stabbed his finger at the water police, "and the whole damn creek is running onto Shorty's meadow!"

"Don't be ridiculous," the water police laughed, but all of the ranchers shoved their hands in their pockets and agreed Shorty would be stealing the whole creek, so the water police agreed to go back up and have a look, and the parade of pickups turned around and drove up the Friendly Creek Road.

Sure enough, Shorty was out walking his ditches, shovel in hand, and all of the foamy brown water in Friendly Creek was rushing through a hole in the ditchbank.

"What's the meaning of this?" the water police yelled.

"Muskrats!" Shorty yelled back. "Thank goodness you're

here! The muskrats came and tore out the creek bank! I'm afraid I may have a flood!"

"That's crazy!" the water police said, and he started across the meadow, lifting his feet up high, as if they would dry off between his steps in the wet field.

"Muskrats," Shorty shook his head, and he pointed his shovel at a huge hole beside the headgate. "Muskrats moved in right after you left! There must've been a million of 'em!"

"Fix that hole!" the water police pointed his finger at Shorty. "You are in violation of Wyoming Statute 41, dash . . . Oh hell, I can't remember the number, but you're breaking the law!"

"I can't fix that hole," Shorty held out his hands. "I've been out here trying to fix that hole all afternoon, but it's just plain too big. I'm just a little rancher. I would need a back hoe or a bulldozer."

"He's lying!" Victor bellowed.

"Why would I lie?" Shorty looked at the water police. "If somebody doesn't help me, my little ranch will be flooded."

"Do you have a bulldozer?" the water police asked Victor.

"Of course I have a bulldozer!" Victor screamed, "but I am not going to come up here and do all of this little tightwad's earth moving for him. He does this every year! *He* dug that hole! Make *him* fix the damn thing!"

"I thought muskrats dug the hole," the water police said, and Shorty nodded vigorously.

"It's an act of God," Shorty looked skyward.

Victor's face was as red as a willow bush, but he stormed back to his pickup and slammed the door, then led a procession down to his ranch, where everyone helped load the bulldozer.

By the time we got back, Shorty was sitting on the porch, sipping on a cold beer and cussing muskrats. His whole ranch was irrigated.

The water police high-stepped through the boggy field while Victor drove his bulldozer into the creek and filled the hole. As Victor was crawling the dozer out of the creek, Shorty asked if he would mind running the dozer through the corrals.

"Just to clean it out a little bit, if you don't mind?" he smiled, and then he launched back into his diatribe about the evil muskrat.

"Muskrats are like fish," he said as he wiped his sweaty brow, "a little pool of water, and they go crazy."

"Are you boys having problems with the muskrats?" he asked, and he opened another cold beer. "It must be a sign of a heavy winter to come, this many muskrats showing up so early."

Victor pushed all of the manure out of the corral and left it on the piles he had pushed out in all the previous years, then drove the dozer back onto the trailer. His face was getting darker all the time, and the red was spreading onto his neck.

"Thank you Mister Wilsz," Shorty waved. "I hope I can call on your friendship again if the muskrats come back."

Everyone was loading up to get back to Victor's headgate when Davey Boyd pulled into the ranch yard and hollered, and then Ira Cusack jumped out of the pickup, madder than a herd bull on the fight. Ira stomped his way across the yard, cold brown water dripping off his hat, jeans and boots sloshing across the dirt, and he stopped in front of us.

"What happened to you?" Joe asked.

"I was crossing the creek with my wagon when the water came up!" he howled. "It almost drowned my team!"

"I found him washed up at the crossing," Davey poked his head out of the pickup and pointed at Ira. "I thought he was dead."

"Who fixed the hole?" Cusack screamed.

Everyone pointed at the water police.

Cusack swung from the hip and caught the water police square on the chin, lifting him a good two feet in the air and depositing him in the rocks, knocked out colder than a clam.

"Who called the water police?" Ira asked, and he pulled his wet sleeves up.

Everyone pointed at Victor, but all that was left to see was the back end of his pickup going over the hill.

"That figures," Ira snarled, and he walked back over to Davey's pickup and climbed inside.

"Take me to Victor's house," he yelled, and Davey slid the truck into gear and headed up the hill, his face as white as a sheet.

Victor wasn't home. While everyone else was arguing over water, Victor sneaked into the Hoosegow and tried to get Shorty drunk so that he could buy his place at the head of the creek. Shorty accepted the down payment and staggered out of the bar at daylight, spent the morning sleeping in his pickup and forgot all about "the deal." Victor fished out a Coors napkin with the agreement all written out and signed by Shorty, but since the agreement was written by Victor and only signed by Shorty, Bobby Baker suggested that Victor could have stolen the signed napkin and written anything.

"I paid that little tightwad a thousand dollars!" Victor bellered.

"I don't have a thousand dollars," the little tightwad said, "and everyone knows that I would *never* sell to Victor."

Bobby said he hadn't seen a thing, and since there were no other witnesses to the transaction, it must have never happened, although Shorty bought a round of drinks and a new shirt the next day, and he sure as heck never did either of those things before.

While all of the devious high finance was taking place in the Hoosegow, and the water police were busy trying to get the creek running level, Red Barnes sawed the ends off all the boards which diverted "legal" water into the Wilsz ditch. That left the water only one place to go, which was straight down Red's ditch and onto his meadows. Davey Boyd was the first to notice the water, but since Red had a better right than Davey, he wasn't actually stealing water from him, so Davey told Victor. Victor drove his bulldozer up the creek and promptly dozed Red's headgate shut.

Red walked out across his meadow and found it dry as a bone, so he took a box of dynamite and blew the dirt out of his headgate. When Victor confronted him, Red lit into Victor before the bigger man could get a word in edgewise.

"*I* don't have the best rights on that ditch!" Red reminded Victor, and he jabbed the bigger man in the chest with his finger. "Figure it out, Victor!"

Victor figured out that Joe had the best right on the ditch, and in the dark of night, Victor buried his bulldozer in the heart of the swamp, no less than fifty yards from Joe's main headgate.

Joe immediately accused Victor of skullduggery.

Victor accused Joe of stealing water, which was senseless, because, as Joe and the water police pointed out, Joe didn't have any more water than Victor did.

That afternoon, Victor guided a pair of winch trucks across Joe's land to claim his bulldozer, and Joe had Buck Martin arrest him for trespassing, which cost Victor twenty five bucks and led him to accuse Joe of stealing his bulldozer.

"I have my own bulldozer!" Joe said, and he looked at Victor's bulldozer, which was being sucked into the gray, boggy swamp at the rate of two feet a day. "Nobody will ever get yours out of the mud bog anyway."

"I'll pay a thousand dollars to any man that can get that dozer out of the bog!" Victor offered.

"I'll do it," Red held up his hand.

"You *can't* do it," Victor spat. "You're incompetent."

"I'll bet you a thousand dollars I can get it out," Red said.

"You don't have any money to bet!" Victor snorted. "You already owe me money as it is!"

"I paid that back a long time ago," Red said, "but if you don't want your bulldozer out, I don't care."

"You get that bulldozer out, and I'll give you a thousand bucks," Victor smiled and crossed his arms.

"Then, I'll bet a thousand dollars I can get it out," Red smiled.

"You don't have a thousand dollars!" Victor waved his arms.

"I got the thousand you owe me for getting it out," Red said, "and I'm betting it all that I can get it done."

"Put your money where your mouth is, Victor," Joe suggested.

"I'll hold the bet," Shorty volunteered, but Victor wasn't about to give Shorty a thousand dollars again, so Joe held the bet. Victor put up Red's thousand for getting the dozer out, then added his own thousand to bet that Red couldn't do it, and Red set the terms.

"No one can watch," Red said, "And the dozer will be out by daylight."

At precisely four-thirty the next morning, Victor's bulldozer rumbled, clanked and roared, then rose straight up out of the mud bog. The pieces were scattered from the Chalk Bluffs to town, and all that was left at the sight of exit was a sucking hole of black bog mud and three empty cases of DuPont's finest blasting powder.

"She's out of the bog," Red smiled.

Joe declared that the terms of the bet had been met and gave Red the two thousand dollars.

While the ranchers were busy rescuing the bulldozer, the water police went out and welded every single headgate shut, then chained, locked, and tagged them all. When they were done with that, they piled sandbags in front of each of them, so that not one drop of illegal water would trickle out of the creek. When all of that was said and done, the water police made a big deal out of opening up Victor's headgate. Satisfied that justice had been done, the water police stopped in at the Hoosegow for a beer, whereupon Ira Cusack recognized him and dropped him with another blow to the chin.

Buck Martin almost had to arrest Cusack and put him in jail, but Buck was quick to point out the fact that Cusack had no water rights at all, and therefore had not violated any water laws, so Cusack was never arrested, and he went home to feed his horses, and irrigate.

The water police called the State Engineer, and the State Engineer called the County Sheriff and the Sheriff went to the circuit judge and the judge called the Highway Patrol. The Governor, a rancher and former water thief, alerted the National Guard, and every law enforcement agent within five counties drove up to Friendly Creek. The ranchers were called into town for a little discussion in the basement of the library. The Governor, State Engineer and other high muckedy mucks flew in from Cheyenne in a chartered airplane, and the Governor asked the irrigators to knock it off.

"Why should I listen to *you*?" Joe snorted at the Governor, "You're a Democrat!"

The crowd bristled at the knowledge that a Democrat might be trying to tell them what to do, and Buck Martin stepped right in front of the Governor and drew his pistol.

"I'm a rancher," the Governor peered around Buck. "I understand your problems here."

"You're no rancher," Shorty scratched his bald head. "You're a Governor. Don't lie to us."

"I used to be a rancher," the Governor smiled.

"Listen to the man!" Victor yelled. "He's the Governor!"

"He's a Democrat!" Joe hissed, and he stood up to leave, a sudden move that Buck Martin mistook for an attack on the Governor.

Buck panicked, and forgetting that he was in the basement

of the library, he pulled a quick draw and fired a warning shot in the air.

The shot quieted the crowd in the basement, but when the bullet zoomed out of the floor upstairs and ricocheted off of the trash can next to the librarian's desk, it scared the bejeezus out of Olivia Cowley, who was shushing people for talking. If talking was a violation of library rules, shooting a gun was way out of line, and Olivia barrelled down the stairs and proceeded to slap the tar out of the water police, who had taken the pistol away from Buck, fearing that violence might break out.

Having been beaten to a pulp by a lumberjack and a librarian in the space of a week, the water police quit his job then and there, and in one of the most brilliant moves in the history of Friendly Creek, the State Engineer looked over the crowd and appointed Ira Cusack as the new water police.

Everyone agreed to share the water, three days at a time, Victor Wilsz first, then Joe Barnes and so on . . . and they all shook on the deal, which made it binding as all get out, and everybody left the library and went home to wait for their water.

From that day forward, there seemed to be plenty of water for everyone on the creek, but there was never so much grumbling and grousing. Nobody waved at each other on the road, and without any water to fight over, there wasn't much reason for anyone to talk to each other at all. Red Barnes allowed as how if everyone was going to be so nice to each other, they ought to just change the name of the creek from Friendly Creek to Lonesome Creek.

Fortunately, one warm afternoon in the heart of springtime, while the water was trickling over the meadows and curlews were dive-bombing irrigators, Carl Loper spied one of Joe's calves in Fred Aspering's corral . . . back up there on Friendly Creek.

Something about springtime always made me feel good. I don't know if it was the longer days, the fact that I could take a layer or two of clothing off or the green on the grass and the trees. Most likely, it was the calves, little guys of every color and size. Every morning when I rode across the creek, their heads came up and they bawled at me, then tumbled and bucked across the meadow with their tails sticking straight in the air. The cows watched the antics of their offspring with patience only mothers comprehend, until the calves suddenly realized how far away from their mothers they were, then turned and ran straight back to Mama.

Then, there was a ritual of sniffing and licking until the cow tucked her baby into her flank and let him suck, converting the tail into a wringing, twisting picture of contented excitement. As I rode closer, the calves would poke their heads out and have another look at me, pink tongues wedged between their lips, eyes wide with excitement, tails suddenly inactive. Some of the bigger calves raised their heads and sniffed at the wind, and maybe they realized who I was, maybe not, but they didn't quit sucking for long. A calf doesn't have too many priorities.

It had been a good calving season, without any heavy snow or really wicked cold, and the calves were big and strong. Most of them were on the ground, but there were always a few old cows that were late, and I checked them every morning. I'd been trying to track down a calf for two days, but his mother was one of those old cows that never lost a baby, and she had the little bugger hid out tighter than Butch Cassidy and the Sundance Kid. This morning, she was laying at the edge of the willows, and she cocked an ear in my direction when I rode up, but her feet were tucked underneath her, and she only opened one eye. I probably could have ridden the willows and spooked the little guy out of his bed, but there wasn't much sense in that. She would bring him out when she was good and ready.

"Where is he?" I asked the old cow, but she didn't act like she was going to answer, so I took my time and worked through the cattle until I found a brand new heifer calf, standing up nervously next to her mother, still wet. I stepped off and slid a tag in her ear; she was probably no more than an hour old. The old cow sniffed at me and snorted a booger or two on my chaps. I pointed the little black nose toward the business end of the cow and checked the pair off in my book.

When I stepped back into the saddle, I noticed a brown station wagon had pulled up at the creek crossing and stopped. There was a skiff of ice on the water, but it wasn't enough to keep the car from crossing, and I wondered what the driver was up to, that far from town, that early in the morning. I angled in the direction of the station wagon, and when we left the cows, my horse broke into a good trot. As he put his head down and picked his way across the creek, a man stepped out and set an old, battered Thermos on the hood of the car.

"Morning," he smiled. "I didn't mean to bother you."

"No bother," I said while I eyed the white license plate.

"Illinois," he grinned. "Chicago . . . the big city."

He held up a cup and I nodded, then stepped off my horse and let the cinch out. The bay lowered his head and picked at the new grass, so I dropped the reins and let him wander around on his own.

"You're a long ways from Chicago." I blew on my coffee and eyed him through the steam.

He was a short, stocky man, in good shape it seemed, which made it tough to guess his age. His eyes were warm and creased at the sides with grooves that sang a song of good humor. I guessed him to be fifty, maybe fifty-five.

"Sometimes," he smiled, "the best thing about being from Chicago is being someplace else."

He sipped at his coffee, soft tanned hands wrapped loosely around the Styrofoam cup, fingernails perfectly trimmed, and his graying hair blew against his forehead. He stared into the hills and mountains across the creek.

"That's Coal Mine Mountain, right?" he pointed, and I followed his finger.

"Yep," I agreed, "that's Coal Mine Mountain."

He grinned, and his mind seemed to settle somewhere above timberline.

"Can you still get to the top?" he asked.

"There's still a good trail up there," I told him, "but not like the old timers talk about, when they were hauling coal with a team and a wagon. The road washed out when the lookout tower burned down."

"The lookout tower burned down?" he asked. "When did that happen?"

"Ten, twelve years ago," I guessed. "The ranger on duty dropped a cigarette on the floor and the whole thing went up in smoke. Burned all the way down Deer Creek before they got it put out."

"Why didn't they rebuild it?" he wondered out loud.

"Said they didn't need it anymore," I shrugged. "Now, they've got computers and satellites and all that. They don't need any lookout towers, I guess."

"How far am I from the Eddleman Place?" he asked.

"It's about a half mile from here," I said, and I pointed up the creek.

"They still call it the Eddleman Place?" He seemed surprised that I would have actually heard of such a place.

"Sure," I shrugged. "What else would they call it?"

"I don't know," he said. "It just surprises me a little bit. There hasn't been an Eddleman around here for forty years."

"Victor Wilsz owns it now," I told him. "It's run down pretty bad."

"It was run down pretty bad when it was new," he sighed, and he poured us another cup of coffee.

"Are you an Eddleman?" I asked.

"No," he shook his head slowly. "My wife was an Eddleman. I was born on this place here."

"Then, you'd be a Keller," I suggested.

"Tom Keller," he held out his hand. "I used to fish from here to the Jacobs' place in the summer. It used to be good fishing."

"Still is," I grinned, "if you can stand the mosquitoes and the willows."

"Are any of the buildings left?" he wondered.

"The house got hit by lightning and burned down about three years ago," I said, suddenly sad that it was true. "But we still use the corrals and the barn, and there's a bunkhouse; I stay there sometimes when the calving is really going fast and I don't have time to go home."

"That barn will never fall down, will it?" he asked, hope in his voice.

"I'd say not," I leaned against the car. "That barn was built to last."

"We hauled the logs off Coal Mine Mountain," Tom Keller stared up at the rocky peak. "My dad picked every log out while it was still standing, measured them to make sure they'd fit, and we left them here to dry. I remember going to school after we cut them. Every morning and night, I walked home and climbed that pile of logs. I thought Papa would never get the barn built, but he did. He stepped out the corrals on a day about like this one, and when I came home from school that day, he had the rocks for the foundation laid. He built the whole thing around a spring, and when the barn was finished, he went in and stole a cup from Mama and hung it on a peg in the barn so that we could all have a drink. Boy, that water was so cold and clear . . . the best water I ever drank."

"When did you leave?" I asked.

"We left in 1935," he stared at the mountains, "one of the last families to go. Papa always thought we were gonna make it, but it just wasn't meant to happen, I guess. Gad, there were families all up and down this creek then."

"I started school over there," he pointed at the Upper Friendly Creek School House. The empty bell tower was leaning to one side and its interior was filled with oats that Carl Loper fed his horses in the winter.

"There were three or four dozen kids in school," he sighed. "There was a family on every quarter-section. There were us and the Eddlemans, and there were the Atchisons, Crowleys, Wilsons, and the Jacobs. Anyplace that looked like you could farm, there was a family. My best friend in all the world was a boy named Billy Barnes. How would he be related to you?"

"That's my dad," I said, and Tom Keller's memories crawled inside of my head and rattled around with the stories my father used to tell me.

"Is he still here?" Tom asked. "I didn't see his name in the phone book."

"He teaches college in Sheridan," I said. "The place he grew up on wasn't big enough for more than one family, so he had to leave. Joe Barnes bought it after my Grandma died."

"How many ranches are left?" he asked.

"Ten maybe," I guessed. "I don't know, really."

I tried to explain the lay of the land from the head of the creek, where Shorty lived, a mixture of the old McGregor Place and half a dozen others that dried up in the Depression.

"Below Shorty, there's Ira Cusack," I said. "It's just a little family place, maybe a section or two. Ira raises work horses and sells some firewood and lumber and stuff like that."

"They're still here?" Keller brightened. "I'd swear that the Cusacks were broke worse than anyone, and they're still here! I'll be!"

Below Ira, Victor Wilsz had the Eddleman Place, the Jacobs Place and the Crowley Farm. He used that ranch to summer some of his horses.

"Mostly work horses," I told the man. "Ira's got a really good Belgian stud, so Victor turns his mares in next to him. Most of 'em foal, too."

Joe Barnes had bought the Keller Place from the bank a long time ago, before I was around, and it fit in with four other little places along the creek, including the one where my dad grew up. There wasn't a lot of grass, but there was protection in the willows and the trees, and the creek stayed open all winter in some stretches along there.

"We calve up here," I told Tom.

I hoped that might make him happy.

"Davey Boyd has a little place above Red Barnes," I pointed down the creek, "and then you're back on Joe's home place. The Wilsz outfit takes up most of the creek, I guess."

"My father refused to sell to the Wilsz family," Tom smiled, and he walked toward the creek. "It's Victor now? At that time, it was Rudy, Victor's father, who was trying to buy the whole creek. My dad said he would've done it, but he couldn't force the Barnes clan out."

"We're still here," I grinned.

"Are the ranchers making it?" he asked.

"I guess so," I shrugged. "It hasn't been too good lately, but things are looking a little better. We've had good calving weather this spring."

"It's amazing." he shook his head. "The country really hasn't changed that much since I was a kid."

"It's still ranch country, if that's what you mean," I stared at Coal Mine Mountain. "What's to change?"

Tom Keller stared at me like my dad did sometimes.

"I just hope that people with money never find this place," he said. "They'll destroy it like they have every other pretty place they've found."

"I don't understand that," I shook my head, but he was staring at Coal Mine Mountain again.

"It was something when I was a kid," he smiled. "We all hayed together, built the school, had hayrides at Christmas, and worked the roundup."

"What do you figure happened?" I wondered out loud.

"The Homestead Act wasn't made for this country," he reasoned. "At the time, everyone was so happy to have a place

65

that they never really sat down and thought about how they could feed a family on a quarter-section. I can see where that might have worked in Illinois, but not here."

"It was always too cold or too hot or too dry to farm. There weren't any jobs, so people loaded up and left with whatever they could take along. We went to California, Oklahoma, Texas . . . wherever Papa could get work. He sold cars, tended bar, swept floors . . . ended up teaching school and coaching football in a little town called Blanchard, Oklahoma . . . a long, long way from here."

His voice was raspy and it trailed off.

I felt myself fidgeting and feeling uncomfortable, and I walked over and caught my horse.

"I've got to go," he sighed, and he opened the door of the station wagon and tossed his Thermos on the seat, then climbed in with it.

I gathered the reins and tightened the cinch on my saddle, unsure of what I might say to Tom Keller. I decided it would be best if I kept my mouth shut and left him alone, so I settled in the saddle and reined the bay around.

"Thanks for the coffee," I waved.

"My father would have loved to see these calves running across the meadow," Tom said, his eyes on the clean white faces.

"It's a great time of year," I grinned.

"I'm sorry to have taken your time," he said and a thin wisp of a smile crossed his face. "I don't imagine you know what it meant to me."

"No problem," I said, and he backed the station wagon around.

I sat tight and watched as the car started down the Friendly Creek Road. I still don't know if I understood what it meant to him, and I still don't know why, but I suddenly spurred the bay and chased the station wagon down the road, until I got in front of Tom Keller and stopped him.

"If you'll take a left through that gate over there," I took a deep breath and pointed at a wire gate, "the road will take you down to the Keller Place. Go in the barn, and you'll find a tin cup hanging on a peg by the door. It's still the best water on the creek."

At four o' clock in the morning, we jumped the horses out of the trailers, pulled our cinches tight in the red glow of the taillights and trotted off into the desert, which was darker than the inside of a cow.

"Nice night," I muttered when my horse staggered over a sagebrush, "We oughta' be able to ambush the cattle while they're still in bed."

"Are you griping?" Joe asked.

"Not really," I said, "I'm actually bitching and whining."

"Whatever you're doing," he said, "don't do it anymore. We've got cattle to gather."

"Right," I yawned. "Black cows in the middle of the night."

My wit was lost on Joe. He had galloped off to holler at a sandstone that resembled a sleeping Angus. The rock chose not to move on to the high country, and the boss, after yelling profanities at the rock and whipping it with his rope, chose not to ride back over and explain.

"Yaaaah," I hollered, and certain that somewhere a cow had moved, I trotted off into the dark to gather her.

By nine o' clock in the morning, while the merchants in town were unlocking their doors, we had trapped four hundred head of assorted bovines and their offspring in the fence corner that divided the land belonging to Joe, Loper, Red Barnes and Victor Wilsz. Cows and calves circled and bawled in search of each other. Yearlings tested the fences, chewed on sticks and wandered back and forth. The bulls tested each other briefly, sniffed a few cows, blew some boogers around and laid down.

Joe and Red and Shorty held a high-level conference around the food and water jugs, slowly flipping the pages on their little spiral notebooks, and the rest of us shifted our weight, stretched our legs and fidgeted, as much as a rider can fidget with his butt draped over a saddle . . . but not one rider stepped off. We were too busy "holding herd."

"What are we doing?" Lee Willoughby asked.

Lee was President of the Friendly Creek State Bank, and he had been wanting to get out of town and see how things worked in the country.

"We're holding herd," I said, and I crossed my hands over the saddle horn.

"How long does it last?" Lee looked at his watch.

"It depends," I sighed. "Sometimes it takes the morning, and sometimes it takes all day, but it always seems like it takes a month or so."

"What do we do?" he asked, and he shifted in his saddle.

After a few hours of riding, I guessed that his butt was probably a little sore.

"Just sit here and wait," I told him, "and somebody will yell at you."

What I really wanted to tell him was that holding herd is a boring, meaningless task assigned to the lowly help and volunteers like him, while the bosses ride around and cut the cattle herd for reasons which are mostly obscure. Holding herd is the most thankless and difficult job on the open range, and it is the children, wives, people from town and hired hands who end up holding herd. In practice, holding herd is a matter of patrolling the outside of the herd, keeping the inside cattle in and the outside cattle out, while at the same time directing the "cuts" to the proper pasture, or portion of the pasture.

"People will *yell* at me?" Lee laughed.

"I don't know a thing about working in a bank," I said, "but, if you wanna' be a cowboy, you'd better get used to getting yelled at. And, if you're gonna' be a cowboy on this outfit, you better get used to getting yelled at a lot."

"I can get yelled at in the bank," Lee whined. "I came out here to get some fresh air and learn a little something about ranching."

"Oh, really?" I looked at Lee. "Everybody else thinks you're out here to count cows."

Lee turned red, but sat his horse quietly.

"Don't worry about it, Lee," I smiled. "There hasn't been a banker around here yet who could count cows, and they've *all* tried."

"What are Joe and the other guys doing?" he asked, and I looked over my shoulder at the bosses.

"I dunno'," I shrugged. "I reckon they're doing whatever bosses do."

By nine-thirty, Joe and Red and Shorty had all had a drink of water, a sandwich and a cigarette, and they mounted up and rode slowly back to the milling herd.

"We'll cut 'em before lunch," Joe advised, "shouldn't take too long."

"What should I do?" Timmie Baker asked.

Timmie was Bobby Baker's daughter, and she was always anxious for a chance to ride her horse, even if it meant holding herd. Timmie was a freckle-faced girl, about my age, I guess, and like her dad, she was usually in a good mood.

"Don't try to cut anything!" Joe barked, and he and Red rode into the herd.

"Yeah," Shorty frowned. "We'll tell you what to do and when to do it."

Joe pushed a black baldy cow and her calf out of the bunch, and Lee sat his horse, holding the cow and calf back, while Joe's horse danced and tried to force the pair outside the herd. Finally, Lee and his horse won out, and the cattle ducked past Joe's horse and ran back into the herd.

"What are you doing?" Joe yelled at Lee.

"Holding herd," Lee said, and he looked over at me like I had told him to screw up.

"You aren't supposed to hold the whole herd!" Joe yelled. "That cow and calf were supposed to go out !"

"Out where?" Lee asked.

"Out there," Joe pointed into the pasture. "These are Seven X Ls. Seven X L cattle go out."

"Right," Lee agreed, but when Joe came back with another pair, Lee sat his ground, and the cow and calf snuck back into the herd.

"Dammit Lee," Joe whined, "Those were supposed to go out!"

"Seven X Ls," Lee nodded, and Joe rode back into the herd, then stopped and looked over his shoulder and came riding back up to me.

"What are those?" he asked and he pointed to a large bunch of cattle that were working their way off the hill toward us.

"I'd say that those are cattle," I advised.

"Must be Seven X Ls," Lee suggested.

"What makes you say that?" Joe snapped.

71

"Because they're out," Lee smiled, "and Seven X L's go out, right?"

"Those aren't Seven X Ls!" Joe pointed at Lee, "Because *you* haven't let us get any Seven X Ls out of the bunch!"

Joe called the other bosses over for a high level conference. It was determined that the cattle coming over the hill were probably some of Victor's that crawled through his sorry fence. One thing was certain; if they got into the bunch we were working, we would have to cut all of the cattle we had, and Victor's to boot.

"Drive those cattle over the hill so they can't see these," Shorty ordered, and a pair of his grandkids rode off like banshees and chased the cattle over the hills to where they couldn't "see."

I thought the idea of moving the cattle over the hill so they couldn't see didn't make a whit of sense. Cows can't see much farther than a few hundred feet on a clear day, but they can hear for a million miles. Moving them over the hill only perked their ears to the sound of calves bawling, creating in their minds an even greater need to join the herd, which they tried to do for the rest of the day. As a result, the bosses held another conference and divided the herd holders into two groups. All of the kids were assigned the duty of keeping the Wilsz cattle "way out," so that they would not be able to join the bunch being cut, and the rest of us were placed at the outside of the main herd to send cattle "out," but not "way out."

"Do you know what we're doing here?" Lee asked.

"More or less," I twisted in my saddle and looked behind me. "I think we're sending Joe's cattle out into the pasture behind us, Red's through the gate to Bald Ridge and holding Shorty's, so he can take them up the creek to his place."

"Why are we doing this?" Timmie asked.

"I'm not sure about that," I said. "I'm just a hired hand, and I'm doing this because this is what the bosses told us to do."

"Why?" Lee asked.

"Never ask why," I warned. "You can ask things like where and when and what, but don't ask a rancher why."

"Why not?" Timmie asked.

"Because," I took a deep breath, "there will either be no reason or they will tell you the reason, and neither of them will be much different. Just trust me on this one."

"And don't ask how either," I added. "Just sit on your horse and do what you're told."

Joe cornered a pair of Herefords and he worked them in my direction, so I pulled my horse's head up and she watched the cattle move toward us.

"These go out?" I asked as they went past, and Joe nodded.

"Hey!" Red yelled from the middle of the herd, so loud that he woke up a bull, "those are Quarter Circle Twos! They don't go out! They go to Bald Ridge!"

"Through the gate?" Timmie yelled as some sort of bovine raced past her.

"Dammit!" Joe bellowed. "You just let a Seven X L through the gate!"

Red Barnes bolted from the herd to chase down his Quarter Circle Two cow and calf, and I charged through the gate in pursuit of the Seven X L cow that was headed to Bald Ridge on a high lope. Timmie sat in the gate and seethed until Red and I came back with the only cattle to leave the herd in an hour. When Joe and Red rode back into the herd, Timmie informed Lee and I that it was her intention to kill both of them as soon as we were finished. Neither Lee nor I had time to help with her plan, because Joe was charging out of the bunch with a dozen wild-eyed cows and calves, running head over heels to somewhere, anywhere, just as long as it was out of the way of the boss.

"The cow and calf in the middle are a pair!" he screamed.

"Seven X Ls?" Lee hollered.

"Seven X Ls!" Joe yelled back. "Can't you read a brand?"

"As a matter of fact, no," Lee yelled, and the cattle charged toward us on a dead run.

"What pair?" I asked.

"Black-faced cow and her white calf!" Joe yelled, and I told Lee that he meant a "white-faced" cow and her black calf.

"How do you know?" Lee asked.

"I've done this before!" I yelled, and I turned back one of Red's cows, then spun my horse and ducked a pair of yearlings back into the bunch.

"What goes out?" I yelled.

"The pair in the middle!" Joe screamed.

"Which pair in the middle?" I begged. In a bunch of four hundred cows and their calves, there's a lot of middle.

"The Seven X L cow and calf!" Joe screamed, and then there were cows and calves all around me.

I let them all go.

"You!" Joe pointed at me. "You were in the wrong place!"

"It was my fault," Lee apologized.

"No it wasn't!" Joe yelled at Lee. "It was *his* fault!"

"No, it was *my* fault," Timmie said.

"I'll decide whose fault it was!" Joe glared at me.

"It was *my* fault," I said.

"You're damn right it was your fault!" Joe yelled.

"I'll go get 'em," Lee sighed and he loped off over the hill, out of earshot.

"Aw, the hell with it," Joe waved his hand. "I think they were all Seven X Ls anyway."

Joe reined his horse and rode back into the herd, and then he turned in the saddle and frowned at me.

74

"You're in the wrong place!" he said.

I looked around, amazed that I could be in the wrong place in a pasture of more than ten sections and still be within earshot.

"Move back," Joe waved.

I turned my horse and settled a few yards back.

"Move to your right," Joe directed, and I eased over to the right.

"Come forward a little," I rode ahead.

"That's too far," Joe shook his head. "Move back."

In the middle of a pasture no smaller than six thousand acres, Joe hollered and waved me and my horse around until he finally decided that I was in the one and only spot where we would be able to work a herd of four hundred cows, their calves, and an odd assortment of heifers, bulls, and steers.

"Could I ask a question?" Timmie suggested when I had been situated.

"What!?" Joe barked.

"Well," she smiled, " I was just wondering if we have a plan?"

"Of course we have a plan!" Joe screamed at her.

"Well, could you maybe tell us what it is?" she suggested.

"I think it would help," Lee added.

"Oh for Pete's sake," Joe galloped over. "How many times do I have to tell you? The Seven X Ls go out and the Quarter Circle Twos and yearlings go to Bald Ridge!"

"Through the gate?" Timmie asked.

"Excuse me!" Joe spun his horse. "Has somebody moved Bald Ridge or is it still through the gate?!"

"Quarter Circle Twos and yearlings go through the gate," Lee smiled.

"And Seven X Ls go out," I added.

"And when we're done," Timmie hissed, "Red and Joe are dead meat."

For six hours, the bosses brought cattle to the outside. Those of us holding herd deftly cut them aside, pushed them out, let them through the gate and raced through the brush to bring the escapees back. Our horses were staggering.

Finally, at five o' clock, we were down to a handful of yearlings and a Quarter Circle Two cow that simply would not go through the gate to Bald Ridge.

Joe vowed to "teach the old rip a lesson she would never forget," and then took her and her calf on an incredibly wild and profane ride to the very top of Bald Ridge, where the cow turned around and outran Joe's tired horse back to the herd. The boss men held a conference and determined that the cow would be allowed to remain with the Seven X L cattle for the summer.

"Do the cows always win?" Lee asked.

"As a matter of fact, I believe they do," I agreed.

"We can cut that cow out this fall," the bosses said.

"If you're still alive," Timmie snarled from the gate.

Red and Timmie followed the Quarter Circle Two cattle over to Bald Ridge, and Shorty poked his cattle through the gate in the corner while the rest of us pushed the Seven X L cows and calves up the hill and ducked them into Joe's pasture. Lee and I held the cattle while Joe counted them, and by the time the last pairs filtered through the gate, Red and Timmie had circled back from Bald Ridge. Shorty and his grandkids were headed up the road with his cattle, and it looked like we were done.

"Well," Joe wrote his count in his little spiral notebook, "that's that."

"Grass looks good," Red observed.

"Yep," Joe agreed.

"Did you get a count on my cows?" Red asked Lee, but Lee shook his head.

"How about the Seven X Ls?" Joe wondered, but Lee admitted he hadn't counted those either.

"You want my count?" Joe asked.

"That's alright," Lee smiled. "I have your count at the bank."

"What is that?" Timmie interrupted, and our eyes followed her finger up the hill. A steady stream of cattle were lined out and kicking up the dust at the far end of the pasture, and as we turned to look, cows and calves ran and bucked through the gate nearly a half mile away. The Quarter Circle Two cattle that had been so carefully cut and sent to Bald Ridge had circled around and crossed the canyon, and they were racing back to join the Seven X Ls.

Red looked at Joe.

Joe looked at Red.

"I thought you closed the gate," Joe said.

"I didn't close the gate," Red shook his head. "It's your gate."

"You've got to be kidding," Timmie snarled.

"Do things always go this smoothly?" Lee asked.

"Usually, we run our cattle together," Joe said, and Red looked at him like he had lost his mind, then looked over at the banker.

"That's right," Red agreed. "We try to share the range. No sense being a hog about it."

No one said a word, and the evening air grew deathly quiet, except for the slow, screeching rasp of Timmie Baker sharpening her pocket knife.

Joe branded last on the creek, and everyone came out from town to help, like they did at most of the other brandings. I suppose branding was as much a social event as it was work; if it was really treated as work, we could have gotten the job done in a couple of hours, but with all the help, it usually took a lot longer.

The town people usually got easy jobs, things like vaccinating and carrying a bucket or cleaning hot irons, but some of them, guys like Bobby Baker and Fingers Filiatreau joined people like me and the little kids and wrestled calves. Fingers and Bobby made up for their lack of status by drinking a lot of beer; it was one of their big brags that they could throw and hold a "big" calf with a beer in their hand and never spill a drop. As tight as he was, I always figured Fingers could rope a full grown bull, brand it, castrate it with his teeth, and ride it to town without spilling a drop of beer.

After a couple hours, we usually stopped for a little break, then finished up before lunch, a big feed that invariably had more grub than people to eat it. And, since the same women made the same dish for every branding, those of us on the creek ate the same thing at every meal for nearly a month.

Dick Wilson usually made it out by lunchtime, and if the weather was good, the game warden would come out with his horse saddled, in hopes that someone might ask him to rope a few calves. Depending on whether or not Red or anyone else might need to buy a tractor or some other piece of equipment, Jerry Watson might show up with a cooler full of beer and the latest brochures from the various implement lines. Any number of other folks from town might show up, especially if they had the grandkids visiting and were about to go out of their minds.

Clouds had been bagging up behind Wilsz Mountain all morning, and while the game warden and Joe sought out the last of the slick calves, everyone else had their eyes on the sky. Joe threw a loop and dallied, then drug a black baldy out of the bunch, and Bobby and Fingers ran over to hold it down. Red pulled an iron out of the fire and trotted across the corral, pulling his old gray hat over his eyes.

"Too much wind!" he yelled. "This rain won't amount to much if the wind's blowing five hundred miles an hour."

"You ever hear of a hurricane?" Bobby Baker yelled back. "In a hurricane, the wind blows a hundred miles an hour and they get about a foot of rain!"

"If we get a foot of rain, I'll kiss . . ."

"If we get a foot of rain, we'll just have a flood and none of it will soak in," Shorty interrupted Red.

"I ain't askin' for much, just one good rain to start the grass, that's all."

"She's sure gettin' darker!" Joe coiled his rope and looked up the canyon. The soft smell of rain was heavy on the wind.

"It's sultry enough to rain." Bobby wiped his brow, and he took a big gulp of beer.

"I sure hope it rains," Fingers whispered to Bobby. "I don't mind coming out to help, but I don't like to come out here and get yelled at all day."

"May be too hot to rain," Loper suggested, and everyone glared at him.

"Shut up, Loper!" Red barked.

"Shut up yourself, Red!" Joe yelled. "This is my branding, and if somebody needs yelled at, I'll do the yelling."

"Thank you," Loper smiled.

"Shut up Loper!" Joe pointed a nicotine stained finger at Loper. "If you can't say something good about the weather, don't open your mouth!"

"I wish Loper would keep talking," Fingers whispered again. "I'd rather have them yell at each other than yell at us."

"They yell at everybody," Bobby drained his beer. "All old ranchers go deaf from yelling at each other."

"Wind's outta the West," I said. "That rain's gotta come down the creek."

"It don't *gotta* do any such thing, Pinhead," Victor Wilsz snapped.

"Probably go down Cottonwood," Loper said. "Once it gets past the lake it's gone."

"They sure do get plenty of rain over on Cottonwood," Bobby shook his head.

I gathered up the branding equipment, and Joe counted the cattle out of the corral, while the rest of the help rallied around the cooler.

"Lookin' up won't make it rain!" Joe walked back from the gate, shoving his pencil and notebook into his shirt pocket.

"I've seen this too many times," Jake Murphy shook his head.

Jake Murphy was about the oldest man in the valley, and while the Murphy Place had sold long before Jake was old, but Jake still figured he was a rancher, and he showed up at every branding, mostly just to gather up stories he could tell at the next branding.

According to Jake, he had a trick knee that could predict snow, a bum elbow that told him when it would rain, and bursitis in his shoulder that would tell him which way the wind would blow.

"Storms like this one always bag up and raise a ruckus," Jake rubbed his aching elbow, and then his shoulder. "They might even throw a few big drops at you, but they always swing north and go down Cottonwood."

As if to defy the old man and his joints, the rain came in gigantic drops, wide sheets of cold and wet. Not one person ran for cover or reached for a coat. Everyone just stood and smiled while the water lashed out of the heavy clouds.

The rain stopped.

"Told you so," Jake spit a stream of tobacco juice on the ground, and beneath a thin layer of caked mud, a little plume of dust rose out of the corral.

The sun seemed hotter than before, and we stared off to the north, listening to the thunder rolling as the rain washed down Cottonwood.

"Aw, heck," Joe sighed, "let's go eat."

I was sitting in the shade of an old cottonwood next to the creek, holding onto a piece of cold chicken and stabbing at a chunk of potato salad when a herd of grandchildren ran through the trees, eyes wide, arms flying. They raced from person to person yelling and screaming, until it was finally more than Joe could stand.

"Whoa!" he yelled at the kids, and they all ran over to stand in front of Joe.

They all started in again, their skinny chests rising while they tried to catch their breath, and Joe reached out and put his hand on a little boy's shoulder.

"What's going on?" he asked.

"There's a horse," the little one caught his breath. "There's a big, black horse in the corral, and it's chasing the pinto mare!"

"Well! *That* oughta piss off the sorrel gelding," Red snickered.

The rest of the crew giggled and went back to eating, but I was watching Joe.

He seemed concerned, and he pulled one of the boys close to him and held the little face gently between his palms.

"What did you see?" he asked.

"There's a big black horse in the krel," the little boy said.

"Let's have a look," Joe stood up.

He pulled his hat over his eyes and looked over his shoulder at me. The kids danced along ahead of us, and old Jake limped along behind, rubbing his shoulder.

"See!" the boy climbed the pole fence and pointed. "There it is!"

A stocky black mare stood in the middle of the corral and eyed us placidly. Most of the other horses ignored her. A few of them blew through their noses at her, but the pinto mare stood at the far gate with her head over the top pole, stamping her front foot and nickering.

"She does that." Joe smiled. "She wants out, that's all."

"Not when Tiger is in," I said, and Joe looked at me.

"By God, you're right," he said, and he looked back at the mare.

"What's the black horse?" Jake asked.

The little boys hung over the fence, as if a gust of wind might blow them away.

"I've never seen her," Joe shrugged. "She might be one of Pete's trader horses or something."

"What would you would trade for that fat old wreck?" Jake scoffed.

The mare was obviously old, maybe twenty-five or thirty. Her tail was tangled and matted and drug on the ground, and her mane was ratty and long. Flecks of white grew together to form patches of gray around her eyes and nose. Her hooves were long and cracked, and one ear was split nearly in half. She drooped in the gut, and her withers were sharp. But, she was square and firm in the shoulders, obviously stout, and her head was still attractive.

"Go get Red," Joe told me. "I'll catch the old rip and tie her up. We can take her back to the ranch and call the brand inspector."

Before I could get Red, Joe let out a howl and I ran back to the corral. Hands, wives, and others jumped up from the picnic and charged through the trees behind me.

By the time I got to the corral, Joe was holding his nose and crawling through the manure and dirt, feeling around for his glasses.

"Stupid damn horse," Joe hissed as he crawled, until Maggie climbed over the fence and handed him the mangled glasses. Joe held them up next to his face so that he could see them, then heaved them into the creek.

"Leave me alone!" he yelled. "I'm fine, *just fine!*"

"You're bleeding bad," Bobby Baker bent down and tried to help Joe to his feet.

Joe's face was covered with blood, and his nose was bent. A black circle was beginning to form under each eye, and his left eye was nearly swollen shut.

"It looks like your nose is . . ."

"Broken!" Joe barked. "Of course it is! It's a long way from my heart, but Jake is . . ."

"Dead," Red interrupted.

Everyone turned to look. Jake was sitting with his back against the fence, grinning from ear to ear.

"Awww damn!" Joe sat in the middle of the corral and threw a wad of dirt in the air. "The rain went down Cottonwood and now Jake is dead."

"Are you sure?" someone whispered.

"Oh, hell yes," Loper said, "When those clouds go north of Squaw Bluff, they're headed for Cottonwood."

"What happened?" Dick Wilson asked.

"I went out and caught that mare," Joe pawed at his face, "and she was fine until I pulled the halter over her ears. Then she went plumb nuts and hit me with her head and knocked me down. I don't know if she kicked me or what, but she sure ain't halter broke."

"What happened to Jake?" Fingers looked over at the dead man.

"He started off the fence," Joe said. "He was laughing at me, and all of a sudden he just fell over. I don't know what happened."

"Heart stopped," Red said.

"Shut up!" Joe stood up. "Don't just stand around here! Go get the truck! Load up your stuff and go home! The branding is over. Get these kids out of here . . . load up the horses and get 'em out of this corral! Somebody give me a ride to the clinic!"

"And you!" he pointed at me. "Get rid of that horse!"

People flew in all directions, except of course for old Jake, who leaned against the fence, still smiling, and still dead.

The women loaded the three bean salad, potato salad, barbecued beef, bread, and beans, and when everyone came running back from the corral, they made a hasty retreat. Bobby

Baker and Fingers ran back and started Bobby's car while Maggie and Red sat Joe in the front seat. Shorty soaked a gunny sack in the creek and smashed it against Joe's face. Victor and Loper loaded their horses in Loper's stock truck while the hands climbed in the back with the horses and a cooler full of beer. The kids piled into the cars they came in, and then Bobby Baker pulled away with the engine roaring. Joe was hollering out driving instructions when they disappeared into the willows. Red saddled his horse and galloped through the trees, and as quickly as the pandemonium set in, it was gone.

I pushed my fingers up under my hat and rubbed my eyes with my palms, wondering what to do with the black mare.

When I looked through my fingers, my belly squeezed hard and I blinked to make sure I was right. The old mare was still standing in the middle of the corral, and the pinto mare had wandered back toward the feed bunk. Joe's horse was rolling around in the dirt, and a pair of magpies were sitting on the fence, their black tails shining green in the hot sun.

Jake was still sitting against the pole fence.

I looked at the yard where everyone had been eating, but every single car and truck was gone.

"Heyyyyyyyyy!" I yelled through the trees, "come baaaaaaack!"

I ran down the road a ways, then ran back and climbed to the top pole of the corral and waved my arms and yelled at each car and truck as they raced through the gate and headed for town; I could hear the hands laughing and drinking in the back of the stock truck, and I could see Joe's mouth moving, and his arms waving, but no one looked back.

"You forgot Jake!" I yelled, and then I slid off the fence and sat down.

Joe expected me to take care of the stupid old nag by the time he got home, and that was trouble enough, without having to figure out what to do with Jake.

"I wish it would rain," I sighed.

I leaned against the fence and stared at the old man. I couldn't just leave Jake sitting in the corral with the flies and magpies and hand him over to the scavengers, but I couldn't very well dress him out like a deer and hang him in the meathouse, either.

"Jake?" I whispered.

"Yo, Jake," I waved my hand in front of his eyes.

"C'mon, Jake," I pushed at his foot with my boot, and before I could grab him, Jake fell over in a heap.

His eyes were still open, and he stared out toward the creek, but he wasn't blinking and he wasn't moving a whole lot.

"Aw Jake," I whined, "you really are dead."

I stood up and wandered around in a circle, then threw a handful of rocks at the magpies, who hopped gracefully a few inches out of range, then settled back on the pole above Jake's body.

"How could a bunch of people leave a branding and forget a dead man?" I asked, and I considered my options.

I couldn't saddle a horse and ride for the nearest place, because when the crew left, they had loaded my horse and saddle. I thought about riding the pinto mare bareback down to Red's place, but if I did that, I would have to leave Jake to the magpies and flies.

"Surely, someone will remember us," I thought, and I turned around to chase a magpie off Jake.

"Yeeuuh," I gagged. "I sure wish you'd died closer to the road, Jake."

I thought about loading him on my back and heading out, but Jake was a big man when he was young and fit, and now that he was old and dead, I guessed him to weigh as much as some of the calves we had branded. Even if I carried him out to the road, there wasn't much chance anyone would come along. But, if I could get him loaded on my back, I figured that maybe

I could at least get him into the old meathouse, where the magpies and flies wouldn't get him.

I rolled him over as gently as I could, until he was lying on his back. Not quite sure what to do next, I put his arms over his chest and tried to push his eyelids shut. The left eye stayed about half closed, but the other one stared at me. I decided not to fiddle around with Jake's face any more.

"Okay, Jake," I warned him. "I'm gonna pick you up and carry you over to the meathouse."

I grabbed his arm and pulled it around my neck, but there was no way I could get him onto my back with one arm, so I tried to lift him up by the belly. I couldn't even get my arms around his big middle. In the end, I had to get down in the dirt and manure and burrow under him until I could rise to my knees, and finally, to my feet.

When I got to the gate, I discovered I couldn't hold onto Jake and lift the latch at the same time, so I leaned him against the gate and lifted the latch and when the gate flew open, Jake's weight spun me around and I lit on my back. Jake fell on top of me, and while I was trying my level best to get out from under him, the pinto mare and Joe's rope horse galloped through the open gate.

By the time I was free, I had lost some of my concern for Jake's feelings, and I grabbed him by the feet and pulled him to the meathouse. I took a minute to catch my breath, then hauled him up the steep steps by the arms and latched the screen door. So much for the magpies and flies.

I wandered back down to the corral, hoping that I might figure out some plan to deal with the old mare, but nothing came to mind. The last thing I wanted to do was catch her, since I would likely end up with a broken nose like Joe or dead like Jake, and there wasn't anyone around to drive me into town or carry me to the meathouse.

In the end, it didn't make any difference.

The black mare was dead too.

"Wow," I shook my head. "This is turning into quite a day."

A big drop of rain hit me on the cheek.

The bank of clouds that had gone down Cottonwood had circled back around the mountain and this time, it looked like maybe they would stick around. I leaned against the pole gate and watched the lightning and thunder work slowly down the creek. A wall of black rain led the procession, and a good blast of wind came in front of the clouds.

Suddenly, I realized that the screens on the meathouse would do a great job of keeping flies and magpies away, but if I left Jake there, he would get cold and wet.

The dark clouds opened and the rain came with a vengeance. I ran back to the meathouse and grabbed Jake by the heels, then turned around and pulled him back toward the barn, where he would stay dry.

Once I got him inside, I tried to rest him in a pile of straw, where he would be comfortable, and then I stuck some boards in the windows so that the magpies couldn't get in. The flies were bad, but it was the magpies that worried me most; magpies go for the eyes first. Finally, when I was satisfied I had protected Jake from the rain and the birds, I started out to the road.

I'd gone far enough to get soaking wet when I thought about what I would say to the occasional passerby who might happen to be out for a drive in the rain.

"I have a dead man up here in the barn. Would you come up and give him a ride to town?"

That would never do.

I turned around, walked back to the barn and plopped down next to Jake. The rain rattled on the roof, and I stared into the gray light until shadows ate the inside of the barn. Old Jake was dead, and I wasn't, but it seemed such a fine line. He was still smiling, and my head was trying to run away from me.

Joe showed up just before dark, his eyes black and his nose as big as a garden vegetable, and Buck Martin and Red Barnes followed along in the county ambulance. It was still raining, a good, steady drizzle that the country needed, and I sat on the pole fence and watched while Buck and Red carted Jake out of the barn. They didn't seem to care that they were letting him get wet, but I didn't say anything. I was pretty tired of taking care of Jake Murphy.

The ambulance pulled out, all four tires spinning in the mud, and thirty miles from town, Buck turned on the red lights and siren, as if maybe they would alert Jake to the problem he was having.

Joe came over and rested his arms on one of the poles.

"Good rain," he sighed.

"Yep," I nodded.

"We sure need it," Joe put his head on his hands.

"Yep," I agreed.

"I take it you're not too happy," he said, and I think he was trying to frown, but with his face all puffed up like a frog, I couldn't really tell.

"Yep," I said.

"Sorry about leaving Jake," Joe apologized. "We forgot."

"How could you leave him like that?" I asked. "How could everyone drive away and leave Jake up here all . . . all *dead*?"

"People have a lot on their mind this time of year," Joe said, and then he took a deep breath and let it out.

"That's no excuse," he shook his head. "We were selfish."

"No kidding," I slid off of the fence and walked toward the truck.

"Tell me something," Joe followed along, half a step behind me. Out of the corner of my eye, I could see him slide his hands in the pockets of his jeans, and he stared at the ground as he walked along.

"What's that?" I asked, looking over my shoulder.

"Are you more concerned because we left Jake or because we left you?"

I stopped, and Joe ran right into me, then caught himself on my arm. We stood there in the rain and mud and looked at each other until I took a deep breath and looked at the ground.

"It was wrong to leave him," I said.

"It was," Joe agreed.

"It was wrong to leave *me*," I added.

"No," Joe shook his head, "it wasn't."

I stared at the ground and the rain rattled off the brim of my hat. Joe stood next to me and let me think for myself. Finally I let out my air and headed for the pickup.

"How's your nose?" I asked.

"I'll live," Joe grinned.

"Good," I sighed. "'Cause I wouldn't know whether to put you in the meathouse or the barn."

The Friendly Creek National Forest was actually a forest for a long time before it was discovered by the government, and the people on Friendly Creek called it a forest for many years before they were probably authorized to do so. Maybe it was just a local forest, but it had trees and grass and other forest things. Before that, it was an ocean or a swamp, but that is mere speculation, since there was nobody around to write about it in the *Friendly Creek Sentinel.*

Maybe the editor got eaten by a brontosaurus or something.

Anyway, it was a forest when the Indians lived there, and it was a forest when the fur traders lived there, and it was a forest when the Barnes and Wilsz families settled the valley. Tiehacks cut the trees, and deer, elk, and moose ate the grass and it was still a forest. Miners picked the coal and panned the gold and it was still a forest.

In fact, after several centuries of actually being a forest, the only difference between being a forest and a *national* forest seemed to be the introduction of the Forest Service, a pack of hands who wore green shirts, Canadian Mountie hats, and apparently worshipped a bear. They moved in, moved up and moved out. They built lookout towers, fought fires, marked trees, built campsites, and graded roads, and when they weren't doing that, they hauled garbage, marked trails, fixed fences and drank a few beers at the Hoosegow. Some of them rode in the annual rodeo, and some were volunteer firemen. They brought their kids out to the brandings, and a lot of them punched cows with the ranchers, just to get a feel for the lifestyle and shoot the breeze. But about the time people on the creek got to know them, they were moved off to some other proud *national* forest.

The rationale behind this official "head 'em up-move 'em out" employment practice was to prevent any of the "unbiased" federal employees from getting to like the place where they lived. Surely, if that were to happen, the federal employees would be rendered totally inept and incapable of decision-making, and there was simply not enough room in Washington for all the inept individuals who couldn't make a decision.

Most of these rangers were foresters, people trained to cut down trees so they could grow new ones, but some were water engineers and others were college educated range managers.

One was an accountant who got lost on the back side of

Wilsz Mountain, leaving unsupervised underlings to spend the entire year's budget hiring helicopters to find him.

He was promptly promoted to Washington, D.C., and a new ranger was assigned to Friendly Creek.

"So, who's the new ranger?" Red Barnes asked.

"Some guy named Woods," Joe said. "Sam 'Smoky' Woods."

"He hates cows," Shorty added.

"How could a man around here hate cows?" Victor asked.

"He thinks they're some sort of varmint," Shorty answered.

"How do you know that?" Bobby Baker demanded. Bobby took great pride in being a purveyor of information, and he had somehow missed the cow-hating nature of Smoky Woods.

"He said so," Shorty said. "I heard him in the mercantile. He was talking to a hippie sort of woman wearin' them funny earth shoes."

"An *environmentalist!* He was talking to an environmentalist?" Joe scoffed. "Here? You mean to tell me that there's an environmentalist walking around in the Merc?"

"I think it was his wife." Shorty nodded.

"His wife!" Victor stood up. "Are you sure?"

"That can't be true," Carl Loper scoffed.

"I'm not sure it was his wife," Shorty confessed, "but she was one of them woodsy, mossy types, wearing them weird shoes with her head covered up in a hippie bandana."

"That's it?" Bobby Baker snorted.

"Nope," Shorty paused for effect. "That ain't it!"

"Well spit it out!" Joe snapped.

"She wasn't wearin' no bra!" Shorty smiled, and he folded his hands on the bar.

Victor slammed a fist on the table. "This woman was wandering around in the Merc without a bra?"

"What about the ranger?!" Joe moaned.

"What about him?" a voice called out from the door, and Sam Woods and his braless wife swung through the door.

93

Everyone jumped up to meet the new ranger, each of them shaking hands and smiling slyly at Mrs. Woods.

"Care to join us?" Loper pulled out a chair.

"I don't drink with *permittees*," Woods smiled. He made the word "permittee" sound vile and wicked.

"Got a place to keep your horses?" Joe smiled.

"I hate horses," the ranger said.

"How can you hate horses?" Red asked.

"You must be a tree man." Victor guessed.

"Attorney," the ranger corrected. "Environmental law."

"I heard you was from Georgia," Shorty smiled

"I'm surprised you don't know more than that, the way you were following me around the grocery store," the ranger hissed and he set a hiking boot up on a chair.

"I'm calling a meeting of the users of the forest for tomorrow night," he announced.

"Well, what the heck!" Victor waved at the other ranchers. "We're the users of the forest. We can hold the meeting right here!"

"The meeting will be at seven o' clock at the library," Sam Woods said, and he picked his tooth, spun on his heel, and walked out the door.

"We got trouble," Joe sighed.

At seven o' clock the next night, the ranchers and the ranger and the ranger's wife were assembled in the library. The only other person in attendance was Ted Phillips, an outfitter who took hunters and fishermen into the timber to chase elk, bears and fish. Ted sat in the front row, his hearing aid in his pocket.

"The last forest I was on," Woods began, "the cattlemen thought they could get away with murder."

Ted Phillips popped his hearing aid back into his ear, not wanting to miss any gossip about murder.

"It was my suspicion there, as it is here, that you are all

94

putting more cattle on the forest than you are allowed," Woods stalked in front of the children's books and glared at everyone.

"That's stupid!" Ted yelled. "I don't even have a cow."

"Then go home!" Woods snapped.

Ted pulled his hearing aid out and left, cussing the government as he went.

"As I was saying," Woods continued, "it is my assumption that you are all either running more cattle than allowed, longer than allowed, or in areas where you are not allowed."

Victor allowed as how he figured this new ranger was a prejudiced son-of-a-bitch.

"Care to share your comments with all of us?!" the ranger whirled and pointed at Victor.

"Sure," Victor stood up. "I said that you ain't been here a day and you're already calling us criminals. I guess I figure you're kind of a biased son-of-a-bitch."

"I have been here *two* days," Smoky corrected, "and you have decided that I am a 'son-of-a-bitch.'"

"Everybody is some kind of son-of-a-bitch," Joe tried to explain the local terminology. "I mean, Shorty here is a Scotch son-of-a-bitch. . ."

"Shorty is a little, tightwad son-of-a-bitch," Victor put in.

"And Victor Wilsz is a fat son-of-a-bitch," Shorty offered.

"And you act like maybe you're a no-good son-of-a-bitch," Red smiled at the ranger.

"I intend to count every animal you try to herd onto the Friendly Creek National Forest," the ranger advised. "And, it is my guess that I will find each of you attempting to cheat me in one way or another, but you can be assured that I know every way that you will try to cheat me, and I will catch you."

He paused to let his threat sink in, but everyone had been expecting something far worse, and no one in the room could think of anything to say. If the ranger had spent just a few more days on the creek, he might have discerned the fact that there was no glory in cheating the government; the real test was in getting a few bites of grass from each other.

"Which of you is Victor Wilsz?" he asked.

Victor uncrossed his arms and held up his hand.

"According to the documentation in the office, you are the first to go onto the forest," the ranger read from a manila folder with a silver clip on top. "Is that correct?"

"First on, first off," Victor agreed.

"You will move cattle to the Wilsz creek allotment on June 15," the ranger continued.

"Well, about then," Victor scratched his head. "unless we get rain or a lot of snow like last winter and it's too wet. Then we wait. If the forest is too dry and we have feed down below, we can wait then too. Come to think of it, we wait most every year."

"That wasn't a question," the Ranger said. "Your permit specifies that you will go onto the forest *June 15,* and that is the day you will go on the forest, and you will turn your cattle through the Bobcat Creek watergap."

"We don't always go up Bobcat Creek," Victor explained. "If we run into a snag, we let 'em drift over Lightning Ridge and work their way up Skunk Creek."

"I am reading *directly* from your permit, Mr. Wilsz," Ranger Sam corrected, "It says those cattle are to be delivered through the Bobcat Creek water gap, *not* over the hill on Skunk Creek or Lightning Ridge. Now, I intend to see those livestock at the Bobcat Creek watergap on *June 15*. When will they arrive?"

"What the hell are you talking about?" Victor blew a gasket. "How do I know what time we'll get 'em there? We've gotta gather 'em, mother 'em, and drive 'em seven miles through the timber!"

"Well then," the ranger retreated, "*approximately* what time?"

"What the hell does it matter when they get there?" Joe asked, surprised to hear himself rise in defense of Victor Wilsz.

"I plan to be there to count the cattle," the ranger paced, "and I see no reason to sit out there all day waiting."

"Well, hell!" Victor yelled. "Saddle a horse and ride along! You can count 'em seven or eight times before we get there!"

"I was not sent here to punch your doggies," the ranger shook his head. "Have the cattle at the gate no later than four."

"You don't know a doggie from a dogie," Red scoffed. "How do you plan to count 'em?"

"I may know a lot more than you think," Woods chuckled, and he declared the meeting adjourned.

On the assigned day, Victor was his usual nasty self. And as his mood grew darker and darker the Wilz crew pushed the cattle harder and harder. Victor had wanted to arrive earlier than the ranger,  but a couple of runbacks and seven miles later, Victor's eyes had folded into beady little slits. The cows were on the fight, and the calves were confused; one wrong move and they would turn and run back down the mountain. Victor and his hands hollered and yelled and kept the cattle moving across the road and down the draw to the gate on Bobcat Creek.

It was three-fifteen.

Victor's Morgan stud was lathered up when Victor charged across the road and let out a scream that sent men and cattle in every direction.

Smoky Woods had his regulation green pickup parked in the middle of the Bobcat Creek gate, and he and his assistant were standing on the hood, hollering and waving and trying to count cows.

The cows had seen all of the humans they cared to in a day, and the green pickup in the gate was all she wrote. Victor and the hands tried to hold them, but the cattle milled, turned and finally raced past the cowboys, down the mountain.

Victor's face was as red as a beefsteak, his teeth clenched and his eyes black, and he rode through the milling cattle on a dead run, until he reached the gate where Smoky Woods stood dumbly on the hood of the pickup.

"You didn't think I'd really be here, did you?" Smoky chuckled. "You had more cattle than your permit allows, and when you found out I was really here, you turned them around and let them go back down the hill, didn't you?"

Victor howled again, jumped off his horse, and chased Woods over the top of the pickup and into the trees.

Victor was at least sixty years old, and Smoky Woods coudn't have been much past forty, but Victor caught him fifty yards into the timber. After that, there was a considerable amount of whining and thumping. By the time he dragged Smoky Woods out of the trees by the collar, Victor was lumbering around like an angered bear, and the Deputy Ranger locked the pickup doors and rolled up the windows.

"Did we park too close to the gate?" he asked.

The question provoked another howl from Victor and probably saved the life of Sam "Smoky" Woods, because Victor dropped him and took a run at the green pickup, nearly knocking it over before he gave up and went off to catch his horse.

Now, even a dude would have racked that little incident up to education and learned something, but about all the new ranger seemed to learn was not to park in the middle of the gate and *never* to underestimate the footspeed of a sixty year old cowboy when properly provoked.

Woods pressed criminal charges, but dropped them for a

number of reasons. First, Victor's oldest daughter was the justice of the peace. Second, the ranger was't hurt that bad. Third, Victor had beaten up a lot of people and none of them ever pressed any charges. And, finally, the only witness to the whole thing was the deputy ranger, who had a good deal more sense than his boss and testified that he couldn't actually see what happened back in the trees. The court ruled that Victor's explanation that the ranger had tripped over a log was reasonable, and suggested that the ranger spend a little more time with the people and a little less with his rule books.

"Why don't you forget counting cows and fix fence?" Bobby Baker suggested to Smoky Woods the next night at the Hoosegow.

"I can tell you they don't have too many cows," the banker Lee Willoughby offered. "I know how many they sold last year, and I'm telling you, the numbers aren't there."

"Look," Fingers suggested, "these guys have sold off a lot of their herds. None of them has as many cows as he's allowed to have."

"You're a local," the ranger sneered. "I suppose you would defend these people if they murdered me."

"I doubt they'll murder you," Jerry Watson speculated. "But if they did, I reckon you'd have a tough time gettin' a jury,"

"We shall see," the ranger said, and he placed his pinched hat on his head and walked out the door.

Two days later we pushed Red's herd through the gate on Dutchman's Creek. Red sat on his horse and counted cows through. On the other side of the gate, faces painted black and green, little clickers in hand, Woods and his deputy sat in a sagebrush fort and counted them as well.

"One hundred and eighty-six head," the ranger announced after the cattle had filed through the gate.

Red took out his spiral notebook and pencil, looked over at the ranger, wrote the correct figure, 275, in his book, and before anyone could offer a correction, declared that there were indeed one hundred and eighty- six head of cattle on the forest.

When Smoky heard about the error, he curled his lip and ordered another count, but Fingers reminded him that the cattle were all mixed up, since the fences weren't fixed.

"Well, then," Smoky said, "I'll fine the permittees who haven't fixed the fence."

"Uh, we're supposed to fix the fence," his deputy advised.

"Who is we?" Smoky asked.

"The Forest Service," the deputy reported.

With that, Woods fired his assistant for not fixing the fence, but he had to hire him back because even a forest ranger with a law degree can't fire a federal employee.

Smoky Woods was determined to count cattle, and equally determined to count the next bunch accurately, but this time, he kept his plans a secret, sending the rumor mill into overtime.

On the last day of June, Joe's cattle were scattered in the meadow below the forest. It was only three miles from the meadow to the gate, but the cows and calves and bulls had to be prodded up a steep sidehill trail, through an old corner of a log and block fence. On a really good day, if the feed in the valley was short and the heel flies were biting, it wasn't unreasonable to start at daylight and be done by noon, but it was a lot more common for the drive to take a full day.

This day was close to perfect. Not a moment after the cattle were gathered, a heel fly bit an old horned Hereford cow and she threw her head in the air and headed for the mountains on a high lope. The other old cows followed, stringing out single file, and within an hour, they had started up the sidehill trail. When they topped the ridge, they eased into the timber and spread out to graze, but they were anxious to get up into the high country.

"I wonder if that forest ranger is up here," Red lit a smoke.

"I doubt it," Joe scoffed. "That boy should have learned his lesson by now. He might be OK with the law books, but he's a damn fool when it comes to cattle."

"The problem," Red suggested, "is that he ain't got that figured out yet."

We worked in behind the cows and jacked them up a little bit. Joe rode up to keep an eye on the lead, and the rest of us fell in behind and made strange noises with our mouths to hurry the calves along. The lead cow was no less than two hundred yards from the gate when Joe waved at me to come up front, and since he wasn't hollering, I figured something was wrong.

I loped around the cattle and caught up. Joe pointed into the timber and I could make out the faint outline of a forest green pickup.

The lead cow had gotten about fifty yards from the gate, but she wasn't trotting; she was standing in a little clearing, ears forward, tail was barely moving. Finally, she took a half step backwards and turned around to bawl at her calf.

"Woods!" Joe yelled, and his voice echoed in the timber.

A few more cows started bawling at their calves, and from the back of the bunch, I could hear Maggie and Red doing their best to keep the cattle pointed toward the forest.

"Woods!" Joe yelled again.

"What in the hell is that idiot up to now?" Red asked.

"I got a bad feeling about this," Joe said. "We'd better push 'em hard."

We rode, yelled, and slapped our legs with our ropes for what seemed an eternity, while the cattle milled and circled and bawled.

Then, when it seemed that we were caught in the middle of a runback, a big old black bull took a jump at the horned cow and she trotted toward the gate where she stopped, sniffed around, looked back at the herd, and then stepped through as neatly as if it were a debutante ball for old cows. The bull curled his upper lip and made bull noises, and the other bulls charged out of the bunch. An old cow followed, and then another, and the herd began to line out through the gate.

"Love conquers all," Joe sighed, and he pulled out his smokes and lit a match on his chaps.

Just as he lifted the match to his cigarette, a bright red blotch bloomed square between his eyes and he fell backwards off his horse.

"Take cover!" I yelled, unsure of who would be ambushing us, but equally certain that some sort of ambush was taking place.

When the shooting started, some of the cows ran through the gate, some ran onto the forest and some ran back down the hill. A bunch of heifers jumped the fence and just ran.

I decided there was no hope in holding the herd so I jumped off my horse and crouched behind a tree. A ball of bright red paint splattered off the trunk in front of me. Red had been hit in the chest and the leg, and he was peeking through the limbs of a deadfall snag. Maggie's colt got it in the flank below the saddle leather, and went bucking down the rock slide. Maggie and the colt would have a wild ride before they hit bottom, but Maggie could handle it. Shorty must have been hit in the head, because he was on the ground, looking dead. I tried to get out to where Joe's horse was standing and took a hit in the gut, then another in the shoulder, and finally crawled back to the shelter of the tree where I had left Joe.

The cattle were long gone, scattered across the mountain like wildflowers.

"What happened?" Joe sat up and pawed at his face.

"We were ambushed," I said.

"*Ambushed?*" Joe looked at me, red paint spread from his forehead to the tip of his nose.

"You've been shot between the eyes with paint," I said.

"We were attacked by painters?" Joe frowned. "Why would painters attack us?"

"Beats me," I said. "All I know is that you got shot, and then they shot the cattle and all hell broke loose."

Joe looked to the sky, and his whole face lit up.

"Woods!" he yelled, and I followed his eyes to the top of an ancient pine tree.

Forty feet above the ground, Sam "Smoky" Woods and three of his deputies were perched in a portable deer hunting stand, pistol barrels dripping.

The rest of the cowboys staggered over and stared up into the tree.

"What are you doing up there?" Red yelled.

"We were trying to mark the cattle," Woods yelled back.

"Why were you doing that?" Joe yelled.

Smoky Woods paced on the little platform while those of us down on the ground stared up at him like baby birds waiting for food.

"I thought if I marked the cattle with paint, I would be able to count them!" the ranger yelled.

"You missed most of the cattle," Red yelled, "but you shot Shorty in the head twice!"

"It was a mistake!" the ranger hollered.

"It couldn't a' been a mistake!" Shorty screamed. "You shot me twice!"

"I'm sorry!" the ranger yelled again. "It was a mistake! I thought it would work and it didn't!"

The forest was silent. Not even a squirrel dared to chatter.

The ranchers looked at one another, then stared up into the tree, and looked back at one another.

"I say we saw 'em out of the tree," Shorty finally suggested.

"That's a horrible idea!" Woods yelled, and his deputies nodded vigorous agreement.

"Well," Joe kicked a dirt clod and looked at the rangers. "What do *you* figure we oughta do?"

"We could meet at the Hoosegow and talk about this!"

Woods screeched. "I'd be happy to buy a round!"

"I'll buy *two* rounds if I can saw 'em out of the tree," Shorty offered, and he looked over at Joe.

Joe furrowed his brow and thought it over. Finally, he caught his horse and swung into the saddle, and the rest of us followed suit. When everyone was mounted, Joe looked up the tree at the ranger.

"There were four hundred, thirty two head," he yelled. "How many did you count?"

"Four thirty two!" the ranger smiled.

Joe stopped, rode back to the base of the tree, then looked up again. "How many?" he asked.

"To be honest, I couldn't count them at all," Woods sighed.

"By God, I believe you'll work out after all," Joe grinned. "We'll be waiting at the Hoosegow."

Sooner or later, every young cowboy reaches that stage where the "glamour" of stringing wire, punching cows, pounding posts and irrigating gets worn pretty thin. When that time comes, there isn't much of anything on a ranch that quite stacks up to the lure of the long old rodeo road.

Usually, this determination directly parallels puberty and a sudden realization of exactly what it is that fills out the tight denim stretched over barrel racer's buns.

For years, I kept the latest copy of "Rodeo Sports News" under my pillow, and every night, I imagined the roar of the crowd in places like Cheyenne, Calgary and Pendleton when a bronc rider topped off a bad one. Eight seconds in the saddle meant another check in the bank, and more importantly, a few seconds on the back of a bronc would pay off in spades in the back seat of a club-cab pickup. If the lure of the rodeo was strong, the thought of a pair of red roper boots on the floor of the pickup was stronger.

Come to think of it, no matter how old a cowboy gets there is nothing in the world as pretty or as powerful as a cowgirl peeking out from under a flat-brimmed hat, lacy white blouse on top, tight jeans and red boots on the bottom.

A big win at Cheyenne was a full year's pay on most

ranches, and if a cowboy drew up right and cashed in at Pendleton, Denver and the other big rodeos, he could be knocking on six figures by the time he was old enough to vote. From one rodeo to the next, it was eight seconds in the saddle, the roar of the crowd, red boots and tight blue jeans.

On Friendly Creek, the only roaring I ever heard was Victor Wilsz. I was supposed to have a little dab of money in the bank, but it was still in Joe's account, and the closest I ever got to a pair of red boots was one time when a pair of barrel racers broke down on the highway. I got their outfit fixed and they apologized for keeping me from my farming.

"Hey!" I yelled at the departing horse trailer. "I'm not a farmer! I'm a *cowboy!*"

Every Spring when the weather got decent, the cowboys on Friendly Creek loaded up their trailers and headed to town for the local "jackpot" rodeos that were held every Saturday night, and some of the better hands took a little run around to towns like Jackson and Cody, where they had real rodeos, with added money and stuff like that. But, the jackpot was about as far as most of the locals went, and nearly everybody around had a job to do on Saturday night.

Joe roped with Shorty, and Red roped with Woody Schmoe, an old hand from over on Horse Creek who couldn't rope a dead bull. He and Red only roped so they wouldn't have to work, and it gave them a reason to stop by the Hoosegow afterwards. Red's abilities at raising and breaking good horses were always evident, and he sold a lot of young horses at the rodeo grounds and even more out in front of the Bar. If nothing else, Woody bought a new heeling horse every year, just to keep up with Red.

"When you get as old as I am," Woody rationalized, "you need a younger horse to keep up with the kids."

Victor Wilsz was the chute boss for the rough stock, and Davey Boyd opened the gate for the ropers. Loper was the arena director and judge, which meant that he scored all of the rides and waved a red flag when people caught something. Maggie Barnes and Edna Loper were the official timers, and Lee Willoughby was in charge of the money.

When they weren't roping, Joe and Red rode around the arena and tried to "pick up" the bronc riders, but most of the time, the bronc riders gave up and let go before either man could get to them, with the end result that Red and Joe ran over more riders than they saved.

Most of the hired hands on the creek seemed to be more interested in rodeo than work, and almost every one of them had a bronc riding outfit, a horse and a team roping partner. It seemed like every new hand on the creek was some bronc rider, bull rider, or roper who had been an ace rodeo hand somewhere else, been "blackballed" on the circuit, injured "real bad over at a perf in Moab" or afflicted with some other malady not caused by themselves. But, out of all the hands around, only Jimmy Wilsz was recognized as a real top hand, and Jimmy rode bucking horses like they were on a merry-go-round.

I helped out wherever I could, but like the dogs on the ranch, I was mostly encouraged to stay in the truck. My break came one night when Davey Boyd got so looped that he couldn't open the timed events chute, and since his whole crew of workers were as looped as he was, I was pressed into service as the chute loader, chute opener and barrier judge. I also held onto a stinking goat in the middle of the arena so that the women could ride up in a big lather, jump off their horses and tie the damn thing down, despite the fact that the goat had been tied up more times than poor Nell, that girl who Dudley Doright was always saving on the cartoons. Every Saturday night, the women galloped up like Snidley Whiplash, jumped off and tied up the goat, then waved their arms in triumph, and every Saturday night, I stood there like old Dudley and rescued the goat so the next girl could tie the poor critter up again.

The women actually did this for money.

When I wasn't rescuing the goat, I herded steers and calves around on foot, untied ropes, rolled barrels into the arena so that the women could race them (the women always won) and sold beer in the Lion's Club beer shack. I wasn't much of a rodeo hand, but my ten percent of the beer sales was more profitable than winning the "All Around Cowboy" for an entire year, so I kept my mouth shut and let Jimmy Wilsz do the strutting.

That all changed when Joe hired an old cowhand by the name of Stovepipe Pilch. According to none other than Stovepipe Pilch, he had been a rough rider down around the Pecos River, where he claimed he had been known as "Bullet," since he threw a loop like it was shot out of a rifle, and never missed.

"There was a time," he told me, "when I woulda' bet a thousand cash that I could toss a loop through a mesquite bush and catch a calf out of the bunch on a dead run."

"Wow," I said, mostly because I didn't know what else to say.

"Back then," he went on, "they called me 'Loop' down around the Pecos, 'cause I was so handy with a rope."

"I thought they called you 'Bullet,'" I reminded him.

"Bullet Loop," he said. "They called me 'Bullet Loop.'"

Stovepipe was pretty handy with a rope alright, and if just

catching calves was all that went into winning, he might have beaten everyone who ever rode into the arena. But, unfortunately for Stovepipe, he was missing an eye, and every time he tried to get off his horse and tie a calf, he fell down. As a result, old Stovepipe had gone into the business of rodeo advising, which mostly amounted to telling me tall tales about his days on the big roundups along the Pecos River.

"When I was younger," he remembered, "all the cowboys called me Bronc, 'cause there was never a bronc I *wouldn't* ride or *couldn't* ride."

After a couple of beers, it was nothing for Stovepipe to give himself a dozen nicknames, and he could ramble on for hours about riding broncs and roping vicious steers that had been wild in the mesquite and the rocks for years. He claimed to have punched cows and chased Senoritas with the likes of Jim Shoulders, Freckles Brown and the rest of the real rodeo hands who rode for the challenge and not for the money, legitimate legends in their own right.

"Old Stovepipe says I'm built just right for the rough stock," I told Joe. "He says I'd make a heck of a bronc rider."

"Stovepipe only has one eye," Joe reminded me.

"He's gonna let me use his riggin'," I added. "He bought it off of Jim Shoulders the year he won the World."

"Why would Jim Shoulders sell his riggin' to Stovepipe?" Joe asked.

"Maybe Jim Shoulders won a new one at some rodeo," I guessed.

"He won a bareback rigging at a rodeo?" Joe scoffed. "They give away a *whole damn saddle* at Friendly Creek Days, and it's too small for guys like Jim Shoulders to bother with. Who ever heard of winning a bareback riggin' at a rodeo?"

"I've heard of people winning buckles at rodeos," he went on, "but never a bareback riggin'. . ."

"Who cares where Jim Shoulders got it?" I snapped. For the

life of me, I couldn't see why nobody would take my rodeo career seriously.

"Did you ever notice that Stovepipe has a different nickname every time he tells a story?" Joe asked. "I'll bet that riggin' is broke or wore out or else old Stovepipe probably *stole* it from Jim Shoulders."

I had to admit the only evidence that the rigging had belonged to Shoulders was Stovepipe's word for it, but since that was the only part of Stovepipe's story that never changed, I figured it had to be true.

"So, when do you ride this bucking horse?" Joe asked.

"Well," I told him, "I'm in training right now. Stovepipe's been coaching me on my rhythm and all, and I've been squeezing a ball of wax and workin' on my spurring action."

"Squeezing a ball of wax?" Joe lifted an eyebrow.

"Yeah," I said. "It makes my forearms stronger. A bronc carries a lot of power."

"That's crazy," he decided.

"Maybe," I stood up, "but, I'm done milking already and you're still rubbing your arms."

"So maybe you oughta' become a milk cow rider," he said.

"You'll see," I told him, "I'm gonna' ride that old barrel up in the barn tonight."

"Oh!" Joe nodded. "Of course! You'll be entering the barrel riding at the jackpots. I thought that was a girl's event."

"It's a bucking barrel!" I said. "It's the best way to get some licks in before I start ridin' bares."

"I thought you was gonna' ride bucking horses," Joe snickered. "Now, you're tellin' me you're gonna' ride a barrel and a bear? What am I gonna' rope . . . pigs?"

"You won't be laughin' when I'm in the money," I said.

"You don't get money for just going to the rodeo," he smiled. "You've gotta' ride the horse first."

"I know that!" I tossed my sock full of resin in the air and

110

caught it, letting the white powder settle on my jeans. "That's why I'm training now, so when I get down on my bronc, I'll have a shot at the cash."

"You make more money selling beer than any of the riders make," Joe shook his head. "Why would you give up a good deal like that to turn out like Jimmy Wilsz?"

"It isn't just the money," I said.

"So you think squeezing that ball of wax and spurring a bale of hay is gonna' do the trick?"

"I may not win it all this year," I said, " but riding broncs is in my blood. I can feel it. Rodeo is my destiny."

"Destiny?" Maggie poked her head out of the kitchen and looked us over. "What is this talk about destiny?"

"Parker's going to become a barrel rider," Joe said, and he poured himself a cup of coffee.

The "cook's helper," a girl named Carol, looked up from a pan of sizzling bacon and stared at me with her big brown eyes, and I wandered over to the table and sat down.

"You're going to ride in the rodeo?" she smiled, and I gave her a hard, bronc rider's stare.

"Uh, yeah, well I'm training right now." I said. "Stovepipe says I'm built just right for the rough stock."

"Stovepipe only has one eye," Maggie yelled from the kitchen, "and when he drinks, he sees double out of it."

"What are you going to ride?" Carol asked, her big brown eyes dancing with excitement.

"Uh, bareback," I smiled, "and saddle broncs too."

"I hope you're going to get this over with soon," Joe sighed. "We seem to be running out of hay in the corral. It appears that most of the bales have been spurred to smithereens."

"What happened to the hay?" Carol asked.

"I've been riding it," I mumbled, "for practice."

"You're riding hay?" Carol looked puzzled, but then, Carol was never going to impress anyone with her wits.

"Not any more," I announced. "Tonight, I'm gonna' ride that bucking barrel in the barn."

"I'll call Casey Tibbs and tell him you're on the circuit," Joe advised, "But before you spur the barrel into submission or kill yourself, would you please set the water in the Big Meadow and open the south ditch and finish that stretch of fence between the Newly Place and Loper's horse pasture?"

Maggie handed me a lunch. I pulled my new hat down over my eyes and stuck my ball of wax in my hip pocket.

"Is that a new hat?" Carol asked.

"Well, uh, yes it is," I smiled.

"Looks kind of like a bronc rider's hat," she grinned.

At least Carol seemed to think I was built just right to ride the rough stock, and she looked a lot better in red boots and tight blue jeans than Joe ever would.

By morning, my new hat had taken a beating, but I had it pulled down over my ears anyway.

"Since when do you wear your hat to breakfast?" Joe asked.

I took the hat off and leaned on my hand.

"What is that on the side of your face?" Maggie asked, and she bent over to have a look.

"Oh that?" I smiled, "that's nothing."

"Don't tell me it's nothing," she scolded. "What have you done to your face?"

"I sort of boogered it up on the barrel."

"How?" Maggie asked, her eyes growing narrower.

"Well," I told her, "I was riding the barrel and doin' pretty good, when all of a sudden Stovepipe gave the cables a big jerk and my riggin' slipped."

"And the barrel hit you in the face?" she gasped.

"Well, yeah, it did," I said, "but that didn't do this. The barrel just cut me above the ear."

I pulled my hair back so she could see the gash where the barrel had nailed me.

"Then what happened your face?" she insisted.

"I'm not real sure," I shrugged. "I think I did that when I slid across the floor. There's slivers in my face."

"Does it hurt?" Carol asked.

"It hurts some," I said, "but not as bad as my arm."

"What the hell happened to your arm?" Joe piped up.

"I fell on it."

"Well, I've heard of a lot of injuries, but falling off a barrel on your arm isn't exactly death defying," he said.

"Oh no," I grabbed a piece of bacon. "I hurt my arm when I fell out the door of the loft."

"How did you fall out of the loft?" Maggie asked, and she took a closer look at my head, perhaps to see if there was anything inside.

"After I hit my head on the post, I wanted to quit, but Stovepipe told me there was never a rider that couldn't be throwed and there was never a barrel that couldn't be rode, so I got back on, and when Stovepipe jerked the cables, I flew out the door."

"That's it!" Maggie wadded a dish towel and tossed it on the table. "Your rodeo days are over and done! And as for that fat, one-eyed, blowhard Stovepipe . . ."

"Don't do that!" I pleaded, "at least not until after Saturday. That's when I ride!"

"This Saturday?" Joe said, "as in the day after tomorrow?"

"Yeah," I announced, "I think I'm ready."

"Could I come watch you?" Carol batted her long eyelashes and smiled, and I began to appreciate Carol for her mind, which seemed to be functioning perfectly.

"Well, sure . . ." I smiled.

Saturday night, Carol and I piled into the feed truck and drove down to the arena for my eight seconds of glory. I had drawn a little pay from Joe and outfitted myself in a fancy orange and green shirt and bought a genuine German silver belt buckle with a little gold blob that looked sort of like a horse and rider. I had been saving a big feather that I plucked out of a road-killed owl, and I wrapped it in rawhide and tied it onto the brim of my bronc riding hat.

Carol was wearing red boots, a white lacy blouse and tight blue jeans, and her blond hair curled around her shoulders.

Most of the other cowboys were hanging around the out-house, drinking beer. I let Carol watch me as I readied up, and she seemed to like it pretty much. According to something I'd read, I was supposed to ready myself in a quiet, introspective manner, so I went about it slow and easy.

First, I pulled my hat down and moved my head from one side to the other real slow. I wasn't real sure why I was doing that, but all of the other bronc riders were doing it, so I figured it must be important. The only thing that bothered me about the exercise was that my owl feather kept hitting me in the face, so I quit doing the head exercise and settled down to my chaps.

"The other guys have prettier chaps," Carol interrupted my preparation. "Look, that guy's chaps are lavender, and those over there are turquoise. Yours are brown."

"I don't figure a guy who wears lavender chaps can be all that tough," I growled.

"They have their initials sewed on theirs," Carol stared at the rear of some cowboy who was bent over. "Isn't that guy with the teal and gold chaps cute?"

The other hands had their big floppy chaps on and they were tying leather strings around their boots.

"How come your boots don't have strings?" Carol asked.

"I'm getting ready here Carol," I groaned, "sorta tryin' to concentrate on my ride. . ."

"Do you want me to go away?" she asked, and she continued to study the cowboy with teal and gold chaps.

"No!" I stood up and the other cowboys gave me the evil eye. "I'm just trying to concentrate, that's all."

One of the other bronc riders jumped up in the air and joined the others who were holding onto their crotches and walking in circles, kicking their legs out and drawing them back like they were spurring the evening air. I thought they looked pretty silly, but I did what the other bronc riders did because, after all, that's what I was.

The horses were being prodded down the long alley into the chutes, and I felt a tightening in my stomach. All of the other cowboys were holding their hats over their hearts and praying, and a scratchy recording of the "Star Spangled Banner" came across the speakers. I bowed my head and walked through the gate behind the chutes.

Stovepipe was sitting on the fence behind the chutes, drunker than a skunk. He pointed at a bay horse in chute four and then closed his eye, weaving and tottering on the fence.

"There's y'r bronc," he slurred.

"Bareback riders! Get ready!" Victor yelled from the other side of the chutes, and I stood beside my chute and stared at the bay horse. He had his eyes rolled back in the sockets.

"Stovepipe!" I shook his leg. "Are you going to help me?"

"Course I yam," he said, and then he fell backwards off the fence into a corral full of bulls.

"This is it!" he yelled, "the sure fire test of a rodeo hand!"

"Who's in chute four?!" Victor yelled, and he looked at his official chute boss clip board.

"Is that you Pinhead?" he sneered. "The mutton bustin' is over with."

"I'm a bronc rider," I said.

"Of course you are," he laughed, and he walked down the row of chutes, yelling at the rest of the hands.

I looked through the bars of the chute at the bay. He was a huge thing, some kind of cross between a Belgian and a saddle horse, and I poked my hand through the bars to stroke his ratty mane. He swung his head toward me, flared his nostrils and kicked the back end out of the chute, then rose straight up and took at swat at me with his front feet.

He appeared to hate me very much.

"That'n's a chute fighter!" some kid with no teeth yelled.

"I see that," I gulped.

Suddenly, my face felt white.

"He ain't never been rode," the kid added. "Jimmy Wilsz won't even git on him!"

"Hard to believe," I gagged, and I climbed on the chute and touched him on the hip.

The horse squealed and jumped, and I crawled right back off the chute and held onto the fence behind me, breathing so hard I was sure my heart would blast through my chest.

"That horse hates ever'thing," the toothless kid smiled. "He'd kick the head off'n his own mama."

"Set your riggin'!" Victor yelled.

I looked around, and Victor poked a cattle stick in my butt.

"You're in the hole, Pinhead!" he hissed, and then he cackled and walked away.

"In the hole?" I squeaked.

The gate next to me swung open and the horse jumped. The cowboy's head banged into the metal gate behind him, and he slid down the chute and rolled into the arena, bleeding and flopping around like a fish on the creek bank. I heard Bobby Baker announce my ride, and then Victor waved up in disgust.

"Well, it looks like Parker isn't ready in chute number four," Bobby said, "so let's go on down to chute number eight for a real top hand . . ."

The cowboy in chute eight made one jump and then his horse pitched him into the arena dirt. While the cowboy was staggering to his feet, the cowboy in lavender chaps set my rigging and declared it tight, and another hand shoved me onto the back of the bay. I tried to remember all of the coaching Stovepipe had offered, and Victor stabbed his stick through the bars and gave me a solid jab in the armpit. A cowboy leaned over the chute and pounded on my hand.

"Ouch!" I yelled, "that hurts!"

"Lean out when you call for him!" The toothless kid advised, "or else he'll bash your brains against the chute!"

"Spurs over the shoulders!" Jimmy Wilsz yelled.

I felt the bronc tense beneath me, and I sat there waiting. The crowd was quiet, and Bobby Baker was babbling on about rodeo, but finally, Bobby ran out of things to say, and everyone sat around and looked at me. I wondered what they were waiting for.

After what seemed like several minutes of heavy suspense, Victor walked over and jabbed me with his stick.

"Nod your head when you're ready," he growled, and he backed off to the end of the rope and waved at Bobby.

"Alright, ladies and gentlemen," Bobby laughed. "It looks like we're finally ready down in chute number four. Watch how he sets that riggin' and gets ready. When he's all set, he'll nod his head and the ride will begin."

I don't remember nodding, but Victor pulled the gate open.

The horse just stood there.

"Spur him!" Jimmy Wilsz hollered, and I reached out with my feet and sort of gave him a little nudge with my spurs.

The horse came completely unglued.

I closed my eyes.

The bay went straight up into the air, then twisted and shook and kicked his back feet. He fell to the left, then caught himself and shook and we were on our way up again. When he came back down, my groin slammed into my fist and if I could have gotten off, I would have thrown up. His hips came up and his head went down and I felt myself flying off to the left, until he turned and jumped back under me. I was trying desperately to let go, but I had twisted around and my hand was caught in the rigging. The horse stood on his hind feet and danced, then crashed his front feet into the ground and took another wild leap, and I felt myself spin around until my hand came free and I hit the ground flat on my back. I opened my eyes in time to see Red ride right over the top of my body, and Joe's horse stopped in time to kick dirt clods in my face.

"What did I score?" I wheezed.

"Score?" Loper laughed, and he held up his chalkboard with a big "zero" written down. "You barely made three jumps!"

"But, I had him rode!" I sat up.

"Get out of the arena!" Victor scolded. "If you're gonna die, go do it somewhere out of the way!"

I wasn't really hurt all that bad, but I stood up and limped like I had been taught, then wandered across the arena, and went out the gate.

Bobby Baker seemed quite pleased to announce that they would not have to pull me out of the arena on a sled.

"You'll do better in the saddle broncs!" Stovepipe threw an arm around my shoulder. "I been thinkin' you're built better for them anyhow."

"I don't think so," I said, but Stovepipe led me around to the chutes again and pointed at a short, stocky buckskin mare known to the audience as "Flicka," better known to the cowboys as "that dirty, rotten buckskin witch."

"You here again?" Victor hissed, and he jabbed me with his stick, barely missing my boy parts.

"Oh, darn," I smiled. "I can't ride this horse! I don't have my saddle or bridle."

"Go home," another hand said. "Please, just go away."

"You can borrow mine!" Jimmy Wilsz smiled, and he threw his bronc saddle over the chute and pulled the cinch tight, then held the hack rein high in the air.

"Aw, darn," I said. "I'm a lefty. This hack is for a right-handed rider."

Jimmy threaded the rein under the horse's neck and stuck it in the palm of my left hand.

119

"How's that?" he grinned.

"Quit jabberin'!" Victor yelled and he jerked the gate open.

Stovepipe let out a whoop, and the buckskin was in the air and bucking. When she pulled her head down, the rein pulled  me forward and I was sure I would go over her head, but somehow, she shifted and I was still in the saddle. The mare stood on one foot and then the other, and she kicked her legs above my head. She shook herself. She fell down. She ran and she spun in both directions. She pulled my hamstrings and my groin and my stomach muscles, but every time I tried to jump off, she ran back under me and gave me another beating.

Suddenly, I noticed a rider on my right, and I looked at him, sure that he must be one of the ghost riders in the sky. If he was, he looked just like Red.

"Let go!" Red yelled.

"I'm not quitting!" I yelled back.

"You made it," Red reached over and slipped the buck rein off and the buckskin took off around the arena on a dead run, with Red riding alongside, prying at my fingers.

Joe rode up on the other side and grabbed me around the waist, and the two of them pulled and tugged at me until I gave up and jumped.

Apparently, my leap caught Joe and Red by surprise, because when I hit the ground, both of them were still hanging onto me, and then the three of us tumbled and skidded in the dirt in front of the announcer's stand.

Loper said I missed the horse out of the gate, and he held up his chalkboard with another big "goose egg" on it. Jimmy Wilsz won the saddle bronc again. I gathered my rodeo crap and threw it all in the back of the pickup with the feed barrels. At one time, I would have carefully wrapped my gear and stowed it in the cab like a treasured friend.

"Pretty good ride," Joe said.

Jimmy Wilsz allowed as how I had been "screwed" by the judge, but then, it's always safe to say the other man has been robbed when the check is in your pocket. It was fairly clear to me that I had not been screwed at all.

Maggie inspected my head for signs of damage, and finally declared me fit, if not totally intelligent.

Carol left with a steer wrestler as big as a bull.

Stovepipe staggered up and threw his arm over my shoulder and started slobbering about how he had seen it all from the very start.

"Yessir," he whooped. "You're built perfect-O!"

I reached into the back of the pickup and grabbed the handle of a good shovel, the kind with a slight curve at the neck and rivets in the handle. The handle was oak, and had been worn smooth by plenty of digging. The blade was sharp; I could see the marks where I had run a file over the curve.

"I'm built just right for irrigating and fixing fence," I said.

"No! No! No!" Stovepipe shook his head, and I could hear his false teeth clattering. "Yerra' rodeo hand! Ever'body's callin' ya Pendleton Parker!'"

"They're calling me Pinhead," I corrected him.

"I can see it now!" he babbled. "You and me at the NFR, you winnin' the world, me and my old buddy Jim hangin' over the fence. I can see it now!"

"Stovepipe," I sighed, "you've only got one eye."

121

Most places, there are four seasons of the year . . . spring, summer, fall, and winter. On Friendly Creek, there are two . . . winter and haying. Some years, there might be a third, but if it happens to come along, summer only lasts for a day. Winter and haying, on the other hand, can last for months on end. In fact, the only thing that ever seems to put an end to haying is winter and the seasons are somewhat dependent upon each other. If the winter is mild and reasonable, then water will be short so that there won't be enough to irrigate, which means hay won't grow. If that is the case, then there won't be enough hay to feed in the winter. If the winter should happen to be "normal," the ranchers will either have to sell cattle or buy expensive hay that they didn't put up with their own equipment.

The only reason it is important to put up hay with your own equipment is that there is usually a large note at the bank against said tractors, mowers, balers and other large, odd-looking machines. While the note accrues interest at incredibly high rates, machinery depreciates at an even swifter rate. The only reason I know that much about banking and banker talk is that I can remember when Joe bought a tractor from Jerry Watson, then went down and took out a loan at the bank.

"I was on the way home," he told me, "when I decided I really couldn't afford the damn tractor, so I turned around and headed back to town to queer the deal. The tractor was worth half what I paid and I owed the bank twice as much as I borrowed."

"What did you do?" I asked.

He shrugged. "I had to keep the tractor a year so I could trade it in and get more than it was worth. Of course, I had to buy another new tractor, and it cost more, but the bank just added the difference onto my note and it came out about even."

Apparently, haying goes back to some brilliant theory that it would be a good idea to store hay in the summer and feed it out in the winter, probably based on observations of squirrels storing nuts for the winter. Anyhow, ranchers went out and conjured up a variety of strange iron machines, hooked them up to horses and spent months cutting, raking and stacking hay. Most of this hay was used to feed the several dozen horses which pulled the haying equipment. Some of the hay that the horses didn't eat went to cows, but most of the remainder was eaten by deer and elk or entombed by massive snow drifts. As soon as the ranchers could get through the snow, the frost had gone out of the ground, and the hay piles were surrounded by mud. This hay was determined to be "extra" hay for a really bad winter, and the cycle repeated itself.

I started in the hayfield when I was six. As if first grade would be terribly expensive, I was put to work so that I could "earn money for school." My job was to wander around miles of meadow and flip bales over, wet side up, dry side down, and I was paid a half-penny a bale. The bales weighed eighty-five pounds dry. I weighed sixty-five wet. I earned about $3.50 a day, and I slept well at night.

When I got older, I was promoted to the exalted position of "shop foreman," which meant that I milked the cow, fed horses, shoveled manure, sorted bolts, coiled wire, filed sections and repaired sickles. I was not only promoted; I was also given a raise. Under the new arrangement, I earned a penny for every section I sharpened or replaced, which came out to about $3.00 a day. When someone pointed out that I was too little to pound rivets with a ballpeen hammer, Joe gave me a bigger hammer.

"Just drop the head on the rivets," he said, "and it'll flatten 'em."

I grew into raking, although Joe had to strap blocks of wood on the clutch and brake pedals so that I could reach them. Raking was the duty of following a trail of mown hay and rolling it into "windrows," aptly named piles of hay which blew away as soon as they were created. Even in a drought, if hay is cut down and left on the ground, it will rain just enough to dampen it, and while the mowing crew races off in front of everyone else, cutting hay down, the rakers and balers wait and wait for the hay to "cure" so they can bale it. Most days, the hay cures at about noon, and then it rains.

In many ways, it is convenient to have it rain in the haying season, because when it rains, it provides an opportunity to fix the balers, which are normally broken more than they are working. Every ranch on Friendly Creek had a graveyard of old equipment, and every graveyard was full of balers. The only reward to being on the baling crew was the opportunity it afforded to watch the raker go around the ranch in her halter top and short shorts, getting tanned.

When Joe appointed me to the baler crew, I wasn't exactly overjoyed, but since the temperature was dropping at night and snow seemed imminent, all of the ranchers were locked in mortal combat to finish first. I knew better than to complain at a time when "the bet" was hanging in the balance. Every year, the ranchers bet a whole case of "good" whiskey on who would finish first, even though there had never been a winner. As far as I knew, nobody had ever finished before it snowed.

"So," Jerry Watson smiled when I walked in the Hoosegow, "I guess we'll be seeing a lot of you in town?"

"Hardly," I laughed. "We're on the whiskey run in the hayfield."

"As I understand it," he smiled. "You're baling."

"Oh yeah," I remembered.

Nothing breaks down more than a baler. The baler crew spends a third of its time running to town for parts, a third installing the parts and a third waiting for hay to dry.

"I think haying was invented by an implement dealer," Red Barnes groused one night when rain had sent everyone to the Hoosegow.

"We are here to serve," Jerry Watson the implement dealer smiled, a gold tooth sparkling even in the low light of the bar. "I notice that you all get even by charging me a King's ransom for horse hay."

"There ain't enough hay in the whole world to get even with your prices," Joe snorted.

"Where else you gonna' go?" Jerry chuckled, and everyone looked away because he was right.

Even if they went somewhere else and bought equipment, they would have to call Jerry for parts when the equipment broke down, which it would do as soon as the parts started moving. Either that, or they had to wait three days to get parts from UPS and pay the additional freight.

In the morning, while I was waiting for the dew to evaporate, I watched the rain clouds bagging up over the mountains and counted seventy-eight little grease zerks on the baler. I crawled over, around and underneath the machine and squeezed grease into thousands of moving parts. When that was done, I cranked diesel into the tank and threaded twine from the box to the knotters. I tightened bolts on the teeth of the reel and checked the tension on the bale chute, squirted oil in the little oil cups and climbed aboard.

The big engine roared as the machine wandered around the meadow in silly little circles, gobbling hay. I perched over the windrows like a hawk in a tornado, carefully watching for hidden dangers, things like rocks and boards and tree limbs and snakes, but I didn't see the skunk until it came over the reel. I managed to extract most of the carcass with a stick, and went back to baling, when I noticed that all of the bales were tied on one side, instead of two. I shut the machine down and replaced the twine, then set out to rebale the hay I had already baled. Actually, things seemed to be going pretty well.

"Ah-mmmmmmm," groaned the engine.

"Swish, swish, swish," swept the reel.

"Ker-chank," poked the plunger.

"Shing, shing," sang the knives.

"Clink-check, clink-check," the knotters worked to perfection.

The sounds of the well-oiled machinery were contenting, and I moved along, quickly, making hay when a new sound cropped up.

"Screeeeeeeeeeeee . . . WHAM!"

The plunger shot through the left wall of the baler like a rocket, then spasmed while knives bashed into it and sent fragments of metal into other internal organs, which crashed and shattered. I kicked the power-take-off lever, and it fell through the floor of the baler. While the machine sputtered and died, a bale fell from the chute and withered there, one twine untied.

It looked like I would need the parts book.

I called the parts numbers in to Jerry Watson, then headed for town to get them. Jerry had four red and yellow boxes on the counter when I got there.

"Good to see you!" Jerry shook my hand. "I appreciate the business. All you have to do is put all of this together like it says in the book, and your baler will be as good as new!"

"The baler is new," I reminded him.

"You probably did something wrong," he frowned. "Company studies have shown that 98% of all breakdowns are a direct result of 'operator error.'"

I shook my head and put a box under each arm and hauled them out the door.

"Actually, you're lucky," Jerry pulled me aside when I came back for the other boxes, and he pointed to the back shop, where three high school kids were busy loading parts onto a flatbed truck.

"Loper bought his equipment in Salt Lake," he warned. "Parts are hard to get, and you need more of them."

"Victor Wilsz has older equipment, and he had to order parts from the factory," Jerry told me. "Do you know what that means?"

I shook my head.

"If you order from the factory, they have to get the parts for old junker equipment made 'special order,'" Jerry said. "Do you know what that means?"

"It costs even more?" I guessed.

"That's right!" Jerry smacked the counter with his hand. "An order like that has to come from the factory in Czechoslovakia! First, you have to get the Communists motivated to make the parts. Then you have to get through all of the secret police. After that, they put the parts on a boat, and after that they have to come to Wyoming on a train. After that, it has to be delivered to my store in a truck!"

"It takes forever," he shook his head.

I signed the invoice and headed for the ranch.

According to the "official" manual, I was to insert a bolt, 60736A, into a 91567 bushing, securing that into a hole in PL-1 with a 5507 nut. I then attached a bar, MFPB12, with a regulation yellow key, YK356, and inserted it into the arm apparatus, MFA978, from inside the machine. This required the use of shear pin MFSP1013, and cotter pin LTC23.

It also required that I climb into the bale chute to get at the whole apparatus.

The bale chute was tight and narrow, a dark place suited to things of the night, and as I scooted along upside down, I heard a buzzing sound, which I assumed was either hydraulic fluid or compressed air, until it occurred to me that the sound was almost identical to that of a rattlesnake.

As a matter of fact, it *was* identical to the sound of a rattlesnake. I flew out of the bale chute, feet first, and stood around and hyperventilated for awhile.

After I shined the headlights of the truck into the chute and removed most of the outside armor from the machine, I crawled back into the bowels of the baler. A large gob of timothy dust fell in my mouth as I tried to roll over to see the parts book, and I dropped my wrench through the only hole in the bale chute. I sneezed and my neck snapped forward until my head met the top of the plunger, which was a neat way of jerking my hair out of the MFS342B spring. I managed to attach the PL-1 to the MFPL1, and I needed only to insert the MF2B76A3118089SBT.

I had no MF2B76A3118089SBT.

I checked my pockets, the boxes and the ground. I looked in the cab of the truck and crawled back into the bale chute. With a parts number like MF2B76A3118089SBT, the part had to be big enough to see, but it was nowhere to be found, and I cussed Jerry for leaving it out.

"I'll bet he didn't forget to charge me for it," I muttered, and I looked an MF2B76A3118089SBT up in the parts book.

It was a stove bolt.

I drove back to the house and called Jerry.

"I need an MF2B76A3118089SBT," I advised.

"We're out," he said. "I'll have to order it from Indiana."

"What do you mean, 'you're out?'" I yelled. "You mean to tell me you don't have a stove bolt?!"

"Not *that* stove bolt," he corrected. "Hafta' order it from the factory. It'll take a week, seven working days."

"This is a brand new machine!" I reminded him. "Parts for new machines are supposed to be carried at the local level. You never need to worry about ordering!"

"That particular part is back-ordered," he said. "It was a little oversight in design. Nobody thought that many of them would break."

"What are you talking about?" I asked.

"That wasn't one of the parts that was *expected* to break," he said. "The machine wasn't designed for that part to break."

"Are you telling me that the baler was made to break?" I asked.

"I'm telling you that we don't have that part," he said.

"It's a *stove bolt*!" I yelled. "I need a three-eighths stove bolt, two inches long."

"I don't have the part," Jerry said. "I'll order you one from Indiana."

"I'll get one at the hardware store," I growled.

"I wouldn't do that," he warned. "It ain't the right bolt."

"What's the difference?" I groaned.

"The MF2B76A3118089SBT is red," he said.

"How much does it cost?" I wondered.

"Thirty-six, fifty," he checked the book, "but I'll let you have it for thirty-six."

"Thirty six dollars?" I asked. "Thirty-six bucks for a red stove bolt?"

"Not just any red stove bolt," he reminded me. "It's an MF2B76A3118089SBT."

I stopped by the hardware store, but Dick Wilson was nowhere to be found. There was a sign on the counter that said,

"OUT OF BALING WIRE." Below that was penciled in a list of other items he was missing, including sledge hammers, needle-nosed pliers, rust buster and 3 in 1 oil. The way it looked to me, without such essentials as those, there would be no hay on Friendly Creek at all.

I wandered back to the bolt bin, only to find it empty. The stove bolt I was looking for was listed at seventeen cents, but they were gone. Another sign advised customers for stove bolts to "ASK AT COUNTER."

"I need a stove bolt," I told the girl at the counter.

"Machinery parts?" she smiled. "What kind?"

"Stove bolt kind," I sighed. "Three eighths by two inches."

"Red, yellow or green?" she asked.

"Red," I sighed.

She fished around in a box under the counter until she found a bright red, three eighths by two inch stove bolt, which she placed in the palm of my hand.

"Twenty-two, fifty," she smiled.

"For a stove bolt?" I looked at the bolt in my palm. "The sign on the bin says they're seventeen cents!"

"We're out of those," she shrugged. "This is a *red* stove bolt. You should be happy. The green ones are thirty bucks!"

I signed the ticket and shoved the stove bolt in my pocket, and then just for the heck of it, I walked to the back and stuck my head into Dick Wilson's little workshop.

Sure as heck, he was back there painting stove bolts.

There's nothing quite like a strange vehicle to stir up folks in the country, and before the dust could even settle behind the "gray pickup," each and every outfit along Friendly Creek had dispatched one or more ranch vehicles to intercept and interrogate the driver.

Edna Loper got credit for sighting the stranger while she was on her way to town. Edna called Faye Wilsz because Faye was the only person she could get ahold of, and in turn, Faye notified the Wilsz Ranch foreman, Spudley McKay, who sent word out to the rest of the outfit on their private radio band. Joe heard about it from Buck Martin, who heard it on the Wilsz Ranch private radio. Red Barnes was bringing a bull back from the Keller Place when Davey Boyd flagged him down and let him know, so he tied his horse to the cattleguard and hopped in the truck with Davey.

Within moments, no less than a dozen ranch trucks were on the road.

Joe ran into Loper and both of them skidded to a halt, then

backed up and hung their milky white arms out the window. Their dark hands tapped lightly on the doors, and both of them looked up and down the road.

"You see a gray pickup?" Joe spat.

"Edna seen it," Loper squinted, and he spit too.

"What would a gray pickup be doin' up here?" Joe wondered.

"Probably rustlin' cattle," Loper guessed, "unless he's a poacher."

"Or worse," Joe growled, but he never got a chance to explain what was worse because Victor Wilsz came around the corner and damn near crashed into both of them.

"What the hell are you doing?" he barked, "makin' some kind of a roadblock?"

"That's right Victor," Loper said. "We finally got tired of you and now we're gonna' hang you."

"Don't give me a bunch of crap, Loper," Victor hissed, and he got out of his truck. "Spud says a gray pickup just went up this road."

"Did Spudley actually see this gray pickup?" Joe asked.

"Don't start!" Victor snapped. "Edna called Faye and she told Spud."

"What do you know about this gray pickup?" Loper wondered.

"I don't know a damn thing about it," Victor snapped, "but I got Spud covering the south side of the creek and Jimmy is headin' off the ridge road."

"Well, I don't guess whoever it is will get very far, then," Joe said. "There oughta' be enough dust to blind him."

About that time, every pickup in the valley came charging down the Friendly Creek Road in hot pursuit of the gray pickup, which had a commanding lead going into the big draw in front of the roadblock. The gray pickup popped over the hill and ground to a halt which nearly caused a wreck, since all of the trucks in pursuit were driving through the dust and couldn't see a thing. A man in a gray suit jumped out of the gray truck, looked at the vehicles on the road, in the ditch, and elsewhere, then smiled and walked right up to everyone.

"Well, if this don't beat all," Joe put his hands on his hips. "Every truck in the country is parked on the Friendly Creek road, and here's some son-of-a-bitch in a suit!"

"Hi there!" the son-of-a-bitch in the suit smiled.

Nobody said a word.

"I believe I'm lost," the man suggested.

"I'd bet on it," Loper agreed.

"I'm looking for a man by the name of Victor Wilson," the man said.

"Never heard of him," Red said.

"What do you want with this `Victor Wilson?'" Victor Wilsz asked.

"Does he live around here?" the man asked. "I was told that he was a big rancher around here."

"Ain't no Wilson's around here," Joe shook his head. "Any of you boys ever heard of some fat rancher named Victor Wilson?"

"Are you from the government?" Victor asked.

"Not at all," the man in the suit smiled. "I'm with Digger Drilling Company."

With that, Victor Wilsz jumped out of the sagebrush like a jack rabbit, shook the man's hand, offered him a fat black cigar and before anyone could get a word in sideways, the man in the suit was halfway to the Wilsz Ranch headquarters, and everyone else stood around on the road, staring at each other. All of a sudden, Carl Loper threw his hat up in the air and let out a big holler. Joe started dancing around and giggling like a girl.

"That oil man can only mean one thing!" Loper panted. "If he's up here, there's oil in this valley! By God, we're all gonna' be rich!"

"Wow!" Red grabbed Davey Boyd by the arm, "Oil! How about that?"

At the prospect of being rich, the ranchers whooped and hollered and danced around on the road, throwing their hats and clapping each other on the backs. They were in the height of celebration when Elmer Eisenhardt came over the hill on the county road grader, quietly pushing dirt and rocks off the road and into the barrow pit. Elmer blasted his horn, then climbed out of the cab and looked at the men in the road. The ranchers quit hopping around and singing, and stared at Elmer. Elmer looked at them nervously, then shifted his eyes and looked out into the brush. Unsure of what to do next, Elmer simply acted like he had never been there in the first place, climbed back on the road grader and went straight back to town, talking to himself all the way.

"You know," Joe grew serious, "we've got to get ourselves a plan."

"Plan for what?" Shorty asked. "If we're gonna' be rich, we don't need no plan."

"Joe's right," Loper said. "If we don't have a plan, we ain't gonna' be rich. That slick operator in the gray pickup is gonna pluck old Victor like a duck, and then he'll skin us."

"I've heard about this before," Joe went on. "I've got a friend over in Douglas who's been through it before. They send these guys in suits, lawyers mostly, into a country where they know there's oil, and they pick the ranchers off, one at a time."

"Why would they pick a jackass like Victor first?" Shorty asked.

"He owns the most land," Loper narrowed his eyes. "Knock off the big piece and you can gather in the little ones."

"As soon as they talk the first guy into a rock bottom price," Joe went on, "they'll claim his price is the going price for everything in the area, and cheat the rest of us out of our oil."

"When they get done with Victor, they'll think we're all a

bunch of rubes," Loper nodded. "What we need to do is have everyone agree that nobody sells until we can work out what the price will be."

"Price for what?" Shorty asked.

"Shorty!" Joe snapped. "Are you paying attention at all here? The price for drilling on our land! The price for driving all over the valley! The price for water!"

"Not to mention the price for oil!" Red reminded him.

"Oh yeah," Shorty nodded, "I forgot."

"The first thing we need to do is find out what kind of deal Victor is cutting," Joe advised.

"That won't be easy," Loper sighed. "If Victor turns them down, which isn't likely, he'll never say a word."

"And," Shorty scratched his head, "if he makes a deal, he'll lie about it."

"Well then," Joe said, "we'll have to rely on Jimmy or Spud for the information."

"Jimmy's the best bet," Loper advised. "If we can catch him at the Hoosegow, we can get him to spill the beans."

"I don't think Victor tells Jimmy that much," Red disagreed.

"Can't blame him for that," Shorty said. "That Jimmy is about as valuable as a magpie in the corral."

"Sooner or later, the truth has to come out," Loper thought out loud. "If everybody just sits around in the Hoosegow and listens, we'll find out what's going on. Fingers Filiatreau will have his nose in this one, and Bobby Baker will hear whatever Victor has to say. Remember how we found out that Missy Jones was pregnant?"

"Missy Jones is pregnant!?" Shorty looked shocked.

"She has three kids, Shorty," Red shook his head. "We're talking about the first one."

"Like I was sayin'," Joe interrupted, "let's all just keep a sharp eye and good ears and we'll know what Victor got, right to the penny. As soon as you hear something, we'll meet at my place and figure out the plan."

Joe was usually right, but this time, Joe was wrong. According to Fingers Filiatreau, Faye Wilsz hadn't shopped at the Merc for two weeks, and Victor Wilsz had dropped clean out of sight. The Postmaster said they hadn't picked up their mail for several days, and the last time they picked it up, it was in the middle of the night. Dick Wilson saw Spud at the cafe one day, and Dick quizzed him, but came up empty handed.

"Spud doesn't even remember the gray pickup," Dick said.

Information was so dry on Friendly Creek that I thought Bobby Baker was going to kiss me when I walked into the Hoosegow. Fingers jumped up off this stool and ran over to meet me at the door, and Bobby had a cold beer sitting on the bar before I could even sit on a stool.

"I'm buying," Fingers waved at Bobby.

"On the house," Bobby waved back, and I had only drunk the beer down to the label when another one appeared on the bar.

"I'm not done," I smiled, but Bobby declared the remaining beer too warm to be ingested, and the second beer was also on the house.

"I take it you boys don't know anything more about the oil boom than I do," I smiled.

"Everything I know as a realtor is strictly confidential," Fingers said, "but I've been hearing plenty over at the Merc."

"What's going on out in the country?" Bobby asked, and he slid another beer under my snout. "You hearing the same things we're hearing here in town?"

Bobby looked at Fingers and winked. Fingers smiled at me.

"I don't know," I confessed. "What are you hearing?"

"You go first," Fingers whispered, and he stuck his finger in his ear to make room for the information.

"I'm just a hired hand," I shrugged. "I spend all of my time working cattle and stuff like that. The management end of things is done when I'm not around."

"I ain't hearing anything!" Fingers yelled, and Bobby slapped his hand on the bar.

"This town is like a tomb," he sniffled, "just like a tomb! The only thing we've heard is that Elmer saw all of the ranchers dancing around in the road, singing and clapping their hands."

"If you will recall," Fingers reminded me, "Elmer once sighted a monkey sitting on a fence post."

Fingers was right. Elmer swore to death that he saw a monkey sitting on fence post, out by the cemetery. Elmer saw a lot of things from his road grader, and fortunately, he didn't report them all.

"I'd say this lends some truth to the story about the monkey on the fence post," I said.

"Jesus!" Fingers knocked beer bottles across the bar. "Why were they dancing around and singing?"

"Same reason the monkey was sitting on the fence post, I guess," I said. "I don't know anymore than you do."

If nobody was going to talk, more desperate action was called for. Joe called Aunt Bess and asked her to attend a meeting of the Eastern Star, her first in at least five years. Joe was sure that with Faye Wilsz being past grandmotherly matron, or whatever she

137

was, there would be plenty of information to be had at the secret meeting.

Edna Loper poked around the Mercantile, listening in on every conversation, until she was embarrassed to death when someone asked her if she was working there.

Davey Boyd had his daughter give a school report on the oil industry, and she even went so far as to get one of Victor's grandchildren as her lab partner.

Nothing.

Now, on Friendly Creek, when gossip dries up, it's bad. But, when gossip dries up about a known event, it constitutes a major disaster. So far, the only rumor floating around was Elmer's tale of grown men dancing a jig behind a roadblock on the Friendly Creek road, but people quickly reminded each other that Elmer had also seen a monkey sitting on a fence post.

Shorty McGregor had been perched on Squaw Bluff since the beginning of the whole affair, and everyone gathered in the shadows of the Bluff to make a plan, but Shorty didn't have any information to offer either.

"What do you mean, nothing's happening?" Loper snorted.

"I mean nothing out of the normal," Shorty said. "Everybody's started calving, except for Fred Aspering."

"Fred doesn't have any cows!" Joe screamed.

"Oh yeah," Shorty agreed. "No wonder he ain't started yet."

"What about the oil?" Joe snapped.

"Oil?" Shorty blinked.

"Never mind," Joe hissed, and the men walked off the bluff with their heads down.

In the entire history of Friendly Creek, no single secret had ever been so well-known, so mysterious and well-kept. In fact, since there was no information, everyone was absolutely certain that there must really be something big going on.

As if to prove it, Victor Wilsz returned to the valley the very next day. Joe and I were headed up the road toward the Keller Place when I noticed an unusual figure out in the sagebrush, a figure which proved to be none other than Victor Wilsz. He was jumping around out in the brush, taking five long steps, then one little hop, writing  in his little spiral notebook, then hopping and skipping again, but he was headed absolutely nowhere.

"Aha!" Joe crowed as he looked through the binoculars, "I knew it!"

"Knew what?" I asked.

"He's out there measuring something," Joe decreed.

I squinted at Victor, and he sure was doing a lot of hopping, but it was beyond me what on earth he could be measuring.

"He looks drunk," I said, but Joe held up his hand and squinted through the binoculars.

"He's figuring out a road," Joe whispered.

"If he's figuring out a road," I whispered back, "why doesn't he just drive his truck through there like the rest of us? Why is he bouncing around like a jack rabbit?"

"Five steps and a hop is a rod," Joe smiled.

"Of course it is," I agreed.

"It is," Joe insisted.

"I believe you," I chuckled. "What is a rod?"

"Sixteen and a half feet," Joe advised.

"Why would he measure in sixteen-and-a-half-foot lengths?" I whispered. "Is that another ranch conversion to metric?"

Joe had explained metrics to me by showing me that the length of the second joint of the index finger was an inch, so the length of the fingernail was a centimeter. This five steps and a hop sounded equally logical to me.

"Shhh," Joe whispered. He was lost in thought.

"I've got to find Loper," he decided, and with that, Joe jumped out of the truck, pulled my horse out of the trailer and sent me to the Keller Place to doctor steers by myself. By the time I got there, I calculated the trip to be no less than three thousand rods.

When I got back, there was action in the big house. All of the neighbors were talking around the kitchen table, and when I walked in for a drink of water, they eyed me like I was Victor Wilsz himself.

"Where have you been?" Joe asked.

"I've been at the Keller Place," I said, "doctoring steers."

"How could you have been at the Keller Place when the truck and trailer are parked outside?" he asked.

"You sent me to the Keller Place on my horse and drove back here! You were muttering and looking at Victor Wilsz hopping around in the brush, and then you said you had to get ahold of Loper and the rest of the neighbors."

"Did you get the steers taken care of?" he sighed, and I nodded.

"Good." he muttered. "Now, leave."

I took one final look at the ranchers huddled around the kitchen table, fairly sure they were plotting some sort of response to something that hadn't happened, and I figured the safest thing for me to do was to take care of my horse, so I let the screen door slam and headed for the barn. I had covered exactly nine rods when a man jumped out of the shadows of the grain bin.

"Hi!" he said.

I jumped, swore and then shook it off the best I could.

"Who are you?" I snarled.

"Name is Jim," he held out his hand. "Sorry about scaring you like that."

"You didn't scare me," I lied. "What do you want?"

"I'm looking for a fellow name of Joe Barnes," he looked around.

"What do you want with Joe Barnes?" I asked.

"Private business," Jim winked.

"You have a southern accent," I winked back. "Are you here about the oil?"

"Uh, no, not at all," his eyes darted back and forth. "I'm here to look at some cattle."

"Oh, good," I smiled. "I'll show you the cattle. Joe's too busy with oil right now."

"Where is Joe?" Jim asked, and he followed me to the barn.

"I'm not sure," I lied, "but I can show you the cattle."

"Do you own the cattle?" he asked.

"Oh yeah," I assured him. "I own all the cattle in the valley now. Everyone else is in the oil business. How many cattle do you want to buy?"

"What about this oil business you keep mentioning?" Jim asked, and he wandered around the barn like a lawyer in jeans. "Have there been people up here asking about oil?"

"So far," I sighed, "you were the only person in this valley not talking about oil, but I see that you have the fever too."

"Just curious," he smiled, and his little eyes darted around the barn. The man seemed very nervous to be around horses, and the horses seemed a little nervous to be around him.

"Joe's in the house," I pointed.

When Jim left, I was pretty happy to be alone with my horse. The horse didn't give a hoot about oil, or at least if he did, he didn't spend all night and day talking about it. By morning, not only was I the only person in the valley who wasn't possessed with oil, I was also the only ranch hand left.

141

Word got out at the Hoosegow that three separate companies were moving in and hiring help, and every hand within forty miles quit being a cowboy and started looking for a high-paying job on a drilling rig. Most of them got hired, and even Davey Boyd hired on with Digger Drilling as a "worm," some position Davey described as being the assistant to the assistant to the boss. It sounded like my job at the ranch.

Joe and the other ranchers started hanging out at the cafe in the morning and the Hoosegow in the evening, just sitting around picking up the latest poop on the oil business and plotting how they would get rich. As soon as it got to town, every one of them picked up a "Wall Street Journal," and hid behind it, except for Shorty, who said he wouldn't read a paper that didn't have cartoons. Talk in the bar centered around Tulsa oil prices, oil futures and OPEC estimates. The ranchers seemed to believe that they were Sheiks in Stetson hats.

Fingers Filiatreau ferreted out the fact that Victor Wilsz had signed up for three thousand bucks for a location and twelve bucks a rod for roads. On top of that, he was getting fifty bucks an acre to let Digger Drilling have exclusive rights to his oil.

When word of this great fortune got out, the agreement to hang together was broken all to hell, and gray pickups, fancy cars and other outfits swarmed the country like a herd of mice. Twin engine airplanes buzzed into the Friendly Creek airport, but since no one ever imagined that kind of airplane flying around on Friendly Creek, Elmer Eisenhardt never had any reason to take his grader over and fill the badger holes in the runway. As a result, the first three oil company planes were scattered across the runway, but the loss of airplanes didn't deter the oil companies; they flew in and out in a fleet of helicopters.

Normal behavior at the Hoosegow slowed considerably. The old crowd disappeared, and was replaced by a steady stream of oil field hands who wandered in day and night.

Bobby Baker put his wife in charge of the Hoosegow and opened up a swanky new restaurant called the "Oily Steer," a joint venture with Fingers Filiatreau.

"Holy Cow," I said when I walked in the Hoosegow. I didn't know a soul, except for Elmer, the county road grader.

"Hey there, Elmer," I sat down next to him. "What do you know?"

"I don't know nothing," he pouted.

"You stayin' busy?" I smiled, and I asked the girl behind the bar to buy him a drink.

"Lemme' tell ya' somethin'," Elmer's eyes opened wide. His eyes were watery and his nose was running, and Elmer hadn't shaved or changed clothes for days; he was looking gaunt and worn.

"Lemme' tell ya' something!" he yelled at me, and he grabbed my sleeve with his greasy hand.

"I'm listening," I pried his fingers loose.

"Therz somethin' goin' on roun' here," Elmer shook his finger in my face, "an' I seen a plenty of it!"

"Yep," I agreed. "There's plenty going on alright."

"You know what I seen?" he asked, and he grabbed me by the sleeve again.

"A monkey sitting on a fence post," I said, and I pried his fingers loose.

"Thass right!" he yipped, "but that ain't it!"

"What did you see?" I asked, and I waved at the girl to cut him off.

"I seen all of them ranchers on Friendly Creek dancing on the road!" he said, "and I seen great big airplanes comin' into the airport! Who ever heard of airplanes like that landin' at th' airport?"

"Elmer," I put an arm around him, "you should go home."

"You know what else I seen?" he yelled. "I seen a dragonfly with people inside of it!"

"That's a helicopter," I smiled.

"You seen it?" his head popped up.

"I've seen it," I smiled.

"Oh good," he put his head on the bar. "Everybody else thinks I'm crazy."

"You're not crazy," I laughed. "Go home."

Satisfied that he wasn't alone in his observation of the dragonfly with people inside, Elmer tottered toward the door, and I studied the anatomy of the new bartender. When Elmer reached the door, he stopped and hollered back at me.

"You!" he pointed in my general direction, and everyone in the bar looked at me.

"You!" he yelled again, and I waved.

"You seen that monkey on the fence post too, di'nt ya"?" he howled, and then he was gone.

In the morning, Elmer's Caterpillar was one of the smallest pieces of equipment in the county. A fleet of gigantic earth beating machines started through every inch of brush and meadow, just driving and pounding and creating a general nuisance to me and the horses and cattle.

Loper was the first to cash in big when he sold the oil companies land for their employee camps, a deal which Fingers Filiatreau claimed to have put together. Normally, everyone would have ignored Fingers, but since they were all going to be rich, Loper paid him a one percent commission on the deal, just to shut him up. When the companies needed water, Loper sold them water, and when they needed firewood, he sold timber.

Red settled on $25 an acre for his place, but he got fifteen bucks a rod for a road and four thousand for the location. It hadn't taken anyone long to figure out what a rod was, because Red's road across half a mile of meadow and a quarter mile of bog turned out to be four miles long. According to Red, the only way not to destroy his farming operation was to go through the main yard, double back to the fence and follow across the upper end of the meadow, then wind down through the willows, but there was no way he would let them chop down his rare and endangered sixteen petal rose bush, so they had to cross the creek and come back again. As it turned out, he got $16,000 for the land and $19,200 for a dirt road to nowhere.

Shorty McGregor wasn't quite so fortunate. One of the oil company men came around early one morning, walked right up, pulled the outhouse door open and caught Shorty in the middle of his morning constitutional. Being a very modest man, Shorty signed up the works for $10,000 so the oil man would leave him alone.

As usual, Joe was the cleverest of all. He sat around the Hoosegow and the cafe, and he wore a suit into the Oily Steer, all the time listening to talk about the deals, and while the thought of taking $35,000 for a road to nowhere was appealing, Joe just knew there was more to this oil business than met the eye. By the time they moved a big old drilling rig onto Wilsz's place, Joe had signed up for free, and he couldn't wait to tell everybody.

"You did what!!?" Loper jumped out of his chair at the Hoosegow.

"I told 'em to go ahead and drill my oil," Joe winked, "I wasn't worried about the cash."

"I always knew you were stupid," Victor chortled.

"Did they catch you in the outhouse too?" Shorty asked.

"I'll get paid when they hit oil," Joe bragged, and he twisted his drink on the bar. "You boys all took the cash, but I get 18 percent of everything they produce!"

Victor Wilsz slammed his hand on the table and glared at Joe, which only served to make Joe carry on about his great scheme all the more. By the time everyone got out napkins and figured out how much Joe would be making on his well, they went home early and sulled up for a full week.

Friendly Creek became a big oil town overnight, and the oil

field hands outnumbered the Mormons, which didn't set well with the Bishop. But he was too busy to protest; he was spending twelve hours a day building a laundromat and pipe yard.

Daisy Aspering whined because she didn't know anyone anymore.

Being the only cowboy in the valley, I was left without a girl to chase, since they were all busy flirting with the oil field crews. When I did stop by the Hoosegow one night to say hello to Mary Petty, some great big guy in a hardhat hit me over the head with a beer bottle, quickly cooling my attraction to Mary Petty, the Hoosegow, and town in general.

The Wilsz family had so much money they bought hay from a farmer over the mountain. Loper left his hay standing, since the tall grass made his meadows look more like residential property than a swamp, and Davey Boyd was too busy "worming" to do any ranch work. Joe and Red decreed that they were still ranchers and since Red had used his entire oil check to buy more cows, Joe wanted us to be in a position to sell him a little hay, oil or no oil.

Cretaceous Corporation moved Joe's well in and within the space of twenty four hours, they had everything rigged up and were noisily boring a hole into the Sand Hill across from Squaw Bluff. Joe checked their progress every day, and every day he grew cheerier and cheerier, until we started cutting the West Brome and he ran the swather into a fence while waving at one of the derrick hands. Undaunted, Joe gave up haying and went into oil geology fulltime. But, there were rumblings of problems on Friendly Creek.

When the Wilsz Number 1 was drilled to its full depth, it was declared a dry hole.

The Wilsz Number 2 hit rock too hard to penetrate, and the Loper Number 1 was backed out before completion because somebody dropped his "tool" in the hole. I suspected it was the worm that did it.

Red's well belched a little tad of gas, which turned out to be poisonous to cattle and moose, so the oil company decided not to produce, advising Red that if there was ever a need for low-grade, high-cost natural gas, and if there was ever a pipeline that ran within a few rods, they might open it up again.

After they had pounded most of Shorty's land, drilled holes and exploded bombs from a helicopter, they decided not to drill any wells.

Most of the former cowboys were former roughnecks, but none of the ranches were hiring. The laundromat and the movie theatre closed up, and the Oily Steer burned down in a rain-storm. The official cause was determined to be too many oily rags near the furnace. I figured it must have taken three or four dump truck loads of oily rags to keep it burning as long as it did in the rain, and it always did seem odd to me that they would be running the furnace in the middle of the summer, but I was no more of a fireman than I was an oil man, so I kept my mouth shut and stacked hay.

Before long, the only hope left was the J. Barnes Number 1, out there in the shadow of Squaw Bluff. Joe was still studying charts and readouts, and he was still certain that there just had to be oil in the ground. After all, he said, if there wasn't any oil, why would these companies be looking for it?

One night just before dark, I threw the last bales on a stack in the Big Meadow, and a pickup owned by the Cretaceous Corporation raced down the road through the heart of the ranch. It was the driller from J. Barnes Number 1, and his eyes were bloodshot. He said he needed to talk to Mr. Barnes in person.

Joe got up from his charts and readouts and Journals of Oil Field Recovery and listened carefully as the driller filled him in, and Maggie and I turned the TV down so that we could hear. The rig was holding, the driller said, because they preferred to hit the oil in daylight! They had just drilled into the "bearing sands" and found evidence of some sort of carboneum or something, and the seismic readouts were giving back a full echo. The mud man was having trouble holding back the pressure, but they had finally gotten the hole stabilized and were cased down to the level where the hole wouldn't collapse. They were going to complete the hole in the morning, and they should be capping it by nine.

It sounded like a lot of jibberish to me.

At daylight, they were fired up again, and the donkey was puffing and smoking. Most of the people on the creek were watching, and Joe was perched on the platform, waiting for his oil to flow. Wendy came out from the newspaper, and word of the eminent strike was going out over the news wires. Finally, at eleven o' clock, the mudman and the driller both yelled that

they couldn't hold it and a stream of greenish-blue oil shot from the top of the derrick.

Joe was dancing with the driller and Red was doing a do-si-do with Loper, and oil was spewing all over. Some of the women were crying, and Victor and Shorty were hopping around like new calves.

"Let 'er blow!" Joe howled, and he threw his good Stetson hat in the air.

A gust of wind caught it, and the Stetson floated as quietly on the breeze as a red-tailed hawk.

The oil stopped.

"Well, I'll be," the driller said.

"What do you mean, you'll be what?" Joe gulped.

"I've never seen anything like it," the driller shook his head, and he pounded on his gauges.

"You've never seen anything like what?" Joe asked, and he pounded on the gauges too.

"It quit," the driller said, and he looked below him to see if somebody slipped a gigantic cork in the hole.

"Well, for hell's sake!" Joe barked. "I can see that!"

"Why'd ya' shut it off?" Victor yelled from the ground.

"I didn't shut it off," the driller yelled back. "It quit."

"What do you mean it quit?" Victor yelled.

"I mean the oil's gone," the driller sighed.

"We hit a pocket," the geologist announced.

"A pocket?" Joe furrowed his brow.

"I've heard of it," the geologist advised. "The oil pool moved off somewhere else, but in all the heat and folding of the earth, it left this little pocket of oil and gas. We just drilled through it and now it's gone."

"Gone?" Joe blinked.

"Sure as hell," the geologist said, and he and the driller both shrugged at Joe.

"Hell of a deal," the driller shook his head.

"You mean to tell me that my oil well is done?" Joe frowned.

"I'm afraid so," the geologist admitted.

"And my oil well has just been shot all over the ground?" Joe looked up at the top of the derrick.

"Looks that way," the driller said. "She's another dry hole."

"Well, I'll be damned," Joe said, and he walked away without another word.

They poked seven more holes around Friendly Creek before they finally found the big oil pool, out on the desert where the Federal Government owned all the land and the minerals.

Loper made out pretty well on his housing, and Red made six bucks a head on the cows he bought.

Davey Boyd paid his place off with his worming wages, and both Friendly Creek and Buzzard Butte became prosperous little oil villages.

Daisy Aspering still didn't know anyone in town, and Shorty installed a dead bolt lock on his outhouse door in case there was ever another boom.

Victor Wilsz bought up the mineral rights on every place he could, but the oil companies weren't interested in them anymore.

Joe went back to ranching, and his humor improved a great deal.

Fingers Filiatreau raised all of the prices in the mercantile and Bobby Baker went back behind the bar in the Hoosegow.

Everyone lamented the fact that the oil boom hadn't worked out better, except for me, I guess.

As far as I was concerned, the best thing about the end of the whole damn oil boom was seeing Elmer Eisenhardt out there grading the Friendly Creek Road again.

a PAIR of LIARS

Joe and I were coming back from the mountain, and I pulled in at the Merc to pick up a can of chew, but before I could get a dollar out of my pocket and onto the checkout stand, Fingers Filiatreau darted around the end of the meat counter and cornered me at the door.

"Looks like big trouble in the swamp," he advised, and he poked his lone finger into his hairy ear and wiggled it around.

"Big trouble in the swamp?" I paid for the chew. "Fingers, I haven't got the foggiest idea what you're talking about."

"The *swamp!*" he tugged at my shirt. "Charlie Binning is raising a big ruckus in the swamp!"

"I'll keep that in mind," I said, and hopped into the pickup.

"What was Fingers jabbering about?" Joe asked.

"He says old Charlie Binning is up to big trouble in the swamp," I laughed.

"Big trouble in the swamp?" he laughed out loud. The thought was preposterous.

The "swamp" was a section of ground that divides the towns of Friendly Creek and Buzzard Butte, a nesting ground for mosquitoes and ducks, curlews and killdeer. On occasion, a few of Loper's horses might wander down there, but other than that, there wasn't much in the swamp but wiregrass. On the west side, there's a fence, the corner post held in place by an old blue car. On the east side there's just an old wooden spool that the Green River REA left behind when they strung the power lines.

I let Joe out at the Post Office, and he came out with his arms full of mail, shaking his head.

"George says Charlie's raising hell in the swamp!" Joe said when he climbed in the pickup.

"Why would he be worried about the swamp?" I wondered out loud.

"Well," Joe rubbed his jaw, "Charlie owns part of the swamp, but it isn't good for much."

I pulled over at Dick Wilson's hardware store and wandered in to pick up some nails and wire.

"How could there be big trouble in the swamp?" I asked myself, and Dick Wilson looked up from his bin of nails and shook his head.

"You heard?" he said. "Word gets around quick, don't it?"

"What's going on?" I asked.

"There's big trouble in the swamp," Dick shrugged, and I walked back out the door.

It seemed to me that the only way to get a question answered was either to be the cause of the problem or to see it myself. If there was "big trouble" in the swamp, I was pretty sure it would stand out.

"Well?" Joe asked when I got in the truck. "What's the story?"

"Beats me," I shrugged again. "Dick says there's trouble in the swamp."

"Let's go have a look," Joe suggested.

"You're not going anywhere," Buck Martin shook his head.

His brown Blazer was parked across the left lane of the highway, lights flashing, and a Green River REA bucket truck was blocking the right lane. Buck was sending cars away, one by one, and a fairly good crowd had gathered, mostly to heckle the Deputy Sheriff.

"What's going on?" Joe yelled at Buck, but Buck was busy flagging another carload of tourists down main street and around the swamp. Behind us, I could see Fingers Filiatreau carrying a table out into the parking lot of the Mercantile, and his hired hands were running along behind with big signs proclaiming that there was a "sidewalk sale."

"There isn't even a sidewalk," I rolled my eyes.

"Darn it, Joe," Buck came over and whined, "You can't park your pickup here! The road is closed!"

"Why?" Joe asked, and he got out of the truck and tried to look through the REA truck.

"Because," Buck waved another car away, "there's big trouble in the swamp!"

"Buck!" Joe followed him over to where he was moving a crowd of teenagers off of the road. "Exactly what is this 'big trouble in the swamp'?"

"Oh for God's sake, what does it matter?" Buck snapped.

"Well," Joe chuckled, "is someone trying to steal the old blue car without a motor or what?"

"Charlie Binning is the cause of all the trouble!" Buck hissed.

"Charlie Binning is eighty years old!" I laughed. "The only person older than Charlie is Granny Wilson."

"I don't care how old he is," Buck growled. "He's sitting down there with a chain saw and he says he's gonna cut the power lines down if the REA doesn't pay him the rent they owe for their power poles by dinnertime!"

"When's dinnertime?" I asked.

"Six o'clock," Buck said looking nervously at his watch.

"So why don't they pay their rent?" Joe asked.

"Because they have lawyers and accountants and company policy," Buck shoved his hands in his pockets.

"So, they don't have to pay rent?" Joe followed him through the crowd. "If you don't pay your light bill, they'll shut your power off."

"You sound like Charlie!" Buck yelled. "That's what *he* says. He says he's gonna' shut off *their* power! They told us in the law academy that there's nothing worse than social unrest, and that's exactly what we got here. Old Charlie is in deep trouble!"

"For what?" Joe asked.

"Conspiracy, inciting a riot, destruction of private property, endangering the lives of citizens . . . you name it!" Buck ticked off the list of crimes. "He's as bad as one of them Black Leopards in San Diego!"

"Black Panthers," I suggested. "And, it's San Francisco."

"They're bad too," Buck snapped, a bead of sweat dripping off his nose and resting on his bushy gray moustache.

"I'm gonna' go on down and see what Charlie has to say," Joe said, and he hopped in the truck and directed me to drive around Buck's Blazer.

"Halt!" Buck held out his hand and blew on a whistle.

"Go around him," Joe ordered.

"Stop in the name of the Law!" Buck tooted the whistle again. "Stop or I'll shoot!"

"Buck!" Joe yelled out my window. "We're going down to see what's going on!"

Joe smiled, and I drove around the deputy.

Charlie Binning was sitting in the middle of the swamp in

a lawn chair, legs crossed, smoking a cigarette. On either side of him stood a power pole, and above him coursed several million megawatts of raw power. Charlie was using the discarded wooden spool as a table, and he had a cooler full of cold chicken, tomatoes and beer. His chain saw was sitting on the ground next to his lawn chair, purring like a kitten.

I stopped the pickup and Joe jumped out and waved at Charlie.

Charlie shielded his eyes and looked up the hill, and his thick glasses bounced light like signals from Indians. I knew he couldn't tell who we were. Joe yelled at him, but he couldn't hear very well either.

"Go down there and see what the problem is," Joe said.

I walked down and stepped over the top wire on the fence, then waded over to the little spot of high ground where Charlie was sitting.

"Oh it's you," he said, "I thought it was some trick them REA boys was trying, but they're afraid to wade out in this bog, so I figured you must be alright."

He squinted up the hill at the pickup.

"Who's up there?" he pointed.

"It's Joe," I said, and Charlie grinned.

"Have a seat," he said, and he offered me his lawn chair.

"I sure picked a hot enough day for this, and the skeeters are God-awful!"

"What are you doing?" I asked, and I leaned against the spool, while Charlie sat down in his chair.

"Gettin' bit by skeeters," he slapped at his cheek. "You want somethin' to eat? I got fried chicken, tomaters and some of them brown rolls they make down there at the cafe . . . I love them brown rolls, don't you?"

"That's OK," I shook my head.

"How about a beer?" Charlie stood up and handed me a can of beer.

"You better have a can of beer in this heat," Charlie warned. "A man could die if he didn't have any beer in this kind of heat."

"It might not be so hot if you took off that wool shirt and your jacket," I suggested, but Charlie shook his head.

"Never know when it might snow," he said.

"What are you doing?" I asked again.

"Stupid REA!" he snarled. "The stupid REA would shut off our lights if we didn't pay our bill, but they ain't paid theirs, so I aim to shut off their power!"

He grabbed the saw and let a few chips fly from off the bottom of the pole, and a cheer went up from both sides of the swamp.

"How much do they owe you?" I asked.

"Six hundred dollars a year," Charlie said, and he handed me a yellowed sheet of paper indicating that he had leased them the ground for their power pole for that figure.

It was dated 1956, the year I was born.

"When did they quit paying you?" I handed the sheet back.

"They ain't paid but once," he shoved the paper inside his shirt, "which means they owe me fourteen thousand, four hundred dollars *plus interest*. I'm tired of messin' with`em, and if they don't have that check down here by dinnertime, I'm cuttin' down this here pole."

I looked at my watch. If Charlie ate dinner at six o' clock, the REA had an hour to save their pole.

"Maybe they thought they *bought* the land for six hundred dollars," I suggested.

"Hah!" Charlie snorted. "If they bought the land, all they have to do is show me the deed, and I'm telling you, they ain't got no deed to show me. You ask anybody who let `em use the land. The deal was fifty bucks a month! That's six hundred bucks a year, *plus interest*!"

"Do they know about this?" I wondered.

"They should!" he said, "They ain't been paying me for

thirty years. If I didn't pay *them* for thirty years, I'll bet they would notice that!"

"Did you send them a letter or anything?" I asked, and Charlie ripped a handwritten flyer off one of the poles

The note warned that if the REA didn't pay Charlie within five days, he would saw down their trespassing poles. It was carefully printed out, and it was signed in his shaky handwriting.

"This has been out here for *five days*," he advised. "I'd say they've had plenty of notice. They shut off my electric once when I was in the hospital and all they done was put a note on my door, so I figure we're even."

Charlie stood up and took a few more bites out of the pole, and another cheer came up from the crowd on the hill.

"Tell the REA they got an hour," Charlie said. "And I want a bank-type check, not one of theirs! *They* take *their* bill out of my social security every month because they don't want *me* to be sending them a bum check. Fair's fair."

"I'll see what I can do," I said.

"Will you shake on that?" he asked, and I grinned. I held out my hand and felt the old man's grip, then looked into the fire in his ancient blue eyes.

"Make *them* shake on it too," he said.

I waded out of the swamp and explained the situation to Joe, then drove back to the roadblock. Buck Martin raced over, pulling on the snap that covered his handcuffs.

"You're under arrest!" he said, and he jerked so hard on the snap that his gunbelt pulled clear up under his armpit. "You have the right to remain silent . . ."

"Knock it off, Buck!" Lefty Carlson yelled.

Lefty was the local man for the REA, and he walked over and shook my hand.

"Crazy old coot," he smiled.

"Oh, Buck's just a little too anxious," Joe grinned.

"No, no," Lefty laughed, "I mean old Charlie Binning."

"Well, Lefty," Joe lifted his hat and ran his fingers through his white hair. "I think Charlie might just be right on this one."

"We paid for that land!" Lefty snapped.

"Then you oughta' have a deed for it," Joe shrugged. "If not, it sure looks to me like it's an annual lease, which means you're trespassing in Charlie's swamp."

"I'm the law here," Buck swelled his chest out.

He looked at the crowd, which was decidedly weighted in favor of Charlie Binning.

"If you own it Lefty, you oughta' have a deed," Buck declared, and the crowd nodded agreement.

"Arrest him!" Granny Wilson yelled from the crowd. "Throw Lefty in jail!"

"Wait a minute. Wait a minute!" Lefty held up his hands. "I think we can work this out, if Charlie and I could just visit about it."

"Charlie put a notice on the pole five days ago," Joe said. "That was your chance to visit about it, and that time's gone ."

"Well, how the hell could he expect me to read a note tacked on that old pole?" Lefty scoffed.

"Same way you expected him to read the notice you tacked on his door when he was in the hospital," Joe smiled.

"Shoot Lefty!" Granny Wilson yelled. "Shoot him or make him pay!"

"What does he say we owe?" Lefty sighed, and he dug out his checkbook.

Joe looked over at me.

"Fourteen thousand, four hundred bucks," I said, "plus interest at bank rates for twenty-two years."

Lefty Carlson's face turned red, then gray, and he snapped the checkbook shut.

"In the first place, that is ridiculous!" he screamed. "And in the second place, I'm not authorized to write a check for that much money."

"He doesn't want a check from you anyway," I said. "He wants a bank check."

"The bank is closed," Lefty smiled smugly.

"I can open it up if it would help," Lee Willoughby offered, and he held up a ring of keys.

"If you open it, can I cash a check?" someone asked.

"Local check?" Lee looked around for the customer.

"No," said a man in Bermuda shorts and sandals, "but I have a bank guarantee card."

"Sure thing," Lee shrugged.

"Well?" Buck looked at Lefty. "What are you gonna' do?"

"This is out of my authority," Lefty crossed his arms. "I am *not* going to be blackmailed by the people of this town."

"Pay up you scumbag!" Granny Wilson bolted from the crowd, and only the quick hands of Fingers Filiatreau saved Lefty from a clubbing with her cane.

"Anybody here think Charlie Binning is in the wrong?" Buck yelled at the crowd.

"Nooooo!" the crowd yelled back.

"I think you better pay up," Buck looked at Lefty.

Everyone trooped off to the bank, and Lee Willoughby calculated the payoff to be $20,004.86 and made the check out to Charlie Binning.

"This check is good?" Joe asked, and both Lee and Lefty assured him that the check was good.

"Will you shake on it?" I remembered my duty, and both of them offered their hand. We drove down to the swamp and delivered the check, and I helped Charlie carry his stuff up the hill. It was five minutes to six.

"We don't want you to be late for dinner," Joe smiled, and I threw the cooler, lawn chair and chain saw in the back of the pickup.

"Let's stop by the Hoosegow," Charlie suggested, "and I'll cash this check and buy a round of beers for all my friends."

Everyone at the Hoosegow shook Charlie's hand and took a look at the check, and even Lefty Carlson stopped by and had a beer on old Charlie. Finally, Charlie looked at his watch and said he had to go on along, because he was already late for dinner, and we walked out onto the step. I gave Charlie and his check a ride across the road to his house, and he stared out of his living room window at the swamp. The power pole was beginning to tilt a little more from all the nicks Charlie gave it with his chain saw, but it didn't look very dangerous.

"You know," Charlie looked at me through his thick lenses, "I lied a little bit in this whole deal."

"Oh God, Charlie," I looked back at the little man, and my throat tightened. "What have you done?"

Charlie looked around the corner to make sure his wife wasn't in earshot, then cupped his wrinkled hand around his mouth and I leaned down to listen.

"We don't eat dinner until six thirty," he whispered, "and I told people we ate at six."

"I'll tell them you were late," I smiled, and we shook on it.

I guess that made us a pair of liars.

According to Red Barnes, the only cause of death on Friendly Creek was "heart failure," and since Red was the Deputy County Coroner, he knew about such things.

"Hell's bells," Red shook his head if anyone ever challenged his logic, "a man can't hardly die if his heart's still pounding away."

Red's expertise in pathology and his appointment as Deputy Coroner for the whole county were both a result of his infamous trip up Coal Mine Mountain in the dead of winter, to claim Fat Jack Calloway's body. Fat Jack was a coal miner, and he lived in a shack at the mouth of his mine, just below timberline. Once a week, summer and winter, Fat Jack would haul a load of coal out of the trees, down the Friendly Creek road and into town, where he would deliver it to the people who had ordered coal. As soon as Fat Jack was done delivering coal, he went to the bar and drank until his belly was full, and then he went to sleep in the back of one of his wagons and let the mules pull him back up the mountain.

When he didn't show up for one week, nobody got too unsettled about it, but when Fat Jack didn't make it to the bar for two weeks in a row, everyone got nervous, and some got cold, since they were out of coal.

The County Coroner, an undertaker from over in the county seat, knew nothing about Friendly Creek, Fat Jack Calloway or Coal Mine Mountain, and he wasn't about to go exploring in the middle of the winter, so he walked in the bar and listened to Red Barnes tell tall tales about what a mountain man he was and deputized him on the spot. At the time, Red was quite proud, and he went so far as to explain his new position in life as being "sort of a County Commissioner for the dead."

Red harnessed his best team, Fibber and Molly, and guided them up Friendly Creek, until the snow was too deep for the team. Then, Red and the Coroner headed up the face of Coal Mine Mountain on snowshoes, until they reached Fat Jack's cabin.

"Fat Jack was dead alright," Red told everyone when he got back. "He was so dead he was lookin' skinny."

The Coroner walked around the inside of the cabin, fretting over how they would get the three hundred pounds of Fat Jack back to the wagon, but Red was ahead of him and pointed to a pair of old wooden skis outside the cabin.

"We'll just tie Fat Jack on these skis," Red shrugged, "and we'll tie a rope around him and let him slide along in front of us until we get to the bottom of the mountain. Then, we load him on the wagon and haul him to town like a load of coal."

"Why not catch the mules and have them pull him down the mountain?" the coroner sighed.

"Because," Red said as he lashed Fat Jack to the skis, "it will take us 'til dark to catch those goofy mules, and then we'll have to grain 'em, water 'em, harness 'em, hitch 'em up and take 'em all the way around the mountain and drive 'em home in the snowstorm."

"What snowstorm?" the Coroner looked out the cabin window.

"The one that's comin'," Red said, and he pushed Fat Jack out the door and tied his lariat rope to a post, then slipped his snowshoes on.

The coroner wasn't overly pleased with Red's methods, but Red was already headed down the mountain, so he put his snowshoes on and followed along. Red made it about a quarter-mile before he got tired, and the coroner sloshed along through the powdery snow to catch up. Red still swears he was handing the rope to the coroner, and the coroner still swears Red did it on purpose, but the fact remains that Red let go of the rope and Fat Jack Calloway shot off of Coal Mine Mountain like a cannonball. By the time Fat Jack got to the head of Bobcat Creek, he was going so fast that he jumped the creek and shot into the timber, out of sight.

"Wow!" Red smiled, "Look at Fat Jack go!"

Red and the Coroner sat on their snowshoes and slid off the face of the mountain. When they got to the rim of Friendly Creek Canyon, they were just in time to see Fat Jack skimming down the frozen creek like a bobsled out of control, and then Fat Jack shot over the falls and slid to a stop in Shorty McGregor's meadow, not more than twenty yards from the house. When Red and the Coroner arrived, Shorty was sitting on the porch, smoking a pipe.

"Howdy Red," Shorty waved. "I see you found Fat Jack."

"Hot damn!" Red grinned. "You shoulda' seen him comin' off the mountain!"

"Yep," Shorty nodded. "That woulda been a sight, alright."

Red was telling the story when I walked in the Hoosegow, and despite the fact that everyone had heard and told it at least a hundred times, they all listened intently. Over the years, the story had grown in significance and scope, to the point where Shorty now claimed to have watched Fat Jack's wild ride off the mountain.

Everyone was standing around the bar, and it looked like they had a pretty good discussion going, so I sat down on a stool and waited for Bobby Baker to bring me a beer.

"What's going on?" I asked when he set one on the bar.

"Oh, Davey Boyd said he figured the most dangerous thing around here was workin' in the oil field," Bobby grinned. "Some guy got hit in the head with a set of tongs, and it was in the paper."

"So, Red's tellin' the Fat Jack Calloway story?" I asked, not quite sure how the two were related.

"Of course," Bobby chuckled. "If there's a subject even close, Red tells the Fat Jack story. It don't matter if somebody says 'fat' or 'snow' or 'skis' or 'trees.' Red tells the story."

"I figure the most dangerous thing around here is freezing to death," Loper said. Ever since the time Loper got stuck one winter and froze the tip off his ear, he wouldn't go out the door without a full tank of gas, a two-way radio, a can of gas and a little pile of wood in the back of his pickup.

"When's the last time anybody around here froze to death?" Dick Wilson scoffed.

"If you understand danger, you don't need to fear it," Loper folded his hands together.

"And, if you only got half an ear, you don't have to worry about freezing it," Red chuckled.

"You know what's really dangerous?" Jerry Watson interrupted, and everyone turned to hear him out.

"I'd say the most dangerous thing is all that old equipment you boys are using," Jerry asserted. "There's lots of people who have lost arms and fingers and legs and stuff on those old mowers and balers. The new line of equipment has protective shields and automatic shut-off features that you oughta check out."

"I think I'd rather lose an arm and leg in an old baler than give you an arm and a leg for a new baler," Shorty said. "How

164

come every time we talk about anything, you try to sell me a new tractor?"

"I'd say logging is the most dangerous thing," Ira Cusack said. "Lots of loggers died in the timber."

"Drank themselves to death," Fingers Filiatreau said.

"Then froze," Loper added.

"The single most dangerous element of life in any town is law enforcement," Buck Martin hooked his fingers in his gunbelt. "Every time I walk out that door, my wife doesn't know if she'll see me again."

"That's because you get lost going to the bathroom," Bobby Baker delivered another round of drinks.

"And your aim is so bad, the only thing you've hit in ten years is your foot," Red added. "If you don't make it home, it'll be because you can't walk without any toes."

"I'd say getting conked on the head with a fence stretcher is pretty dangerous," Victor Wilsz pulled a toothpick out of his mouth and stared at me.

"Moose are dangerous," Shorty said. "I had a cow moose chase me into the middle of a big willow bush up at my place last week and I couldn't get out for two hours."

"A moose?" Dick Wilson asked. "Did you say a moose?"

"He could be right," Bobby Baker said. "I saw where there's a worm that a moose gets in its head that eats its brain and makes it go plumb nuts."

"That's insane," Victor scoffed.

"That's right," Bobby rattled on. "I saw in the National Geographic where the worm makes the moose insane and they do all kinds of weird things."

"I want to know what Pinhead thinks is dangerous," Victor challenged me, and I swiveled my stool around and smiled.

"I'd say the most dangerous thing around here is Daisy Aspering," I said.

Nobody said a word.

"Daisy Aspering?" Victor stood up.

"Sit down, Victor," Ira said. "I want to hear this."

"I'd say your brains got rattled when Victor hit you with that fence stretcher," Loper shook his head.

"He's got that moose worm!" Shorty suggested.

"How can you say that?" Joe asked me. I think he was a little embarrassed to hear it come from my mouth.

"Number one, Daisy is almost deaf, right?" I asked.

They all nodded.

"And she can't see, right?"

"That's right," Shorty agreed. "She's as blind as a bat."

"Well," I raised my eyebrows, "every morning, I drive up the road and meet Daisy Aspering somewhere, and she's driving straight into the sun. She can't hear and she can't see and she scares the begeezus out of me."

"That's crazy," Loper shook his head.

"It ain't crazy!" Red stood up. "Daisy gets in the car in the garage and revs the engine up until *she* can hear it, and then she drops the clutch . . ."

"And comes out of the garage going ninety miles an hour backwards!" I said. "Fred has a cattleguard fifty yards wide and she still knocks the corners out!"

"By God," Joe shook his head, "he might be right. I met her on the corner above the creek today and had to pull clear up the hill to miss her."

"I was moving bulls to the mountain one day and she came around the corner at about a hundred miles an hour and drove right through the whole bunch," Loper laughed. "She never hit a bull and she never hit the brakes. I asked her about it later, and she didn't remember seeing me."

"Well," Buck Martin sighed, "I know she can't hear. I've followed her around with the siren going a dozen times and she never stops."

"Neither does anybody else," Fingers reminded him.

"Pinhead," Victor stood up, "you have finally proved just how damn stupid you are. In fact, I think . . ."

Victor was interrupted by the roar of a car racing past, and everyone stood up to look out the door. A brown Ford Galaxie careened off of the porch and bounced across the vacant lot, then headed straight for the Masonic Lodge. A collie dog hung its head out of the driver's side window. Behind the errant Galaxie, the shrill voice of Daisy Aspering pierced the air and then her squat body came into view, running as fast as she could behind the Ford.

"Stop Lady!" she yelled at the dog. "Lady! Stop!"

The collie dog hung its head out of the window and looked back, and then the Ford Galaxie crashed through the wall of the Masonic Lodge, sending Worthy Matrons of the Eastern Star screaming out the back.

"Stupid darn car!" Daisy snorted, and she limped up the steps and walked into the Hoosegow. Buck Martin looked at Daisy, then at the hole in the Masonic Lodge, then back at Daisy.

"What happened?" he asked, and Bobby Baker set a jigger of bourbon in front of Daisy.

"Hey!" Victor looked across the street. Victor was some sort of grand, exalted, honored something-or-other of the Masonic Lodge, and there was a car sticking out of his building.

"Dammit Buck!" he yelled at the Deputy, "This woman has run her car into the lodge! Are you going to get over there and investigate or not?"

"I can't," Buck shook his head. "I'm not a member."

Victor ran over to attend to the worthy matrons, and the rest of us retreated to the bar to tend to Daisy.

The upshot of the disaster, according to Daisy (who would never, ever tell a lie), was that she was delivering some Avon for Edna Loper and thought she put her car out of gear and into neutral. She said she had even put her foot on the brake and listened to make sure the engine was running and the car wasn't moving, and when she stepped out of the door, the car took off without her.

"I just don't like these new automatic transmissions," she whined, and everyone nodded agreement.

Buck Martin understandably cited the cause of the accident as "mechanical failure."

I offered to give Daisy a ride home, and Bobby Baker handed me a bottle of his best Kentucky Sour Mash to help her unwind. Daisy was never much of a drinker, but after her dog drove through the Masonic Lodge, she was pounding them down fast enough to catch up with most of the regulars in the Hoosegow.

And, when all was said and done, I figured I must have made my point, because Victor Wilsz quit calling me "Pinhead" and started calling me "Smart Ass". . . at least for a day or two.

"Well, well," Bobby Baker smiled when I walked into the Hoosegow. "Long time. No see."

"No kidding," I pulled up a stool. "Joe's had me building fence from daylight to dark."

"So I hear," Bobby punched the buttons on the register, "What's going on out there?"

"Joe's making a subdivision, isn't he?" Fingers Filiatreau interrupted. "You know, I'm the only licensed realtor in town, so if he plans to sell those lots, he'll be needing to call me."

Fingers handed me a business card with his name on it, as if I might forget who he was or where to find him.

"I get calls from all over the United States," he winked. "There's lots of people who want to buy land around here."

"You haven't sold a piece of ground in fifteen years," Dick Wilson scoffed.

"It's a seller's market," Fingers said, and he took his beer back to the end of the bar and had a seat.

"Joe better not be subdividing," Victor sneered at me. "He needs a permit from the county, and he doesn't have one. I did a little checking on that."

"Relax," I said. "He's not subdividing."

"Well, what the hell is he doing?" Shorty asked.

"I'd say it's none of your business," Dick Wilson suggested. "Whatever Joe wants to do on his private land is his business."

"That's easy for you to say," Jerry Watson said, "You're selling him all the wire and posts. I'm thinking about adding a new line of fencing supplies at the implement store, just to keep you honest."

"Go ahead," Dick said. "I'll start selling tractors."

"What kind of tractors?" Joe walked through the door.

"Hey there, Joe," Fingers walked over and handed him a card with his name on it. "Let me know if you aim to sell any of them lots you're making. You know, I'm the only licensed realtor in Friendly Creek and I get a lot of calls on property."

"What lots?" Joe looked around the bar.

"What are you building all the fence for?" Red asked.

"Savory grazing system," Joe smiled, and he turned his back to wait for questions.

"What the hell is a Savory grazing system?" Victor asked.

"I've heard of it," Jerry Watson said. "It's an intensive grazing management system based on the grazing patterns of animals in Africa."

"We're a long ways from Africa," Victor scoffed. "You gonna' start raising giraffes, Joe?"

"Laugh all you want," Joe smirked, "but, when you see how

well it works, you'll all be wanting to get in it, except for maybe you, Victor."

"Why wouldn't I want to do it?" Victor asked.

"You have to fix fence to make it work," Joe said, "and you haven't fixed a fence in your life!"

"Are you making your ranch into a pie?" Jerry Watson wondered. "I read that you have to make a pie to make it work."

"What the hell does making pie have to do with a subdivision?" Fingers asked. He had certainly learned no such thing in any of his real estate classes.

"You don't have to make a pie to make it work," Joe told Jerry. "All you do is keep the cattle moving from pasture to pasture so they don't camp out in one place. If you move them, it keeps the land disturbed and lets the seeds find a place to settle and you get more grass."

"When do you move `em?" Shorty asked

"Depends on your plan," Joe said. "You move 'em when they've had the proper impact on the range, or when it rains. No matter what, if it rains, you move 'em."

"Sounds like a lotta' riding to me," Red snorted.

"It sounds stupid to me," Victor agreed, "like most of the ideas you drag around, Joe. You can move cows in the rain if you want, but I'm a little smarter than that."

"You call the cows with a whistle," Joe said. "Just sit in the pickup or get on a motorcycle and lead them around. Horses get in the way."

Everyone looked at Joe like he had finally lost his mind.

"He's not kidding!" Jerry Watson said. "I've heard about this! You blow a whistle and the cows all come running, like dogs."

"My dogs don't come when I whistle," Red sighed. "How the hell would I get my cows to come?"

"I suppose you name all of the cows so you can call them," Victor snickered. "Here Buffy! Here Bosco! Here Bully, Bully!"

"Nope," Joe had a sip of his drink. "You train the cows to come to the whistle, because you reward them."

"Sure you do," Victor nodded. "What do you do, open a bank account for every cow?"

Everybody had a pretty good laugh at that, including Joe.

"You train 'em," Jerry Watson said. "A lot of guys use old cake and pour molasses on it to get the cows used to coming around when they blow the whistle."

"Sounds like a pretty good deal for the feed store," Shorty thought, "as if the price of feed ain't high enough already."

"They learn that the whistle means better grass," Joe said.

Victor smiled. "That's the same thing as honking the pickup horn in the winter. I've known about that for a long time."

"How come you haven't done it then?" Joe asked.

"Never needed to," Victor crossed his arms. "My pasture is in good enough shape as it is."

"How do you know?" Joe pressed him.

"I can see it!" Victor said, and he pointed at his eyes. "I use my eyes, for Christ's sake!"

"Okay," Joe shrugged. "You guys do whatever you want."

Joe and Jerry fell into an enthusiastic discussion about the merits of holistic resource management, using the animals as a tool to harvest the grass, and the rest of the ranchers snuck over to another table and giggled and smirked about the whole thing. When Joe got up to leave he looked at me.

"Try to answer their questions, will you?" he winked.

I doubt if Joe had his pickup started before Shorty and Red wandered up to the bar and started to quiz me about this whistling business, and I pulled my whistle out of my shirt pocket and blew it for them.

"Look out boys!" Victor yelled. "Pinhead's callin' in his cows!"

"I'd give 'em a week," Bobby Baker whispered.

Ten days later, I was standing in the Post Office when

172

George Bracken, the Postmaster, reached his hand through one of the big boxes and grabbed me by the sleeve.

"Jeez, George!" I peeked inside the mailbox. "You scared me to death!"

"Come over here," he said, and I followed him past the sign that said I was invading official government property and could be arrested. George led me back through a row of shelves and finally stopped in front of a metal cart with a pile of big, brown envelopes on top.

"You ever hear of this?" he said, and he handed me one of the packages.

The return address indicated that the package was from a Center for Holism. He shook one of the packages next to my ear, and I could hear a faint rattle.

"You think it's porno?" he asked, and he held it up to his ear and shook it some more.

"It's range management," I laughed, and I handed the package back to George.

"Are you sure?" George asked, and when I assured him that it was not a violation of the mail, he took a deep breath.

"Good thing," he shook his head. "I got one for everybody but Joe."

"Joe already has one," I said, and George shook his head and pushed the cart over to the row of mailboxes.

Jerry Watson decided not to test Dick Wilson's fence prices and instead, added a nifty line of automatic post pounders, wire stringers and other equipment, most of which would only fit on a brand new tractor, and Fingers Filiatreau stocked three lines of leather gloves.

Even the Rural Electric got in the act and started to advertise electric fence. The high school Future Business Leaders made a killing selling fence posts, until Buck Martin arrested the kids and their advisor for cutting down federal trees without a permit.

Sam "Smoky" Woods showed up at the court hearing with a permit he claimed the kids had applied for but never picked up, and the charges were dropped, despite the fact that one kid insisted they had never even talked about a permit.

The Judge declared the kid in contempt of court and made him leave the hearing, and his parents took him home and grounded him. The Hoosegow was abandoned. Night after night, only Fingers Filiatreau and Bobby Baker were there to keep the lights burning, and Bobby Baker growled that he would have to start selling wire and posts if he ever wanted to see another customer again.

When the fences were finished, the ranchers streamed back into the bar. Wild discussions broke out over what type of cattle were best suited to this new management scheme, but no matter the plan of each individual rancher, they were fully committed. Even the Forest Service and the Bureau of Land Management were taking a good, hard look at the plans. The merchants huddled around the bar and calculated what kind of money they would make if this holistic management actually translated into more cows, more feed, more equipment, more income and more to spend, and there was general agreement that this was about the best thing that ever happened on Friendly Creek. While it was agreed that it would not be as good as the Great Friendly Creek Oil Boom, it was certainly a boom in its own right, and nobody complained.

On every ranch, the cattle moved according to schedule, and the results were almost immediate. If nothing else, the cattle spent more time eating; the calves were as fat as anyone could ever remember. Joe took a big chance and divided up one of the meadows with electric fence and let the cattle graze the meadow down, then move to the next pasture, and it looked like there was more feed when they returned than there was when they first started eating.

On Sunday, a light drizzle came over the mountains and

settled on Friendly Creek, and Joe walked out to the barn and told me to forget about whatever I was doing.

"It's raining," he reminded me. "We've got to move the cows."

We hopped in the pickup and headed for the east end of Squaw Bluff, and when Joe pulled off the road, I jumped out and opened the gate.

Some of the cows looked up from their grazing and eyed the truck anxiously, and Joe grinned from ear to ear.

"One toot on the old whistle and they'll be here," he smiled, and he let go with a blast that bounced around the cab and made my ears ring.

The closest cows bawled and trotted toward the gate, and even the cows on top of the hill looked up and mooed, then started for the gate, looking behind for their calves. The calves had come to learn that the whistle meant mama would be leaving, and half of the little guys ran to the gate and waited for their mothers to catch up.

"Works like a charm," Joe grinned, and he puffed out his cheeks and let go with a really good blast.

"You know, I wonder how far away a cow can hear that whistle," I said.

"Beats me, Joe replied. "Cows have pretty good ears."

Joe blew on his whistle and honked the horn, and the whole bunch of cattle ran down the hill and started going through the gate.

And then, as if by magic, they raised their heads, and the tail-enders started back over the hill.

"What the hell is going on?" Joe asked, and he blew so hard on his whistle that his face turned red.

The cows turned around and looked back, but they were starting to circle the pickup and stream back out the gate. I turned around to see what it was that was bothering them.

"Oh no!" I yelped and I grabbed Joe by the arm.

175

Every black cow on Victor Wilsz's ranch was coming over the hill behind us, running ahead full steam and bawling. Victor was driving through the sagebrush behind them, blowing on his whistle, to no avail. To the west, Red Barnes and Shorty McGregor were trying to get around their cattle, but the cattle were trained to follow, and no amount of chasing did a lick of good. Every time the two cowboys fell in behind a little bunch of cows, the cows ran around behind them, anxious to follow them to better feed. Behind Red and Shorty, Fred Aspering's milk cow loped over the hill, running as fast as a horse, her bag swinging as high as her hip bones.

"Wow!" I said, "What a mess!"

Suddenly, every cow raised her head, and then they all raced past Red and Shorty. Fred's milk cow jumped the fence and bounded through the sagebrush like an elk, and then the whole mass of bovine life on Friendly Creek galloped over the hill toward Carl Loper's place. Shorty and Red stopped at the crest of the hill and watched the cattle stream past, their whistles hanging limp around their necks. Victor gave Joe an ugly look and drove up to where Red and Shorty were sitting. Joe followed, whistle still clenched between his teeth.

The cattle had swarmed into Loper's meadow like bees, and Carl was sitting on his motorcycle, still tooting absently on his whistle while thousands of cows and calves streamed past.

"Howdy, Joe," Red folded his hands on the saddle horn.

"Hi Red," Joe nodded.

"You and your stupid ideas!" Victor yelled, and he slammed the door on his official blue Wilsz Ranch pickup. "I say you should have to sort those cows!"

"Nobody made you blow a whistle, Victor," Joe stared at the cattle.

"Nobody makes me do anything!" Victor said, and then he realized that he was agreeing with Joe and slammed his fist on the hood of his pickup.

176

"Looks like we got us a mess," Shorty suggested, and he tugged absently at his rope.

"Yessir," Red agreed, "It looks like we got ourselves a real mess."

"It ain't that bad," Joe said. "This is kind of like the old days on the roundup."

"The roundup was a mess," Red said.

"I suppose you're right," Joe decided, and then his face lit up like he was a little boy, "but doesn't that whistling work slicker than heck?"

SOLD OUT

Ira Cusack got sold out two days before the rest of the valley went crazy over the Friendly Creek Days Rodeo and Mike Thomas set the county bulldogging record with a run of three-point-two seconds.

Ira didn't have a lot left to sell. He'd already taken his little bunch of cows over to the sale barn. The cows weren't all that great by any means, but not one person bid on them and the sale barn had to buy them all. They put his name on the check right after the bank's, and then sent the check to some attorney in Casper.

I stopped in at the Hoosegow before I headed up to Ira's, and Bobby Baker set a cup of coffee up on the bar.

"You want breakfast?" he asked.

"You don't serve breakfast," I said.

"I will this morning," he said. "Somehow, I don't think this is going to be a very good one."

"Thanks," I said, "but I've eaten."

"So," Bobby wiped the bar. "You goin' to Ira's for the sale?"

"Figured I would," I said, "but I ain't exactly lookin' forward to it."

"What do you figure Ira's gonna do?" Bobby wondered.

"I don't know," I thought. "What does a guy do when all he knows is cutting timber and raising horses and he can't do that anymore?"

"You know," Bobby sighed. "I could've bought some boards from him a time or two and I never did it. I went down to the lumber yard in Salt Lake and thought I got a bargain. I feel like maybe I didn't do my part to help old Ira out."

I left the bar and stopped by the Post Office to check the mail. Fingers Filiatreau was standing inside, and he followed me out to the pickup, then leaned inside the driver's side window, his single finger tapping on the door.

"You goin' up to Ira's?" he asked.

"Figured I'd stop by," I nodded.

"Listen," he looked up and down the street. "If there's anything that looks like it's something Ira really needs, buy it for me."

"You'll have to do that yourself," I bristled. "I'm not about to . . ."

"Hey!" Fingers grabbed my sleeve. "Don't be a damn fool. I've got enough money to cover things like that, and those of us in town agreed that we won't go to the sale. Nobody wants to buy Ira's things. I just don't want somebody from out of town buying his stuff. Understand?"

"I guess not," I hung my head. "I guess I don't understand at all."

"Well," Fingers let go of my sleeve. "Just be damn sure

nobody wrong buys Ira's stuff. Nobody likes to see it come to this. God, this is bad."

Up at Ira's, Abe Rose sat on the back of a flatbed truck and did the auctioneering.

Ira stood behind Abe like a wooden Indian while everything he had was held up and sold, one item at a time.

The State Bank of Friendly Creek bought the land and buildings, but not before Joe and Red ran the price up to the point where it would cover Ira's note. At first, I couldn't figure out what they wanted with Ira's place; neither of them needed the land, and the Cusack Place didn't fit either of their ranches worth a hoot, but when it looked like the bank was about to back out, Joe and Red quit bidding. I thought about that and it wasn't so hard to figure out.

Joe was on the bank board, so he knew exactly how long Lee Willoughby would keep raising his hand to cover the loan. He also knew that Victor Wilsz would buy the land back from the bank as soon as the paperwork was finished, but, there was no way he or Red were going to stand by and watch Victor take it for one red cent less than what it was worth, so they stared Victor straight in the eye and took turns raising their hands.

Every time Joe raised his arm, Victor turned a deeper shade of red, until he finally pushed through the crowd and grabbed Joe by the wrist.

"I told you I wanted that piece of ground!" Victor hissed.

"You'll get it, Victor," Joe pried the bigger man's fingers loose and stared back at him. "But, you ain't gonna steal it."

When the bidding finally got out of Victor's reach, Joe and Red crossed their arms and let the bank have it. Victor's eyes were as hard and dark as steel bearings.

There were only two bids on Ira's best team, a pair of perfectly matched four-year old Belgians he called Edgar and Charlie, after Edgar Bergen and his puppet. Victor ponied up two hundred bucks, but before anyone else could make an offer,

Shorty McGregor offered two thousand, which pretty well backed everybody off.

"They're worth a thousand apiece," Shorty declared as he walked through the crowd. "Ira broke 'em."

"That ain't all he broke," Victor smirked.

Shorty never said a word, and without breaking his stride a single step, Shorty reached down inside himself and slugged Victor on the chin, as calmly as if he was hitting a badger with a shovel.

Victor folded up and crashed to the ground in a heap, and then jumped up, his fists doubled so hard that his knuckles were white, but the crowd closed around Victor, and Shorty walked up and wrote out his check for the team.

Joe bought the colts, four sorrel geldings that were coming two year olds, and Davey Boyd bought a pair of mares that Ira favored more for color than size.

Red bought two old brood mares, and Fred Aspering took an old gelding that Ira used to train colts to the harness.

A pair of fillies that everybody wanted almost sold to some guy in a pig hat, but I remembered what Fingers told me, and he ended up getting himself a fine pair of yearlings for eight hundred bucks apiece.

Fingers also ran the price of Ira's Belgian stud up to four thousand before he let Victor take him, and I'm not sure Fingers wouldn't have gone a little higher, but Joe grabbed my arm and told me enough was enough.

Red split the harness with Fred Aspering, and Daisy Aspering bought every single keepsake, outbidding at least a dozen antique dealers who had shown up to make off with some bargains.

Just as soon as she bought one of the Cusack family treasures, she would direct Fred to walk over and get it, and then she carried it over and placed it on the front seat of Ira's pickup. Her blue eyes weren't sparkling like usual, and she stared at the antique dealers every time they offered a bid, until finally, she just held her hand in the air until they were worn out. The antique dealers huddled together and glared at Daisy's outstretched arm, then finally crawled back to their cars and went away.

Loper bought the equipment, despite the fact that he had no need for any horse-drawn implements, and Fred took the milk cow. After Shorty knocked Victor on his keester, prices held up pretty well.

The auction didn't last long. I guess when a man is stripped of his land and his horses, it tends to quicken the finish, and if it weren't for some strange, quiet obligation that everyone felt to bid at least once on everything, the sale would have ended long before it did.

Through it all, Ira never sat, never smiled, never shed a tear. When it was all over, he walked up to the clerk's table, signed the papers and stepped off the porch.

"Thank you," he put a big arm around Shorty. "You've been my friend."

"Shoot, Ira," Shorty looked at the ground. "I don't want the team. I bought 'em back for you."

"I have no use for them now," the big man shrugged. "Maybe someday I can come and drive them."

"Any time," Shorty looked at the ground and his lower lip shook.

"I know what you were doing," he smiled at Joe and Red.

"I got me a bunch of colts," Joe offered. "Figure I might need me a horse hand to break 'em right."

"Thank you," Ira nodded, "but, not now."

"You paid too much," he shook hands with Davey. "All I

try to teach you and you pay too much for the oldest, shortest team I had?"

"They got good color," Davey reminded him.

"I'll tell Fingers what you did," Ira shook my hand. His brown eyes were soft and sad.

Daisy ran up, her head about as high as Ira's belt buckle, and started babbling about how sorry she was, and for the first time all day, Ira laughed out loud.

"Daisy," he wrapped his gigantic frame around the little woman, then held her face in his hands. "You always was the best thing on this creek."

That much done, Ira walked over to the corral, shoulders square, until his brown hands rested on the poles. Unlike the other corrals on the creek, Ira's were crafted of poles identical in size; every one of them as straight as a string, evenly spaced, notched at the corners, and fitted as tightly as a set of dentures.

The rest of us let him go. His whole body sagged against the poles.

The colts trotted over and nuzzled at the big man, and Ira reached into the pocket of his jacket and slipped each of them a chunk of cottonseed cake that had managed to escape the liens and the auction block. The colts rolled their upper lips back and shook their heads and Ira touched each of them on the soft part of the nose, then climbed in his old red pickup and drove off down the Friendly Creek road. He never looked back.

In the long run, Victor Wilsz absorbed the acreage, but for the rest of us, Friendly Creek will always be a quarter-mile shorter.

The Gather

The cattle market reached a forty-year low on the very day Victor Wilsz sold his calves, and Victor walked out of the meeting at the Friendly Creek State Bank and headed straight for the Hoosegow, where he stood at the end of the bar and poured four Old Charters into his head. His thirst apparently tamed, he smashed his huge fist on the bar and sent a white Hoosegow ashtray rolling across the floor.

"There's a band of rustlers been working my herd!" he declared to Bobby Baker, who was busy washing out beer glasses.

"You don't say," Bobby smiled.

"Sons-of-bitches!" Victor yelled again, and he smashed his fist onto the bar when I walked through the door.

"Howdy, Victor," I waved.

"Don't you 'howdy' me, Pinhead!" he yelled. "For all I know, you could be one of the dirty, little, stinking, brush-crawling, lowlife scumbag snakes who's stealing my cattle."

"Victor just came from the bank," Bobby said. "He's in a bad mood."

"No kidding?" I sat down. "I thought he was like this all the time."

"Let every man be on notice!" Victor barked, and he twisted a beer napkin into little pieces. "If I see *anyone* messing around my cattle, I'll smash 'em like a jackrabbit on the highway!"

With that, he turned to assess the impact of his tirade on the other patrons in the bar.

"Hey, Victor!" Davey Boyd waved from the corner.

"You're the only person here?" Victor whined.

"Yep," Davey nodded. "But, I'll tell everybody what a fine speech you made."

"That wasn't a speech," Victor screamed, "It was a threat!"

"Well, whatever it was, it was sure good." Davey grinned.

"Howdy there Victor!" Shorty wandered into the bar. "You buyin'?"

"Spread the word!" Victor snapped. "I aim to ride every damn herd on the creek this fall!"

"Hot damn!" Shorty grinned. "That'll be a big help. I'm gonna gather next week. Can you bring along some extra hands?"

Victor stomped across the wooden floor and slammed the bathroom door.

"Wow," Shorty whistled, "That Victor sure gets cranky. I hope he's in a better mood when he comes to help me gather cows."

"Shorty," Bobby Baker groaned. "Victor just came from the bank. He claims he's losin' cattle. Says there's rustlers workin' his herd."

"Oh, hell," Shorty laughed. "Victor says that ever' year. He counts a thousand cows at the bank, five hundred through the gate and fifty on the tax rolls."

"What's the matter with Victor?" Red walked in the door.

"He just came from the bank," Bobby repeated himself. "Says there's rustlers working his cattle herd."

"Oh," Red perched himself at the bar. The notion of rustlers didn't seem to bother Red. He just sat up at the bar and sipped on his beer, but everyone else had plenty of rustler stories to toss around.

Joe had a theory that the rustlers were most active when the market was up, since there was more money in a higher-priced product. As evidence, he pointed out some trivia he had heard that more robbers stole from jewelry shops than they did from grocery stores.

"That thing about jewelry stores is wrong," Fingers disagreed. "People steal from me all the time, and they don't steal jewelry."

"You don't sell jewelry," Joe reminded him, "except for those overpriced watches you keep under lock and key."

"Nobody ever tries to steal those!" Fingers said. "They all steal candy."

"So what are you saying?" Loper asked. "You think these rustlers are third graders?"

"I was talking about thieves," Fingers advised, "not rustlers."

"I still say they steal cattle when the price is high," Joe said. "Why would someone steal something that ain't worth a damn?"

"Same reason they steal highway signs and towels from motels," Loper thought. "Thieves are just thieves. They *like* to steal."

"That's crazy," Joe scoffed. "People who steal towels from motels don't try to sell them."

"Neither do all the rustlers on this creek," Red growled.

"What are you getting at?" Shorty asked, and Red swung around on his stool and faced the rest of the crowd.

"Every fall," Red said, "Victor ends up with a dozen of my cows, and every damn one of 'em is a dry. And, every year, he ships a dozen damn good black baldy calves. Now, you tell me how he can end up with a dozen baldies out of straight black cows, and I end up twelve calves short."

"How is it that these rustlers steal from Joe in the good years, Victor in the bad year's and everybody else all the time," Bobby wondered, "and none of them ever come in my bar and spend any of the loot?"

"Because when they're in town, they're busy stealing stuff out of my store!" Fingers yelled.

Actually, I thought Bobby had a pretty good question there. He had never seen any of them in town, and I'd never seen any of them on the road, or for that matter, rustling around behind any of the bushes I had ridden around.

"Where do you figure all these rustlers live?" I asked.

Every head turned to look at me.

"What are you saying?" Loper frowned.

"I just wonder where all of these rustlers live," I shrugged. "That's all."

"Where the hell do you think they live?" Victor roared from the bathroom door. "I suppose you expect 'em to paint a sign on the door of their pickup so we'll know when they're here!"

"Nope," I shook my head. "I just haven't seen anyone anywhere that looked like a rustler, and it seems like if they were stealing all the time, sooner or later you'd see something."

"They're professionals!" Victor groused. "They aren't gonna let some pinheaded kid like you just sit around and watch 'em, for Christ's sake!"

"This whole ring of thieves could be an 'inside job,'" Loper thought out loud. "It could be somebody from around here that's doing it."

"Well, Glory Hallelujah! Red stood up. "It's about time you figured that out!"

"I've had it with this jabbering!" Victor decreed, and he rose from his seat, vowing to get to the bottom of the rustling, "come hell or high water!"

From that moment on, lacking any other possible suspects, just about everybody on the creek accused everybody else of being a dirty, rotten, lowdown, conniving, slinking, night-riding, long looped, thieving son-of-a-bitch.

Even Fred Aspering, whose lone bovine critter was an old milk cow, was watched closely. Victor called Buck Martin, the Deputy Sheriff, to arrest Fred for stealing a bull for one day to breed the old rip, and while the basic charge was true, the idea that Fred would steal one of Victor's black bulls was laughable. Fred always used Red's Shorthorns or Joe's Herefords.

Buck finished his investigation and refused to throw Fred in jail, and Victor blew sky high, cursed everyone whose name he could remember and hired himself a "range detective."

After Victor announced that the range detective had been hired, no one saw hide nor hair of him, but there was plenty of grumbling about this phantom, and even the people in town were pretty indignant that anyone would stoop to such a level of distrust.

That, coupled with Victor's threat to "ride every herd on the creek," hung over the valley like a cold, wet fog.

I tried to stay as far away from the subject of rustling as possible and went on about my job, fall irrigating, which, in fact, really didn't amount to much more than stealing water.

The fact that the valley was obsessed with rustling made my job much easier than usual, and I was chuckling at my good fortune when I blew over the sand notch on Squaw Bluff. I had the throttle on the dirt bike wide open, and I caught some air, then made a perfect landing on the back tire and ran right over the top of Victor's range detective.

He was sitting in a hole he had scratched out of the sand, and his horse was hidden in a little corral built out of sagebrush. From where he was hiding, he could see most of the valley below him, but he hadn't seen me coming until I had left a knobby track down his chest and crashed into the rocks down the hill.

The noise spooked his horse, and the last I saw of the broomtail was its butt headed over the ridge, hobbles and all, stirrups flapping at both sides.

"Hey!" I yelled up the hill. "What do you think you are? A badger?"

He poked his head out of his hole and squinted at me.

"I think you should reconsider what you said," he whispered, real low and mean.

"What?" I cupped a hand to my ear. "Speak up!"

"I don't take kindly to bein' called a 'rodent,'" he said.

"A badger isn't a rodent," I said. "It's a member of the dog family, more or less."

"I don't like bein' called a dog neither," he added, and he hauled out a big pistol and pointed it at me.

"Hey!" I hollered, "put that gun away before you hurt somebody!"

"Stop right there," he hissed, and he crouched into some weird stance, like maybe he had to go to the bathroom or something.

"Hey, wait a minute," I stopped. "Are you a rustler?"

He shook his head vigorously, and his long moustache flapped against his cheeks.

"Well, then," I said, "if you aren't a badger and you aren't a rustler, I'd guess you must be Victor's range detective."

"What makes you think Mr. Wilsz has hired a range detective?" he asked.

"His speeches in the bar and his ad in the newspaper," I said.

"You seem to know an awful lot about all this thievery," he squinted, and he hoisted the gun again.

"Put that away!" I yelled.

"I aim to find them rustlers," he slid the hogleg into his holster. He worked his cheeks around and shot a stream of tobacco spit right next to my boot, so I moved over a little bit.

"That's great," I smiled, "but I think it would be a good idea if you did your burrowing and gunplay on Victor's land. You're right in the middle of the Barnes outfit."

"I know where I am," he said, and he crouched down again.

"What are you doing up here?" I asked.

"I'm jest watchin' and waitin'," he stood up and stared at my bike.

He seemed to be confused.

"Why don't you ride a cayuse?" he asked.

"A what?"

"A cayuse!" he snapped. "You know. A cayuse, mount, bronc, pony."

"You mean a *horse*?" I asked.

"I mean a cayuse," he insisted.

"Four legs, whinnies, tail like a broom?" I described the creature for him. "We call those horses, and yes, I ride one."

"Then why you ridin' that Jap pony?" he pointed at the dirt bike.

"That," I informed him, "is a Husquavarna. It is not your run of the mill Japanese dirt bike. It's Swedish. And I ride it because it will go sixty miles an hour uphill and it won't jump out of a sagebrush corral and run home without me."

"You seen any thieves?" he changed the subject, and he looked around us skulkily.

"Water thieves, cow thieves, horse thieves, candy stealers or some other kind?" I asked.

"A thief's a thief," he said.

"Well then, everybody you see on this creek is a thief," I advised.

"Who's the biggest one?" he wondered, and he flipped out a little note pad which must have contained all of the clues he was getting while he was hunkered down in his little bed.

"I'd say Victor Wilsz outweighs 'em all," I smiled.

"I believe I'm gonna hafta shoot you right in that smart mouth of yours," he said, and he hauled his big pistol out again.

"I've had enough of this," I said, and I walked down the hill and pulled the bike onto its wheels, then headed home to report this development to higher authorities than myself.

"He was doing what?" Joe asked.

"He was sitting in a little hole up there below the sand hill," I explained, "and he had a big pistol."

"Sitting in a hole," Joe thought. "Like a gopher?"

"More like a badger," I suggested.

"You sure he wasn't a rustler?" Joe asked.

"Beats me," I shrugged. "I've never seen a rustler."

"What did he look like?"

"It was the biggest hat I ever saw," I remembered, "sort of a cross between a sombrero and a forest ranger hat, and there was a big crease right down the middle of the thing and a string around his neck, like I used to have when I was a little kid."

I added that he was wearing a green silk scarf, and a red and white checkered shirt, and he had a leather vest with a watch chain hanging out of it, faded jeans and short little chaps.

"Like shoeing chaps?" Joe asked.

"Kinda like that," I nodded, "and he had on a pair of boots with high heels and big red tops with eagles on them, and he wore 'em on the outside of his pants."

"He was wearing spurs, too," I added. "They looked like some of the stuff we pull behind the tractor. He had leather cuffs on his sleeves, and he had a big pistol."

"Oh yeah," I remembered. "He had the longest moustache I ever saw. He looked like that cartoon guy . . . Yosemite Sam."

On top of the hill, a vehicle rattled across the cattleguard and Victor pulled up in an official blue Wilsz Ranch pickup with the brand on the door. He was pulling a trailer, and the sorrel inside looked familiar.

"You seen my range detective?" Victor asked.

"Nope," Joe said. "What's he look like?"

"He's a buckaroo," Victor said.

"A bucket of what?" Joe asked.

"A buckaroo," Victor repeated himself, "from Nevada."

"Does he look like Yosemite Sam?" I asked.

"Who's Yosemite Sam?" Victor glared at me.

"He's a friend of Bugs Bunny," I said. I didn't know exactly how to explain it any better.

"This guy is a rough character!" Victor held his hands about three feet apart. "He's got a pistol this big . . ."

"He looks like Yosemite Sam," I whispered to Joe.

"Why are you lookin' for this buckaroo?" Joe asked.

"His horse came home without him, and I'm pretty sure he's been drygulched by rustlers," Victor sighed. "That's the only way anybody could take him out."

"Halloooooo the camp!" came a holler from the ridge behind the barn. "I'm friendly and I'll be moseyin' in!"

"What the hell was that?" Joe asked.

"Sounds like Claude," Victor said, and he halloooed back.

"Where is he?" Joe asked.

"He's moseyin' on in," Victor bristled.

We waited patiently, but there was no sign of the buckaroo.

"How long does this moseyin' take?" Joe finally asked.

"He's prob'ly checkin' out the lay of the land," Victor suggested. "There ain't no sense a man walkin' into a trap."

All of a sudden, a little yip came out of the Wilsz buckaroo, and then there was the sound of crashing metal and iron.

"Sounds to me like that buckaroo just moseyed into the junk pile," Joe said.

A few minutes later, the guy who looked like Yosemite Sam came sneaking around the corner of the shop, from the opposite direction that he had hallooooooed us. Apparently satisfied that we weren't going to dry gulch him right there in the yard, he stepped into the light and rested his hand on his hogleg.

"This," Victor pointed at Claude. "is my range detective."

"I see." Joe said, but I'm not sure he saw.

Victor and Claude whispered to each other for a moment then jumped into Victor's pick-up and drove away.

"Yosemite Sam?" Joe laughed.

"Yosemite Sam." I nodded.

When daylight woke the valley, it was Shorty's appointed day to gather cattle, and as he promised, Victor was there to ride Shorty's little bunch of cattle. There were no less than forty people assembled in Shorty's yard; half of them to ride his herd, and half of them to watch. The cows were standing at the gate, just waiting to come home, but there were enough pickups, trailers, horses, and cowboys to have a jackpot roping.

While the rest of us stood around and yawned, Claude checked his cinch and grabbed the headstall, then pulled a long rope out and tied it from the neck of his horse to his waist.

"What is that?" Joe asked.

"Runaway rope," the buckaroo advised. "I ain't gonna let my cayuse dust me off and run away."

"What does he do with the rope?" I asked.

"If he gets unloaded," Victor advised, "he'll be able to grab onto that runaway rope and catch his horse."

Claude was pretty fired up by all of the attention, and he swung aboard the bronc, which took about three jumps and twisted him around like a sack of oats, then deposited him in the rocky yard. His runaway rope snuck around his back and came straight up through his legs, and then the horse was off and

193

running, and Claude was bouncing along behind with the rope slapping upward between his thighs.

"I'd think that would hurt," Joe suggested.

The last we heard of Claude was a high-pitched "whoa" and the rattle of his fanny raking over the cattleguard.

Shorty walked out of his little house and looked at the people, animals, and vehicles assembled in the yard, then started giggling.

"This ain't no laughing matter, McGregor!" Victor yelled from the back of his horse. "I aim to cut strays all up and down this creek until I find my cattle!"

"Well, boys!" Shorty pointed up at the cows, "The cows are up there at the gate, waitin' to come home. You wanna draw straws for who gits to herd which cow?"

With that, Shorty convulsed with laughter at his own great wit and led his horse over to the trailer.

"What the hell is he doing?" Victor asked Joe.

"I have no idea," Joe sighed. "As I recall, this whole mess was your idea."

Everyone sat grimly and watched, and Shorty opened the trailer gate and slapped his favorite buckskin mare on the butt. When she was loaded, he sat down on the fender of the trailer and shoved a chew in his mouth.

"What the hell are you doing?" Victor finally snapped.

"Go on now Victor!" Shorty growled back. "You're so sure that everybody around is stealing cows you never had. Now, get in there and gather my cows!"

"I aim to do just that!" Victor yelled, "But I want to know what it is you plan to do with that horse!"

"Well," Shorty grinned, his eyes twinkling, "I figure while

all of you Fearless Fosdicks are out checking my cows, I'll just ride on down and steal all of yours!"

"You old son-of-a-bitch," Victor whispered, and then all of the outfits tried to hide their sheepish grins behind their hats, and they loaded their horses back into the fleet of trailers and pulled them home with the fleet of pickups.

Shorty sat on the fender and giggled, and when the dust cleared and the sun was high in the sky, he went out and gathered his cows.

Nobody knows what possessed Edna Loper to call a meeting of the Friendly Creek Cattlemen's Association, but she darn sure did it, and it pretty well caught everyone by surprise. For one thing, it was only the third meeting in the ninety-year history of the organization. The first was an organizational meeting back in the 1890s, and the second had turned into a wild riot known locally as the "massacre," in which everyone divided up the treasury to make it through the Depression. By the time everyone agreed to the division of assets, the bank had closed up and allocated the account for other purposes, and while nobody got any of the treasury, they did fire the banker as their "unbiased" treasurer, thereby setting a long-standing policy that no bankers would be allowed to hold the funds of the FCCA ever again.

Now, forty-odd years later, without any apparent reason, Edna just mailed out notices and put an ad in the newspaper.

If the notices were a surprise, the advertisement in the *Friendly Creek Sentinel* touched off a wild run of gossip and speculation in four counties. A contingent from the other side of the mountain declared that they would be in attendance, and several ranches over on the river sent in their dues so they could vote. Everyone in town began to speculate on the purpose of the meeting, and everyone was nervous enough that finally, Bobby Baker and Lee Willoughby offered to pay for the booze so that they would be invited. Not to be outdone, Fingers and the other merchants donated about three hundred door prizes, all of which could be given away after dinner.

By the time all of the associated gossip and rumor got back to Edna, she was fit to be tied and Carl was more than ready to tie her up. For more than a week, Edna had fretted as the meeting grew to demonic proportions, finally reaching such monumental import that there was a little blurb about it in the Casper newspaper.

"All I wanted to do was have a nice little potluck supper," she fretted while she straightened her dress, "and now, everyone in town is planning to be here."

"What possessed you to do this?" Carl asked, and he tried to remember how to tie a knot in his tie.

"Well," she sighed, "I don't really know."

"For God's sake Edna!" Carl gasped. "If you don't know what you're doing, why don't you just go out and murder the children? I could explain that!"

"You can't wear that tie," she scolded. "It's stained."

"Where?" Carl held the tie up and looked it over.

"By the horse," she pointed. "You probably spilled booze on it when you got so drunk at the Carter girl's wedding. Throw it away. The tie is ruined."

"How the hell did we get to a commentary on my necktie?"

Carl asked. "If you hadn't gone out and called this stupid meeting, I wouldn't have to wear a necktie in the first place!"

"The last time you wore one you got drunker than a Lord," Edna turned around so that he could zip her dress. "I hope you won't do that tonight."

"Edna," he zipped, "the last Association meeting turned into a riot! There are people coming who don't even live here!"

"Good," she stuck her face close to the mirror and looked at her lipstick. "Maybe we'll make some new friends."

"Maybe nobody will come," Carl fished in the closet for another tie.

"Oh Carl," Edna whined. "Don't say that. I have RSVPs from two hundred."

"Two hundred!"

"Well, every ranch is bringing their crew and then there's all the people from the bank, and the river people and the folks from over the mountain, and the gas company asked if they could come along, and..."

"Edna," Carl whispered, "if we live through this, I'm going to kill you."

"Don't be silly, dear," she smiled. "You were elected President at the last meeting. It's up to you from here."

Carl handled it well. When the first car arrived, he was on the porch, waving and smiling, and he helped Bobby serve drinks in a most gracious manner. Everyone brought along a roaster full of beef, salad or potatoes, and the folks from over the mountain must have baked a thousand pies. Content that there would be no riot, the bankers, gas company, newspaper, merchants, and others left right after dinner. Carl gave away all of the good door prizes right at the first, and when the ranchers from over the mountain and down on the river didn't win any, they took their pie plates and went on home.

The third meeting of the Friendly Creek Cattlemen's Association moved into the living room.

"Well, hell," Carl called the meeting to order. "I'd like to thank you all for coming. We haven't really got much of an agenda here, being's Edna was the one who called this damn thing, but I guess we oughta go on ahead with the meeting anyway."

"Point of order," Jimmy Wilsz waved his hand.

"Yeah, go ahead," Carl shrugged.

"How come you're the chairman?"

"I was elected at the last one," Carl explained.

"That's right," Shorty agreed, "and Victor was elected Vice President."

"When is the next election?" Jimmy asked.

"Well," Carl tried to smile, "if you would let me get the meeting started and quit interrupting with things that happened before you was born, I was planning to have the election at the beginning."

"I nominate my dad," Jimmy crowed.

Spudley McKay, the Wilsz Ranch foreman, seconded.

"Now, wait a minute," Red raised his arm. "I don't see where it's fair that the Wilsz outfit can nominate the chairman and second it too."

"You don't have to second a nomination," Joe advised.

"I nominate Shorty McGregor," Red said.

"Second," Spudley said.

"You don't have to second a nomination," Joe reminded them.

Shorty declined the nomination.

"Hell, Shorty, make a run at it," Red told him.

"No way," Shorty shook his head. "I was secretary at the last meeting, and I'm too old to make it another forty years to the next one. I say we give it to Victor. Let *him* die in office."

"I'll second that," Red offered.

"Let's vote," Loper suggested.

"Wait a minute!" Davey Boyd interrupted. "Are we voting

199

on whether Victor is gonna be the President or whether he should die in office?"

"It's the same thing," Shorty advised.

"Is he president, or is he chairman?" Jimmy asked.

"Who gives a damn?" Joe growled.

"All in favor say aye," Carl begged, and Victor was made chairman or president of the Friendly Creek Cattlemen's Association.

After a great deal of debate and nomination, Red Barnes was elected Vice President and Edna Loper was elected Secretary, prompting her to offer a thirty minute acceptance speech that was totally incomprehensible.

"Just don't go calling a lot of meetings," Carl suggested, and every head nodded approval.

"First order of business here," Victor said, "is to change the by laws to say that the officers aren't responsible if we get sued by somebody."

"You got some girl in trouble, Victor?" Joe asked.

"What Victor means here is that there's too many lawsuits all over the place," Carl jumped in. "No sense anybody losin' his place because the officers do somethin' wrong."

"Well now, what the hell have these new officers got cooked up?" Red asked.

"Just a minute!" Victor yelled. "What this means is that if something happens at one of the meetings, then some fool can't come in here and sue the officers personally."

"That isn't what it means at all," Loper clarified the matter. "What it says is that if Edna called this here meeting and then fed everybody a fine beef dinner, and the cafe prepared the meal and then everybody got sick, somebody couldn't sue Edna. They'd have to sue the cafe. Now, on the other hand, if Edna had insisted that we all come here and eat fried chicken, and she cooked all the fried chicken and we all got the Salmonelli bug and died, then we could go on ahead and sue her."

"Well I can tell you this!" Edna chimed in. "I do not serve chicken at our home! As past-president of the Cowbelles, I have never served chicken to guests."

"Sure," Red chuckled. "You and Loper sneak off and eat it when nobody can see."

"You never minded a good fried chicken," Red's wife hollered from the kitchen.

"That was when I was raising the chickens," Joe piped up.

"Are you calling me a chicken rustler?' Red bristled.

"Shut up!" Loper yelled, and he banged a spoon on the back of a chair to get the chatter died down.

"Now, we've had a fine meal and a good meeting here, and I agree with Victor. We need to change the Bylaws and adjourn this damn fool thing. And Edna, for God's sake.....nobody here is questioning your virtue when it comes to serving beef."

"As President of the Friendly Creek Cattlemen's Association," Victor orated, "I believe we'd ought to have some resolutions come out of this historic meeting."

"I resolve that we shoot all rustlers on sight!" Jimmy Wilsz crowed.

"I second that resolve," Davey waved his hand, and a spirited discussion ensued, with the resolution being amended to smithereens and finally passing unanimously.

"I resolve that everybody vaccinate everything for every disease there is," Joe said.

"I don't think you really want to do that," Jack Jackman advised. Jack was the local veterinarian, and it surprised most of the people that he would offer an opinion that didn't cost anything.

"Why shouldn't we do that?" Joe asked.

"I think you should name the diseases you want to control," Jack said, "not just pass a resolution that says to vaccinate for everything they could get."

"You sell us vaccine for every disease a critter might ever

get," Shorty said. "Why shouldn't we pass a resolution like that?"

"Just a minute!" Victor pointed at Jack. "You haven't paid dues to this outfit, and you aren't a rancher, so you can't talk."

"I'm an associate member," the veterinarian said. "That costs more money than it does to be a member."

"You make it up on vaccine," Shorty suggested.

"Like I said, I'm an associate member," Jack pouted.

"Then you can't talk and you can't vote," Victor decided, and he hit the antique table with a gravy spoon.

"What the hell can I do?" the vet asked.

"You can sit there and be quiet," Joe said.

"Unless somebody calls on you to answer a question," Victor said.

"I'd like to ask him to explain what he meant," Fred Aspering announced.

"*You* can't ask him," Joe insisted. "You're a *sheep* man and this is the 'Friendly Creek *Cattle*men's Association."

"I paid my dues," Fred said. "and I own a cow *and* a calf."

"Where did you get the calf?" Joe asked. "You don't own a bull."

"It looks like the calf is a Hereford this year," Red advised. "Usually, he steals one of my Shorthorn bulls, but this year it's a Hereford looking thing."

"I make a motion that we allow associate members to vote," Fred said.

Davey seconded.

"That's out of order," Joe said. "You don't make a motion. You move."

"Besides that," Red agreed, "that takes a change in the Bylaws and it has to go out for thirty days before the next meeting."

"I think if we take their money, they oughta get to vote," Fred suggested.

"They oughta at least own a cow!" Joe crossed his arms.

It was pointed out that the veterinarian owned more cows than Fred, and he was only an associate member, whereas Fred had been allowed to talk and vote.

"Next meeting the banker will want to talk about interest rates," Joe yelled. "I say this outfit is a cowman's outfit and the rest of 'em can pay their dues and shut up!"

"If we wait the normal period for the next meeting," Shorty reminded them, "we'll all be old and dead."

"Oh for Pete's sake," Victor said, and he directed the doctor to answer the question.

Doctors being doctors and science being science, the veterinarian took forty minutes to explain his point of view, and when he was done, the ranchers voted unanimously to ignore his advice and pass Joe's resolution.

Red offered a resolution that Victor would quit stealing Red's cows, but that one failed, either because the majority didn't think that Victor was stealing Red's cows, or because nobody thought the resolution would do a bit of good.

Each resolution was preceded by a glorious oration of varying quality, and in the true tradition of democracy, somebody rose to oppose each and every proposal.

Other resolutions called upon Congress to balance the budget, to get rid of the Federal Reserve, to sell the BLM lands for a "reasonable" price, and to allow the President a line item veto. There was a resolution calling for a return to interest rates where a rancher could make a living, and there was another opposing the wolf, coyotes, grizzly bears, and environmental impact statements in general. In all, there were twenty-two resolutions, not counting the one to thank all of the bankers and merchants for donations and liquor.

"Is there any other business?" Victor looked at his watch.

"Yeah," Red raised his hand. "What are we gonna do with all these resolutions?"

"Well, now," Victor thought that one over. "I guess I don't really know."

"I say we send 'em to the President and the Congress!" Jimmy Wilsz hollered.

"I say you've been sittin' too close to the beer cooler," Joe snorted. "What is the President and the Congress gonna do? Fold up tent because we sent 'em a passel of resolutions?"

"Now hold on!" Victor said. "I'm gonna ask the secretary to tell us what to do."

He looked over at Edna, and she smiled sweetly.

"Oh dear me," she held her hand to her mouth. "Did you want me to write all of that down?"

"What the hell were you doing?" Loper screamed.

"You mean we don't get to shoot all rustlers on sight?" Jimmy Wilsz whined.

"How could you do this?" Victor asked Edna.

"I'm so sorry," Edna said, "but I guess I'm so used to hearing you all rattle on like this, I never knew it was 'official' business."

Well, nobody knew what the hell to say about that, and Victor twisted the gravy spoon in the palm of his hand.

Finally, Shorty stood up and smiled at Edna.

"Hell, Edna," he grinned. "I wouldn't worry about it. By the time you have to read the minutes, we'll all be dead."

LITTLE BUCKY

The news that Congressman Sam Wilson was coming to visit Friendly Creek put everyone into a lather. As far back as any of the old-timers could remember, no Congressman has ever been to Friendly Creek. The *Friendly Creek Sentinel* had an editorial and a news story on the impending visit. The Republican Women scheduled a parade and a visit to both the High School and the Senior Citizen's center, and of course, there would be a luncheon and an awards ceremony, and the Mayor would give Congressman Wilson a plaque in recognition of his devotion to the people of Friendly Creek.

All of a sudden, everybody on the creek was sporting Sam Wilson buttons and there were bumper stickers all over the valley. Every old lady in the county was filing her nails with a Sam Wilson fingernail rasp, and some zealot tied Sam Wilson balloons to the water tower.

I could never figure out where people got all that Sam

Wilson junk, unless they *kept* stuff like that. If they did, I wondered what on earth they planned to do with it. Personally, I never found much value in a political bumper sticker, except Shorty McGregor's "Don't Re-Elect Anybody."

"When is he going to see the drought" Joe asked when he read the paper. "There's parades and speeches and lunches and a bunch of that crap, but when is he gonna' see the damn drought?"

"Why is he getting a plaque?" Red asked. "I've lived here for sixty-six years, and nobody ever gave me a plaque."

"You're not a Congressman," Davey Boyd reminded him.

"Well, if I was," Red stiffened, "I'd sure take time to see the drought."

"He came one time and we all voted for him." Loper said. " What does he want from us now?"

"He wants a plaque," Red sulked.

"Maybe he's coming up here to see me!" Davey said.

"Now that," Bobby Baker yelled from behind the bar, "is the dumbest idea I've heard so far."

"Oh yeah?" Davey stood up.

"Yeah," Bobby laughed.

"Well, it just so happens that I have a letter here from my personal friend Sam Wilson inviting me to sit at the head table with him at lunch!" Davey said, and he pulled out his letter, complete with a blue Congressional crest at the top of the letterhead.

"That's a photo copy," Joe scoffed, and he held the paper up to the light. "Hell, it says `Dear Friend.'"

"We're old buddies," Davey said, and he folded his letter and put it back in his wallet. "Me and Sam go way back."

Whatever it was that Sam Wilson wanted, he arrived right at lunchtime on the appointed day, and the people in Friendly Creek and Buzzard Butte turned out on the streets with their instamatics and took pictures as he raced past. Right behind his car came another, this one full of photographers from national publications, and behind that one came a van full of staff members. When Sam arrived at the Senior Center, every deputy in the county stood in front of him, just in case some sort of threat might be posed, and Sam Wilson waved and blew kisses.

"He's been in Washington too long," Shorty shoved his hands in his pockets. "He acts like some kind of fairy."

Red counted up all the staff members and decided that if he had that many hired hands, he could ranch the whole county and still have time to rope every night.

Sam waded into the crowd and shook hands, and as Eloise Carter, the local chairman of the Republican women, whispered in the ear of an aide, the aide whispered in the ear of Sam Wilson, and like magic, he seemed to remember the name of everyone in town.

Finally, the Congressman stood up on the porch of the Senior Center and waved. Eloise Carter introduced her husband and the members of the Executive Board of the Republican Women, and then she introduced Johnny Dunphy, the county committeeman, who introduced all of the precinct people and finally, Congressman Sam Wilson.

"My dear, dear friends of Happy Creek," Sam blew a kiss. "It is so good to be here on such a fine day! Thank God it isn't muggy and rainy like it is in the nation's capitol."

"What do you mean?" Joe yelled. "We've got a drought here!"

"Please hold your questions until later," an aide suggested, and one of the deputy sheriffs walked over and stood in front of Joe.

"I was visiting with the President the other day," Sam said, and people nodded approvingly at each other. "He and I were reminiscing about how much we both love the true Americans who live in towns like Happy Valley and Buzzers Bluff."

"Where the hell is this 'Happy Valley'?" Loper squawked.

Johnny Dunphy whispered in the Congressman's ear, and Sam Wilson beamed with delight.

"Just like I told the President," Sam pounded on the podium, "you don't see that kind of pride unless you've been out among the people!"

The crowd actually cheered.

"I remember my first trip up here," Sam went on. "One of the first people I met was a young fellow named Buck. He was out riding a beautiful tan horse, and he told me that horse controlled his life."

"Who's this 'Buck?' " Joe asked.

"What is a tan horse?" Victor wondered.

"I told Little Bucky that if he voted for me, he could take control of his own life!" Sam yelled, and he held both hands in the air. "I told Little Bucky if he would vote for me he would see the day when I would go to Washington and clean up this country for people like him and his horse!"

The crowd clapped and cheered, and old Sam held his hands in the air and smiled from ear to ear.

"Not a day goes by that I don't think about little Bucky and his pony," he wiped a tear from his eye. "And I believe, in my heart of hearts, that the job I am doing is a job to make this nation a place where little Bucky and his tan pony can run free, free, free like the wind!"

Bobby Baker worked his way through the crowd and caught Joe by the arm.

"Who is this Bucky kid?" Bobby whispered.

"He's making it up," Joe said.

"Sam Wilson is a straight shooter!" Davey hissed. "He ain't makin' it up!"

The Mayor handed Sam Wilson his plaque, and Sam said he would cherish it as one of his most prized honors of all time. He gave it to an aide, who handed it to another aide who handed it to a young girl who ran out and threw it in the trunk of the car.

A line formed, and the people shuffled along to shake hands with Sam Wilson, who shook two hands at a time, gently pulling the people along their way, bobbing his head and winking. I stood at the base of the stairs and watched as Davey got in line, got up to the Congressman and held out his hand.

"I've got a problem I need to talk to you about," Davey said.

"Great to see ya'!" Sam said, and he pulled Davey right on down the line and grabbed Shorty's hand.

As soon as Davey realized what had happened, he ran out the back door of the Senior Center and got back in line, and this time, he didn't offer a hand for the Congressman.

"I'm Davey Boyd," he said. "I gave you a ride to Shoshoni when your wife drove off and left you. I've been writing to you for three months about a problem I've been having."

"I remember the letters," Sam frowned. "I'm right on top of that problem and I'll be getting back with you."

The Congressman reached out and grabbed the next person in line, turned at the very moment the flash went off, then jerked the old lady along out of the way and grabbed another, and Davey ran out the back door and got in line again.

"Hey!" Sam Wilson smiled when Davey came around again, "I remember you! Boy, it sure is good to see you again!"

Davey was careful to keep his hands in his pockets so that Sam Wilson couldn't pull him away, but Buck Martin came over and led Davey out of the way, and then Sam Wilson was hustling off toward the big, black car.

"Sorry we can't stay," an aide told the crowd. "The President is on the car phone. It looks like the Congressman will have to get right back to Washington."

"Can't say no to the President!" Sam waved, and he ran for the car with Davey hot on his trail.

"Hey you!" Davey yelled. "I gave you a ride to Shoshoni! I told people you were a good guy! I *voted* for you!"

"He appreciates it very much," the aide smiled, and he gave Davey a polite little shove.

Suddenly, the Congressman's car skidded to a stop and Sam Wilson jumped out and ran into the crowd.

"Bucky!" he yelled. "Bucky, my boy!"

Everybody looked around for this mythical doofus who was the owner of a tan pony, and the next thing I knew the Congressman had thrown his arms around me and he was shaking my hand and mauling me.

"Bucky?" Bobby Baker looked at me.

"You're Bucky?" Joe yelled.

"I remember the day I met you on the road," Sam Wilson said, and he drug his wife out of the car to have a look at me. I'd bet that I looked like an idiot.

"I'm not Bucky!" I insisted, but Sam Wilson was hugging me, and he didn't listen.

"Ladies and gentlemen!" he yelled to the crowd. "Right here is the young man I think of every day! Little Bucky! Every day I think of this frail child and his tan pony!"

"What the hell is going on around here?" Joe yelled at me.

"Bucky," Sam grabbed my shoulders and smiled, "I want to give you something. You've been an inspiration to me, and to the people of this nation. Every where I go, I talk about you."

"You have the wrong guy," I insisted.

"Shut up!" the aide hissed in my ear.

"This is for you, Bucky!" Sam smiled, and he handed me a heavy package.

"What's going on here?" Joe asked.

"Who the hell ever called you `Bucky?'" Shorty asked.

"Where did you get a tan pony?" Joe asked.

"I think he has me confused with that big buckskin gelding," I suggested.

"That buckskin is no tan pony," Joe said, "and your name isn't Bucky."

"You're really not Bucky?" Sam asked, and he took his arm off my shoulder.

"No," I said. "I think you have me confused with my horse. I'm the guy who picked you up on the road and gave you a ride to the bar when your wife drove off without you."

"Do you realize how important it is for Bucky to exist?" the aide whispered in my ear. "Go with the flow."

"You made it up," I said, "and my horse isn't named Bucky either."

The Congressman frowned at me, and his aide gave me an evil, nasty look. I thought about that day when I had first seen Congressman Wilson campaigning on the Friendly Creek road.

"Let's get out of here," the Congressman said, and Sam Wilson sped off down the highway.

I looked at the package he had placed in my hands . . . It was a plaque from the people of Friendly Creek and Buzzard Butte.

The way the old timers tell things, every ranch on Friendly Creek used to work together, including the Barnes and Wilsz outfits. They started in the spring, when everyone gathered and helped each other brand, then kept it up through the busiest seasons of the year. Benevolent historians try to make people believe that the help came of a certain sense of community obligation and heritage, and that may be true in some places, but on Friendly Creek everyone showed up at the other guy's branding to make sure there weren't any Double Mill Iron calves sucking Seven XL cows.

In the fall, they rode the roundup together, sharing the summer grass, the water, and the work when the grazing season was finished. They would gather in the mornings, cut cattle and brand in the afternoons, and argue in the evenings. After the cattle had filled on the hard, yellow grass of fall, they drove them to the railroad, seven hard days on horseback. When that was done, the bosses rode the cattle cars to Omaha and Chicago to watch the cattle sell and settle up, but mostly, to celebrate until the Stockyards Inn ran out of decent whiskey.

"Ah, but that was back when we sold cattle by the head, not by the pound," Red shook his head.

I stepped off my horse and opened the gate, and Red folded his hands over his saddle horn.

"That was back in the days before the railroad abandoned the spur lines up to the little towns and quit hauling steers and heifers, or for that matter, anything that wasn't coal," Red sighed, and his horse walked through the open gate.

After that, the big commission companies in Omaha, Kansas City, Chicago, and other places sent men out in the spring to line up calves for fall delivery. The buyers always showed up right after the calves were branded and turned onto green grass with their mamas, and the buyers came into the valley one right after the other, offering a penny here and there, maybe a half-penny more if the calves looked especially good. The name of the game was filling the sale ring every week through the fall run, and high country calves like those from Friendly Creek were a big draw. The farmers in the corn belt liked to feed those big, framy calves, and they sat in the bleachers with their hands in their overalls and their chew in their cheeks, nodding or wiggling their long eyebrows when they were interested.

I could remember the ranchers laying in wait for these eastern boys, estimating weights and sharpening pencils, and scratching out the "bottom line" on Big Chief tablets. If the cattle weighed up a little heavy, the ranchers came out ahead; if they were light, the commission man made a little bit. The bottom line moved a little bit every day, depending on what they heard on the radio, read in the newspaper or picked up on the party line. They chuckled and cackled and grunted and groaned because it was hard work trying to outwit the cattle buyers, but that was only half the challenge. The real test was being able to say they got a half-penny more for their calves than the other guy got for his. At the time, nobody paid a lick of attention to weight, breed or anything other than half-pennies, except for maybe the banker, who only paid attention to the dollars the calves brought and the dollars that made it into the bank against the note.

"I miss the old days," Red claimed as he pulled out a pack of cigarettes and fished around for a match. "Things were better when we could all ride the train and watch the cattle sell, then have a drink with the farmer that bought 'em."

I smiled and jumped back on my horse, and we lit out for Squaw Bluff, looking for a bunch of cattle that had taken their time coming off the mountain.

"If we had a normal Fall, them cows woulda come out by now," Red groused. "This hot weather ain't good for nothin'."

"Sold your calves?" I asked.

"Nah," he shook his head. "Hell of it is, it's gettin' to be so confusing to sell the damn things, I may just keep 'em all 'til they die."

"I heard Victor sold his calves for ninety cents," I said, more than a little bit proud to be able to offer some information.

"Victor always sells first," Red shrugged, "and he always gets the highest price on the creek, and he always acts like he's cut a fat hog in the butt."

"Think you'll get ninety?" I asked.

"Never have," Red smiled. "Prob'ly never will. But, my calves'll weigh eighty pounds more than Victor's, year in and year out, and they'll put more money in the bank."

"I hear there's been some buyers up here snoopin' around," I kicked the mare to keep up. "You gonna sell to one of them?"

"Price is right, and the check is good," Red winked, "I'd sell 'em to you."

He galloped down a big draw south of the Bluff and picked up a little gang of cattle, and I chased a pair of heifers, one of Joe's and one of Shorty's, from a pocket in the sand rocks. Red rode up and pushed them into the bunch, and I headed back up under the rim. I was looking for errant yearlings, but not very hard. Mostly, I was looking for answers.

According to most of the knowledge on Friendly Creek, Victor *always* sold his calves first, and he *always* sold them the first week in September and he *always* sold them to the same buyer, none other than Magnet Martin. Magnet Martin *always* loaded them up and hauled them off to some sale barn in South Dakota and made a damn fortune on them. Victor always got the highest price too, but then, according to the other sellers, that was because all of Victor's calves were worthless little pee wees.

"Ninety cents times three hundred pounds don't add up to much," Joe scoffed one time, but the way my pencil worked, it added up to more than seventy cents times four hundred pounds after you got the freight and yardage out.

Davey Boyd *always* loaded his little bunch up on the first Tuesday in October and hauled them over to Riverton for the sale because that was the biggest sale day of the year and all of the buyers would be there. Only once did Davey deviate from his set ways, and that was the year he decided to "hold out" for a higher price and sent them to Riverton the second Tuesday in October.

Woody Schmoe, who ranched over on Cottonwood, *always* loaded his calves on the trucks at the end of October and sent them to Omaha, then drove out there in his Lincoln Continental to watch them sell.

His calves still topped the market, but the trucking about ate up the difference. When you got right down to it, Woody

215

didn't seem to gain much from topping the market in Omaha, but he was the only one who got to drink whiskey at the Stockyards Inn, and Woody was always good enough at that to make up quite a bit of freight.

Shorty McGregor *always* waited until the first of October before he sold. The way he had it figured, September was too early, because the farmers were trying to count how many bushels of corn they would have to feed to cattle. The middle of October was too late, because the middle of October was Yom Kippur and that meant all the Jews wouldn't eat, and if all the Jews weren't eating, they wouldn't buy any meat, even if it didn't come from a pig. It was Shorty's absolute knowledge that the Jews controlled all of the meat markets in the world, not to mention the money supply, and the way Shorty saw it, if the Jews hadn't eaten for a whole damn day, they would be crabby. Furthermore, by the time Yom Kippur was over, all of the Gentiles would be thinking about Thanksgiving, and that meant they would all be wanting to buy turkeys.

"It's OK to deliver calves then," Shorty advised, "But they better be sold and you better have a deposit, because too much religion at once can make people do some pretty rotten things."

Joe Barnes *always* sold to the same feeder in Iowa, unless the feeder in Iowa wasn't interested, and then he sold to a feeder in Colorado. If the guy in Colorado wasn't interested, Joe panicked and called the buyers and asked them what they would pay, which wasn't much. When that happened, Joe got mad and hauled his calves over to the sale barn in Torrington right after Thanksgiving, unless it snowed, which it usually did that time of year.

Red Barnes *always* hung on and waited because the way he had it figured, when the market went up, the buyers would find him, and if the buyers weren't looking for him, the market wasn't good enough to be worrying about in the first place. More than once, that theory wound up putting Red into the

216

yearling business the following summer. Of course, Red always claimed that was his intention in the first place.

And Loper . . . well, Carl *always* had some scheme rattling around in his head that was going to make him rich and make all of the other ranchers look stupid. The hell of it was, nine times out of ten, for whatever reason, that's the way it worked.

One year, Loper came up with a hair-brained scheme that he would hold onto his calves and actually pay some guy he didn't even know to feed his cattle until they were fat. Everyone tried to explain to Loper how silly his idea was, but Loper was a whole lot bigger on giving advice than he was on receiving it, and on the first day of November, the calves were on their way to Ault, Colorado, to eat their little bellies full of corn silage and other goodies.

Between a surge in the overseas dollar and a tremendous campaign to buy beef on Father's Day, the fat market was higher than a kite when Loper sold, and he pocketed a cool three hundred bucks a head profit. The next fall, every ranch on the creek but Loper went to the feedlot, and while Loper sold his calves for nearly ninety cents a pound, the boys in the feeding business lost two hundred bucks a head when the early spring mud created a "corn panic" and caused the buyers to spook.

About all I learned from that was that cattle buyers are about as skittish as a yearling filly.

I poked ten head of yearlings down the hill while Red went on ahead to open the gate. We let the cattle drift into a corner where we could cut them, six for Red, five for Joe, two for Loper, four for Victor, one for Shorty and a big, slick milk cow calf that about had to belong to Fred Aspering.

"Where did you hear that Victor got ninety cents?" Red asked when we were done.

"Brand inspector," I said.

"Prob'ly a lie," Red decided, and he took his six head and poked them over the hill.

By the time I got Joe's two yearlings into the corral, the entire creek was in a lather, and Joe came running out to the barn without his hat.

"Red said you told him the brand inspector said that Victor got ninety cents for his calves!" Joe nearly shouted.

"That's true," I said.

"It is?" Joe rubbed his bald head. "Victor got ninety cents?"

"I don't know about that," I said, "But it's true that I told Red what the brand inspector told me."

"How did he know?" Joe questioned.

"He said that he heard it from one of the truck drivers," I shrugged.

I had been more than a little amazed that Red could have acted so calm and disinterested when I told him, but he had to have taken his yearlings home on a dead run to get on the horn and report my rumor.

"How did the truck driver know?" Joe asked.

"Said he heard Victor talking with Magnet Martin," I shrugged.

It all seemed pretty simple to me.

"Humph," Joe frowned, then hustled back into the house and gathered up all of the market reports for the last few weeks.

For three days, Joe fell into a vile humor, and he scoured the papers and dialed the telephone, only to find out nothing of the big cattle sale that had happened right under his nose. Morning, noon and night, Joe was on the phone with Red or Shorty or Loper or some friend from over the mountains, but there was no word on the cattle market save the bleak reports in the cow papers and Evan Slack's daylight report, in which Evan had to admit that he hadn't heard much about the cattle market situation either.

Finally, in a fit of desperation, Joe actually called up the farm reporter and told him he had heard of a string of calves going down the road for ninety cents. With all of the calling that was going on, it was no small wonder to me that nobody could buy any calves at any price. All the lines were busy.

Finally, on the fourth day, a break came. Jimmy Wilsz got liquored up and spilled the beans to Bobby, who promised not to tell a soul, then walked down to the other end of the bar and whispered the information to Fingers Filiatreau, who went back to the Mercantile and told Red Barnes's wife.

Victor had sold his calves for ninety cents alright, but he had to give a six percent shrink and pay a sliding penalty if they weighed over three hundred pounds, which they did. Victor also got stuck with the freight to get the calves to the state line, and he had to pay for the vaccination, brand inspection and health papers.

By the time you calculated in all of the deducts for crooked noses, bent knees, hump backs and runts, then took out the penalties, freight, and other charges, Victor's calves had brought exactly seventy-nine cents a pound.

"No wonder he ain't talkin'," Joe chuckled. "I can haul mine over to the sale barn and get eighty."

"But," Red scratched on a napkin, "if you do that, you'll have to pay freight and yardage and feed and then you'll only get about seventy-five."

"Plus," Shorty warned, "you'll be right between Yom Kippur and Thanksgiving."

"And," Davey reminded him, "if you send 'em to Riverton, you'll want to go along, stay in the motel, and drink a lot of whiskey and that'll mean you'll only get about seventy-two."

"I didn't say I was going to the sale barn!" Joe snapped. "I said I *could* go there and get more than Victor did!"

"Victor got ninety cents," Davey whistled. "I don't think you'll beat that."

On the first day of October, Shorty walked into the Hoosegow and bought a round for the house, and everyone crowded up to the bar to see what the market was doing.

"I got 'em sold," he said, and he downed a straight shot of the expensive scotch whiskey, the kind that comes in a funny bottle and costs more than ten bucks for a half-gallon.

"Well?" Loper asked.

"Eighty-four cents," Shorty smiled, "with a three percent shrink at the ranch."

Everyone grabbed a napkin and started scribbling.

"What'll they weigh?" Joe asked.

"When do they go?" Davey wondered.

"Who bought 'em?" Loper asked.

Victor and Woody sat back and watched. After all, Victor had gotten ninety for his and Woody was headed to Omaha to top the market. There was absolutely no sense in getting all worked up over the news that Shorty had sold his calves, but when Victor thought Woody wasn't watching, he tried to guess the weight of Shorty's calves and fiddled around with his pencil and a napkin.

Woody wasn't watching because all the time he was pretending to blow his nose, he was actually punching out the numbers in a little calculator he got for free when he opened an account at the State Bank of Friendly Creek.

Shorty let the information drop out a crumb at a time, and when they had enough to calculate the net, he announced it for them.

"Three hundred and fifty bucks a head," he smiled.

That set the crowd to more calculations, to see just how many more dollars a head Shorty had gotten on Victor, and since Victor knew he had ended up with two hundred and eighty bucks a head, he bought a six pack and left. As far as he was concerned, ninety cents was still ninety cents, which meant he had beat Shorty by six cents.

Davey's calves left the next Monday, and on the first Tuesday in October, after deducting yardage, feed, water, commissions, and other costs from his eighty-four cents at the sale barn,

Davey drove home with a check for three hundred and twenty dollars a head and bought another round at the Hoosegow.

Joe's calves would have sold on Yom Kippur, but the buyer was fasting and couldn't come to the phone, so he sold them the next day. We loaded them out on the first of November, and the steers weighed right at five hundred pounds. Despite the fact that Joe only got seventy-seven cents, his check turned out to be for three hundred and seventy-five bucks a head.

Loper heard that the market was going to hell in a bucket, so he called some big city broker in a black suit and sold futures contracts on his calves. Shorty pointed out that the holidays were all over, and Joe warned him that the futures markets were manipulated and controlled by people with computers and inside trader information. General concensus held that Loper would be broke and asking for handouts so he could buy Christmas presents for his wife and his girlfriend who waited on tables in the Mexican resturant in Rock Springs.

"You wait and see," Shorty shook his head.

Two days after Christmas, responding to "negative vibes" in the oil market, the Middle East, Central America and Texas, the cattle market went into a nosedive that lasted for two weeks straight.

Red went home and drank whiskey while he was waiting for the phone to ring, but all of the people in the world were getting rid of cattle. Loper sold his at the sale barn for sixty-five cents, then quietly pocketed an additional twenty cents on his futures contract, so that after all was said and done, he scratched up three hundred and sixty dollars a head. He was nervous as a cat for the week it took him to get the check from the broker-age firm, but the check was good.

With that, everyone but Red forgot all about the cattle market. It wasn't that nobody was sympathetic to Red's woes ... it was just that they had seen him caught with his pants down plenty of times before.

221

"It's a wonder he can stay in business at all," Victor shook his head.

"Well," Joe sighed. "The market is coming back up a little. Maybe he'll salvage something."

"I doubt it," Loper advised. "I'd say he was back in the yearling business again."

Red holed up for a month before he came out, and when he did, it was only to plow a track for the big trucks to get in and haul away the calves. Everyone looked up from the feed sleds as the trucks hauled Red's calves away, and nobody said much that night when Red wandered into the Hoosegow. In fact, everyone bought a drink for him, and Red drank them all down.

It was almost clsoing time before Red offered to buy a round.

"You don't have to do that," Bobby said, and he handed Red his money back.

Red shuffled over to a table and sat down.

"How about a little game?" Fingers smiled, and the boys all played pan until Red cleaned them out, and with a little cash in his pocket, Red again offered to buy another round, but everyone politely declined.

"But, you've been buying all night!" Red insisted.

"Don't worry about it," Victor scoffed. "Everybody can't get ninety cents for their calves. I can afford it."

"You been to the bank?" Joe asked, and Red nodded.

"What did they say?" Davey wondered.

Davey had an inherent fear of banks and bankers, and was sure that if Red had been to the bank, he must be in deep, deep trouble.

"Why, they didn't say a thing," Red smiled, and he climbed in his pickup and drove home.

In the morning, just before daylight, Even Slack's farm report was on the air, and he reported that Spring was traditionally a good time to sell calves.

"But this year, hooooooo boy!" he yelled in the microphone. "With the panic last fall leading to a biiiiiig run on cattle, calves are in short supply, and the market is a *barn burner*!"

Only Evan Slack could make a down market sound good, and when the market hit a lick, Evan went plumb nuts, and when Evan Slack went nuts, I swear, you could hear every person on Friendly Creek stop and listen.

"Yesiree Bob!" Evan was yelling louder. "Just yesterday, a big string of one-iron calves weighing *five hundred and fifty pounds* went out of Friendly Creek, Wyoming, for a dollar a pound!"

Victor spit his toothbrush through the wall.

It was snowing like usual . . . sideways.

The radio announcer said that the combination of a temperature of thirty below and fifty mile an hour winds added up to a chill factor of about ninety degrees below zero and constituted some sort of "winter chill warning," which was probably the reason nobody was wandering around the streets. I had been up on the mountain for two weeks, picking up stray heifers and dodging hunter's bullets, but the cold and snow drove me out of the hills in a hurry. If those heifers wanted to stay up there in that kind of weather, I didn't figure it was my place to stop them. My only intention was to stop by the Hoosegow and drink as much beer as I could hold, then go home and take a hot shower and climb into bed.

The only signs of life in Friendly Creek were a dim light in the window of Bud's Sinclair Service and the dome light in Buck Martin's police truck. Despite Buck's diligent efforts to curb excessive speed, he always waited on the east side of the Friendly Creek bridge, behind the same willow bush with his dome light on, and he rarely caught any speeders.

"I'm a deterrant," Buck said. "People around here have found out that they can't get away with speeding in my town."

Actually, as long as people didn't speed across the Friendly Creek bridge, they could speed around anywhere else they wanted, and as a matter of fact, they did just that.

I checked the gas gauge and pulled in below the big green dinosaur, right next to a sign which said, "Full Dino Service Day or Night. Honk Horn." There was no sense honking the horn, and there was no sense expecting Bud to come out and deliver any "Full Dino Service." The only time Bud left his swivel chair behind the cash register was if a motorist swerved and tried to run over his dog, and as cold as it was, the dog was sure to be inside with Bud. They were probably sharing a candy bar.

I got out and started the pump, then looked over my shoulder when I heard the station door creak. I knew Bud had seen me, because I saw him wiping the frost off the inside of the window with his green Dino rag, but I had never seen either the man or the mutt move very fast, so I was more than a little surprised to see Bud standing at the door, holding it open for the black, car chasing dog he called "Oily."

"The hell with ya" Bud told the dog, and he was halfway across the gravel driveway when the dog stuck its black nose to the glass door and yipped.

"Dumb dog," Bud said, and while he wandered back to let the mutt out, I pulled the nozzle out of the tank and hung it back on the pump. I checked the oil, and by the time I was done, Bud wandered back outside while the mutt stood on his swivel chair and panted on the window.

"Check that oil for ya?" Bud sneered.

"No, thanks," I smiled. "I got it."

"Fill 'er up?" he pointed at the pump.

"I got that too," I said.

"Then you owe me seventeen bucks," Bud said, and he held out his hand.

"Charge it," I said, and I shook his hand.

Bud looked to see if I had put any money in his palm.

"You owe me seventeen bucks," he said, and he wandered back to the door.

"Right," I followed him. "So what's been goin' on?"

"Plenty," he shook his head.

"Seems pretty quiet," I smiled, and Bud looked up at me from under his dirty green Dino hat.

"Either you ain't been around or you're dumber than a post," Bud growled, and he dug around in a steel box and hunted the ranch's charge record. His dog sniffed at my leg.

"I've been up on the mountain," I explained. I didn't want him telling everyone in town that I was dumber than a post.

"You may wish you were still there," Bud sighed. "If this crime wave doesn't pass, there won't be anybody left to buy gas."

"Crime wave?" I frowned. "I haven't heard anything about any crime wave.

"Of course not," Bud snorted. "You've been up in the hills."

"What happened?" I asked.

"Victor lost ten bales of hay," Bud rolled his eyes.

"That's a crime wave?" I asked.

"It ain't the ten bales of hay!" Bud waved his arms. "It's who took it!"

"Who took it?" I asked.

"Well, you know that Jimmy Wilsz has been messin' around with the ditch rider's wife," Bud chuckled.

I nodded. Jimmy had been messing around with the "ditch rider's wife" for four or five years. Her name was Mary Bodine, and she hadn't been the ditch rider's wife for about eight years. In fact, the ditch rider of reference left Friendly Creek six years earlier, but Mary Bodine was still the ditch rider's wife, and Jimmy was still messing around with her.

"Well, you know that ditch rider's wife, she likes them horses," Bud said, "but they've always looked pretty thin. All of a sudden, Jimmy moves in with her and gets to snortin' her flank and just like that, she's got the fattest horses on the creek, and Victor is missing ten bales of hay. I ain't sayin' that Jimmy took the hay, but two and two is still four, ain't it?"

"Why doesn't Buck arrest Jimmy?" I shrugged.

"Tracks don't match," Bud said. "Buck went out to the haystack to investigate, and he made some of them plaster of Paris models of the tracks and matched them up with all the vehicles in the valley."

"Who made the tracks?" I asked.

"Victor," Bud said. "Now, why would a man steal his own hay?"

I had to admit that one was a real stumper.

Bud said that Victor refused to press charges against himself, and without any further evidence, Buck refused to arrest anyone else.

"On his way back to town," Bud continued, "Buck pulled Edna Loper over for driving without a headlight, and when he got to the car, he could tell that she was drunk as a skunk."

"Wow," I whistled through my teeth. "What did he do?"

"Well, he did what he always does," Bud said. "He took her to town to get some coffee and sober her up. She didn't want to go to the Cafe, and she had already been to the Hoosegow, so he took her to the jail."

Bud giggled and shook his head.

"Edna finally keeled over and Buck packed her into a cell to lay her down, but he had to wake her up to make room for Fingers, Joe, Red, Shorty and Bobby Baker."

"Joe was in jail?" I couldn't believe it. "Why was Joe in jail?"

"The way I heard it, Joe was out in the shop when a whole

herd of elk ran through the yard and stopped in the swamp,"
Bud said. "So, he calls up Bobby, 'cause Bobby didn't get him an
elk, and Bobby tells the other guys in the bar and they all go
charging out there and shoot two or three elk apiece, and that
ain't legal."

"How much was the fine?" I wondered. I could imagine
Shorty, tight as the bark on a tree, having to pay a fine for
shooting an elk.

"There wasn't a fine!" Bud giggled. "The warden let the
guys all wash up before they came to jail, and while he was
hauling them to town, Maggie gathered up Davey Boyd and
they hauled the elk off somewhere and buried the guts. The
judge came down to set some sort of bail, and she asked the
game warden for some proof, but he couldn't come up with any,
so she let 'em all go."

"What happened to the elk?" I wondered.

"Well, now, that ain't been figured out yet," Bud laughed
again. "The warden got a warrant to look in Joe's barn, but they
weren't in there, so he got a warrant to look in Davey's shed and
they weren't there. They were in Jerry Watson's shop for a day,
and then Dick Wilson had some of 'em, and they was in the
ladies room here for a couple of hours. The game warden has
most of the places staked out, but everybody's got *him* staked
out, and when he goes to sleep, Fingers cuts up elk to beat the
blazes. I'd bet by now the elk are cut and wrapped and scattered
all over town."

"God, I love this place," I smiled.

"I guess you heard about Archie Aylward beatin' Jimmy
Wilsz with a shovel?" Bud clucked.

"Archie beat up Jimmy with a shovel?" I asked.

"Went right into Jimmy's house and tapped him on the
head with one of them good, curve-handled shovels," Bud
assured me.

"What was that about?" I asked.

"Well, like I told you, Jimmy was sparkin' the ditch rider's wife and stealing hay for her," Bud leaned over the counter. "It turns out that Archie was sparkin' her too, and when Jimmy moved in with her, she quit Archie like a bad habit."

Bud cackled like an old hen.

"That Jimmy Wilsz has needed beat with a shovel for a long time," he laughed. "I sure would like to have seen that."

"How bad was he hurt?" I asked.

"He wasn't hurt," Bud snorted. "Archie was hittin' him on the head. You can't hurt a Wilsz hittin' 'em on the head."

"Besides, Jimmy was talking to that buddy of his, old Steve, on the telephone when Archie walked in the house and started rapping him with the shovel. Steve figured it out in time to save Jimmy's bacon."

Bud laughed out loud, and he wandered over and poured us both a cup of coffee.

"To hear Steve tell it, he heard a big, loud 'clang' and then he heard Jimmy holler, and then Archie'd clang him with the shovel again. Jimmy'd yell 'help' and Archie would clang him again. It took Steve ten minutes to figure out what was happening, and then it took the ambulance two hours to get there."

"Why was that?" I wondered.

"Caught on fire," Bud said.

"The ambulance caught on fire?"

"Yep," Bud nodded emphatically. "Most of 'em catch on fire and burn right up, but they got the fire put out in this one and headed up to the hospital with Jimmy in the back before it caught on fire for real, and that time, it burned the sucker down to the rims."

"What happened to Jimmy?" I wondered.

"He'll live," Bud smiled. "He sure sucked up a lot of smoke though. Buck was busy with Edna, and Red was in jail, so some new guy was driving. He got so excited about the fire, he forgot he had Jimmy in the back."

I shook my head and turned to leave.

"Fred Aspering got arrested," Bud said.

"Fred?" I turned around. "For what?"

"Pulled a U-turn on main street," Bud shrugged. "The highway patrol pulled him over."

"Since when is it illegal to pull a U-turn?" I asked.

"You sound like Fred," Bud said.

"Is it illegal?"

"I don't know," Bud admitted. "but, it ain't legal to keep a pistol behind the seat of the pickup."

"How do you know that?" I wondered.

"When Fred hopped out of his truck and started cussing the highway patrolman, his pistol fell out from behind the seat and the patrol gave him a ticket for carrying a concealed weapon."

"I'd better get home," I smiled, and I grabbed the handle on the door.

"It's Loper who's in real trouble, though," Bud sighed, and I turned around again.

"What did Loper do?"

"He had a bunch of Mexican whores," Bud whispered. "That's why Edna got drunk. Everybody in town heard about the Mexican whores and *she* didn't know a thing about it. Man, was she *hot!*"

"Wait a minute," I stopped him. "What was Loper doing with a bunch of Mexican whores? I never saw any Mexican whores."

"What are you? Blind?" Bud asked. "They've been here all summer. Loper's had 'em working on that farm of his down on the river all year long!"

"Those aren't Mexican whores!" I laughed. "They're Mexican hoe-ers."

"I don't care how you pronounce it," Bud scoffed. "A whore is a whore."

"No, no," I laughed harder. "They hoe Loper's potato patch! They aren't whores!"

"You tell Edna that," Bud raised his eyebrows. "Loper told her the same thing, and she told him if he liked them Mexican whores workin' his potato patch, he could keep 'em. That Edna has no sense of humor at all when it comes to Mexican whores."

"Where is Loper?" I asked.

"He's still in jail," Bud said. "Edna told Buck to keep him there until he got over his midlife crisis and gave up the Mexican whores."

"I'm going home," I laughed, and I pulled the door open.

"Be careful!" Bud warned.

"I'll do that," I agreed, and I held onto my hat as I walked across the driveway.

Above me, Dino the dinosaur beckoned to any traveler who might be bold enough to stop in such a crime-ridden place.

"Don't drink and drive. Don't steal cattle or horses. Don't write hot checks, and for God's sake, don't get caught up with a bunch of Mexican whores," I said to myself when I turned the key, "and you'll do just fine on Friendly Creek."

I was still laughing about Loper and thinking about a beer at the Hoosegow when I crossed the bridge, and then there was a flash of red and blue lights in the rear-view mirror.

". . . and don't speed across the Friendly Creek bridge," I sighed, but it was too late.

A major cold front had been camped out on Friendly Creek for nearly two months, and according to the National Weather Service, it was going to stay there forever, maybe longer. The highest reading on the thermometer at the airport was twenty below, and that came on a day when the sunshine beat on the thermometer for nearly an hour.

At first, they closed the schools because the buses wouldn't start, but after a week of that, the Superintendant decided that they would open the schools, whether anyone could get there or not. It was rumored that he only kept the schools open because he and the other teachers would have to make up the days in June, and everybody knew that a bunch of them had an Alaskan fishing trip lined up for the week after school got out, so it was probably true.

All of the merchants in Friendly Creek and Buzzard Butte shoveled snow and opened at the regular time, but when they got the first heat bill from the REA, they changed their hours to cut costs. As far as I know, there were no complaints. Nobody was too anxious to get out of the house and go shopping in Friendly Creek or Buzzard Butte when the weather was good.

After six weeks of cold and snow though, people were beginning to get a little dose of cabin fever. A man named Walt Tanner ran out on main street as naked as a jaybird, then walked in and out of the stores until Buck Martin rolled out his Deputy Sheriff blazer and hauled Walt home.

Buck served him up a stern warning about the dangers of freezing certain parts of the anatomy in such weather, and Walt Tanner stood there and shivered through it all.

"Aren't you going to arrest me?" Walt asked when Buck was done with his lecture on nakedness.

"Hell no!" Buck yelled. "If I was to arrest you, then I'd hafta heat the danged jail to keep you warm, and the county can't afford it. You go on back inside, and if you want to freeze your tallywhacker, open up a window and do it at home."

For once, I appreciated the construction of the little log bunkhouse. As small as it was, and as carefully as the logs were laid together, it didn't take the woodstove long to heat the room, and once it was heated, it stayed warm all day. By dark, I was about the only person who could come home to a warm house, even if the bed did take up half the room.

Every morning, Joe rolled out of his bed in the big house, looked out the window at the crystalline air, read the thermometer and the gas meter, then launched into a ritual of swearing until he wandered down and turned the TV to the weather channel, whereupon he sat and cussed until his mouth was so dry that he would put on a pot of coffee.

By the time I finished the chores and showed up for breakfast, he was worked into a genuine fit. Today was no different.

233

"You clear a hole in the ice for the cattle?" he asked.

"Ice is close to two feet thick," I nodded, while I warmed my hands on a cup of coffee.

"Harness the team?"

"Both of 'em," I said. "Today's a full feed day."

"We'll use Roy and Dale first," he decided. "Ranger and Tonto have been out every day."

"I harnessed Tanya and LaCosta," I blew on my coffee. "I figured Ranger and Tonto could use the rest."

"You harness 'em, you drive 'em," Joe shook his head. "Tanya and LaCosta are a pair of idiots."

"I just figured they wouldn't be too bad in this snow," I said. "If you don't like 'em, why don't you sell 'em?"

"I might," he poured more coffee, but I knew damn well that he wouldn't. They were the last team of Ira Cusack horses on the creek, and they were dandy mares, even if they were a little skittish.

"You find that '77' cow?" Joe asked, the same question he had asked every morning since fall, when his favorite cow didn't show up coming off the mountain.

"She's got to be dead," I shook my head, "I've looked...."

"She ain't dead!" he yelled, and he walked in a little circle around the kitchen.

"She's just independent. If she's dead I want to see the head, so you find her, dead or alive! That cow is the first heifer calf out of the best cow that I ever bought in Canada, and she's raised more good bull calves than all the cows in this herd. If she's dead, I want to see the bones. Got it?"

"Got it," I sighed, and I looked outside.

"I'll take care of feeding," Joe decided. "You saddle a horse and find that cow."

"It's forty below zero," I reminded him. "Couldn't I look for her in the pickup?"

"You're a cowboy," he reminded me. "Cowboys ride horses.

You wanta be a cowboy, get your butt in the saddle and find that cow."

"Besides that," he finished his coffee, "there's only one pickup that'll start and I plan to take it to town."

I took a deep breath and stood up.

"Any calves yet?" he asked.

"Got one yesterday," I said. "The cow and calf are in the barn at the Keller Place, that big space heater is running full blast, and I added more sawdust and straw to the pens."

"Good boy," Joe said. "Now, find that cow. She breeds early and I don't want to lose her or her calf."

That much settled, I settled my cold butt in the saddle and Joe settled into the Hoosegow with Victor Wilsz, Carl Loper, Red, Shorty and the rest of the management types.

"What was the high yesterday?" Victor asked.

"Twenty below," Bobby Baker yelled from behind the bar.

"In town," Red shook his head. "It was twenty-eight below at my place when the sun came out."

"I think it's warmin' up," Shorty announced. "It was thirty-five below at my place, seventy-five below the other night."

"Shoot," Loper scoffed. "It doesn't get that cold at the North Pole."

"The North Pole is lower," Shorty explained. "It never gets as cold at sea level as it does at my place."

"I'd think it would be warm at your place," Victor said, "with all the hot air you keep blowing around."

"I've never seen it so damn cold in my life," Joe said. "Hell, when the sun comes out, it just gets colder."

"There's a dome of hot air laying over the mountains from here to the river," Bobby Baker drew a dome in the air with his right hand. "The hot air blows across the top of the valley and keeps the cold air locked in. If the frost would go out, it might have enough impact to break the layer of hot and cold air, but it might also create an inverse dome of heat that would . . ."

"Shut up, Bobby," Joe moaned.

"Yeah," Loper agreed. "Who do you think you are . . . Willard Scott?"

"Ever since you got that weather channel and that dish you've been a pain in the butt," Victor said.

"You got one of them dishes?" Davey Boyd brightened. "Can you get that poontang channel?"

"I'll bet the old fart watches that poontang every night," Joe laughed.

"I don't watch the poontang channel!" Bobby yelled, and he rinsed out a coffee cup.

"Do ya get it?" Red asked.

"Of course I get it!" Bobby said.

"How do you know you get it if you don't watch it?" Joe asked.

Bobby shook his head and turned the heat up.

"You guys calvin' yet?" Victor changed the subject.

"Got one yesterday," Joe said.

"I got two," Red sighed. "The kitchen is full."

"None up at my place," Shorty said. "But, up at my place it's colder, so the cows aren't hurrying anything."

"We're goin' strong," Victor smiled, and he stood up. "I gotta go ride Squaw Bluff to see where we're missin' a cow."

"I'm missin' one too," Joe said. "Let me know if you see her. It's that old '77' cow, the one with the funny head."

The ranchers moved over to the Cafe where they all had the "lunch special" of chicken fried steak, mashed potatoes and gravy, and plenty of hot coffee.

I ate my lunch under a willow bush along the creek at the Keller Place, and I ate it fast. I was working up a talk for Joe on how I was certain that his favorite cow was dead, and how I would find her head in the Spring, if only he would let me check the cows in the pickup for one day.

I had ridden the willows for so long that I was crossing my

own tracks, and every time I rode up on a cow, she seemed to be bored to see me. They were beginning to calve pretty heavy, and I tagged the new ones and rubbed them off with my "monkey fuzz" gloves until I was sure they were alright. Their mothers could have done the job, I know, but there was something special about rubbing the little buggers down when they were still wet and warm, so I waited until they were on their feet to leave them.

There was plenty of feed, and the cows were fine, but it seemed to be a hard way for a calf to enter the world. And yet, even as cold as it was, the cows seemed to know what to do with their babies. When it was wet, the old cows knew the only places on the creek that were dry, and when it was cold, they knew those spots where the sun would shine, where the willows and sagebrush would offer shelter, and when the time was right, it was in those places they settled and gave birth. With or without me, they licked their babies warm and dry, then tucked them cozily inside their warm flanks and waited the cold weather out. The calves didn't seem to mind the weather, as long as they were with their mothers. When you got right down to it, I figured those calves weren't so dumb after all.

I was riding a good little sorrel gelding and when he slowed to climb the ridge. I pulled my numb cheeks out of my sheepskin collar and looked ahead. My eyes were watering, and my fingers felt like sticks in my wet gloves. I was anxious to be back in the warmth of the bunkhouse, but I pulled my horse up and let him blow, then turned in the saddle and looked back.

There was a single track through the snow, a line of tiny shadows in the white landscape. The track ran along the break in the hillside, and I was sure it hadn't been there in the morning.

I rubbed the water out of my eyes and tried see where the track began and ended, but there was no way to tell, so I turned my horse back down the hill.

It was a single cow track.

"I'll be," I thought out loud. "That rip really is alive."

I followed the track up the draw, hoping I could find the old girl before dark, when my horse raised his head and let out a long whinny. Not far away, another horse answered. My horse began to dance and trot, and I wiped my eyes and tried to see through the cold.

The other horse was a bay mare, and she was standing on top of a knob at the head of the draw. She had a Double Mill Iron branded on her left hip, and the bridle reins were tied to a low sagebrush. One of them was looped around the mare's right front foot, and from the look of the ground around her, she had been there a quite a while. There was no sign of a rider, but she was saddled.

I caught the mare and pulled the rein off her foot, then sat on the knob and wondered what to do next.

I stared at the hillside until I was sure that I hadn't missed something obvious, but there wasn't a sign of movement. The wind was really picking up. About the only thing I could think to do was to forget about Joe's precious cow and backtrack the mare. She had obviously been carrying someone across the basin, and someone was obviously not riding her now, so I settled back in the saddle and led the mare back off the hill.

When the horse track crossed the cow track, I got nervous.

None of the signs made sense. The cow was obviously headed up the draw, and the rider had been following her, and then the horse track headed off up the hill and the cow track kept going up the draw. If the rider was following the cow, why would he leave her?

I rode back to where the horse and cow track first crossed, then followed them back to the point where they parted. My only option was the cow track, and I followed it up the draw.

It was the '77' cow, and she was laying in a soft patch of sand, out of the wind and cold, protected by the sagebrush, rocks and a massive drift of snow and ice. In that one warm spot on Friendly Creek, the sun crossed from east to west across the southern sky, keeping it warm and dry for the whole day, and it was impossible to see unless you were right on top of it.

Victor Wilsz was on top of it, sort of. The old cow was laying on her side, her back downhill, a pair of legs poked out of her rear end, and she was straining hard, to no avail. There was no way she could stand up, and the calf was a big one, so there was no way she could deliver.

Victor was pinned under her hip bone, his overshoes poking out beneath her swollen udder, head barely visible over the top of her yellow back.

"Well, I'll be," I said.

"Who is that?" Victor croaked, his voice worn from yelling.

"Hello Victor," I looked over the cow's back. "What's up?"

"Pinhead!" he rasped. "You little son-of-a-bitch! Get this cow off of me!"

"I thought you would be happy to see me," I wandered around the cow and looked at Victor. "What are you doing down there?"

"Get this cow off me and give me my horse!"

"What are you doing to that cow?" I asked as I tied the horses to a sagebrush and walked over to have a look at the calf.

"Hey!" Victor screamed. "Get this cow off of me!"

"She's trying to calve," I advised him. "Looks like it's a big bugger."

"What are you doing?" Victor fumed. "Get the cow off me!"

"Yep," I reached inside. "It's a big one alright. He's got his head back. That's the problem. Let me see if I can get a hold and get him out of there."

"You little bastard!" Victor hissed. "Get me out of here or I swear to God, I'll kill you deader than hell!"

"This is Joe's favorite cow," I told him. "Boy, is he gonna be glad I found her."

"I found her!" Victor screamed.

"Oh yeah," I looked at Victor. "You did find her. So what the heck are you doing down there?"

"I tried to pull the calf," he moaned, "but I got her off balance, and then I slipped and she fell downhill on top of me. I'm mashed down in the sand. I can't move."

"Remember that time you conked me on the head with a fence stretcher?" I asked.

"Oh for Hell's sake, I'm sorry!" he yelled. "Is that what you want?"

"Actually," I chuckled, "I'd give about anything to have a fence stretcher right about now."

"You little smart ass!" Victor panted. "Get me out of here now, or I swear I'll kill you!"

"Victor," I smiled, "I think you're a little too worked up right now. You can't kill me where you are, and I don't want to die just yet, so I'm gonna let you cool off a little bit."

"You little Barnes bastard," he hissed, and he shook his head around until I thought *he* might calve.

I slid the calf's feet back into the cow, then pushed until I could get the head turned into the birth canal, and when the old cow pushed, I pulled.

"When did you find her?" I asked.

"How the hell do I know?" Victor screamed. "My watch is on my wrist, which is on my arm, which is under the cow!"

I looked at my watch.

"It's quarter to five," I smiled.

"It's been an hour or two then," Victor grunted.

"Well," I puffed, "she's about out of gas and I'm not sure I can get him pulled by myself."

"Then pull me out!" Victor suggested. "I'll help."

"You said you were going to kill me if I let you out," I reminded him.

"I didn't mean it," he whined.

"I think I can get this calf," I said, and I reached back inside. "If I try to move the cow, I'll screw everything up."

"She's just a cow!" Victor snarled. "Let her die, and let me up!"

"You had a chance to let her die," I thought, "but you didn't do it. Why not?"

"Oh, for Christ's sake," he groaned, "get me out of here!"

I pulled hard on the calf's legs, but he didn't budge.

"Where's the calf?" Victor asked.

"He's in the birth canal," I panted. "but he's a big sucker. It feels like he's hanging up on the shoulders or something."

"Where is his back?" Victor asked.

"It's straight up," I felt inside.

"Straight up to her back?"

"The calf is pointing up," I said.

"He's sideways," Victor said. "You need to turn him right side up."

"Up to the sky?" I felt around.

"Turn his back up to the cow's back," Victor wheezed.

"I can't move him," I said. "She's straining too hard."

"Listen to me," Victor sighed. "The cow is laying upside down. The birth canal is screwed up as Hogan's goat. Get the calf turned over."

"She's straining too hard," I told him again, and her muscles locked down hard on my arm.

"It's not her fault." he said. "Your timing is all screwed up. When I tell you to turn him, you turn the calf."

I reached inside and got ahold of the calf and waited, and Victor and the cow breathed together.

"Now," Victor said, and I pushed and twisted the calf until he was straight up, and then Victor yelled at me to "pull" and I leaned back and braced my overshoes against the old cow's hips and all at once, there was a slippery, sloppy, groggy bull calf on top of me. The old cow kicked and rolled, and while she pulled her back feet under her, I grabbed Victor's hand and pulled him to his feet.

Victor promptly fell on his butt.

"My legs are asleep," he explained, and while he rubbed the feeling back into his legs, the old cow licked off her calf and nudged him to stand.

I untied the horses and handed Victor the reins to his bay mare while the calf wobbled up and found his way to his mother's flank. The old cow sniffed him, licked him hard, and wandered up the draw until they were far enough from us to be comfortable, and then she directed his wobbly little body between her legs and let him suck.

"Good calf," Victor grinned.

"Joe'll be happy," I said, and I watched the little guy as his eyes rolled back and he sucked hard.

The old cow was slowly moving her baby away from us, and while the little guy wasn't very certain about his feet, he was definitely certain that he was going to follow his mama, wherever she went.

"Thanks for the help," I said.

"I could've died out here." Victor took the reins to the bay mare. "I saw the old rip having trouble, and like a damn fool, I tied my horse up and walked down here to help her. If I'd known that she was one of Joe's, I wouldn't have wasted my time."

"Is that really true?" I asked, and Victor turned around like I had conked him with a fence stretcher.

"Let me tell you something," he snapped, then he looked at his pointed overshoe and pulled a cigarette out of his pocket.

"I suppose I've been 'telling you something' since the day you were born, haven't I?" he asked.

"I don't remember what you said when I was born," I admitted, "but you've sure been hammering at me plenty since then."

"Well," he slipped a foot in the stirrup, "you're a Barnes."

"Quite a crime," I sighed, and I swung onto my horse and gathered his head.

"Why is it such a big surprise that I might actually care about a cow or a horse?" Victor asked after we'd made a hundred yards, and there was a strange, hollow sound in the angry voice I had always known.

"I guess you never seemed to care much about anyone else." I said. "You've never said a decent word to me in your whole life."

"That started a long time ago." he said.

"You weren't here. I wasn't here," I shook my head. "I really don't care if your grandfather did eat our family milk cow."

"So that's it?" he laughed. "You live on the memory of a damn milk cow?"

"You've hated me since the day I was born," I frowned. "At least I got to know you a little before I decided you were a jerk."

"You don't know a thing about me," he bristled.

"I got a pretty good idea," I touched the spurs to my horse and let him trot. "You've spent so much time trying to look hard and mean that you've become that way inside."

"This country will do that to you," he said, and he reined

the big mare in and smiled. It was the first time I had ever seen him show an emotion other than anger.

"There are times when I wish I could sit down with people like Joe and spit things out, have a cat fight, whatever . . . but it'll never happen. We've all been here too long. We're still fighting over things that happened before we born, and it ain't gonna change."

"That's a shame," I thought out loud.

Victor and I pulled our necks into our heavy coats and thought our own thoughts while the horses headed for home. When we hit the main road. Victor stopped and lit a cigarette. In the flare of the match, I could see a softer light in his eyes, and I took a deep breath and let it out.

"I'm sure glad you came along," he sighed, his breath and the smoke mixing in a white cloud above us.

"Me too," I smiled.

The big man stared across the inky night at me, then let his eyes drop to the saddle horn.

"I guess the Barnes outfit got one on me today." he tried to smile. "I can't wait to hear this one in the Hoosegow."

Out there in the cold night, Victor's voice was strangely quiet, and I was struck by the realization that beneath all of his bravado, there really was a heart inside of Victor Wilsz.

"I'm freezing to death," I said.

"Me too, Pinhead," he smiled. "Me, too."

Victor started down the Friendly Creek Road and I cut through the sagebrush and headed for the corner gate, but after about twenty yards, I turned my horse and hollered at Victor.

He pulled the mare around and sat there in the darkness, the tip of his cigarette burning like a beacon under his hat.

"What is it?" he yelled back.

"You won't hear about it in the Hoosegow," I smiled, and let the sorrel have his head

According to the speedometer, we were screaming down Highway 26 at about eighty-five miles an hour . . . five hours from leaving Billings and still six from arriving on Friendly Creek. From the passenger side of the pickup, some girl named Jill kept up a rather rattled commentary on men, women, music, scenery, and sex, interrupting herself only when she found it necessary to critique my driving. I wasn't doing very well in any of Jill's categories, but when it came to driving, she seemed to rate me the poorest of all.

"How fast are we going?" she asked, and then she leaned over and peeked around the steering wheel to see for herself.

"Good God!" she pulled the seat belt tighter around her waist. "Does everybody in Wyoming drive like you do?"

"Nope," I said, and I checked the mirror. "Some of 'em drive like a bat outta hell."

A blue Chevy pickup pulled out behind me, then passed us like we were backing up. Jill looked at me out of the corner of her eye, then shook her head in disgust.

"What's the hurry?" she wondered.

I shrugged. "If you drive too slow, you can't keep up with the rotation of the earth and you'll never get anywhere."

"Good God," she shook her head, "that is the stupidest thing I ever heard."

"Maybe so," I smiled, "but I had a friend who left Cheyenne one time, trying to get to Salt Lake. He drove straight west, going fifty-five miles an hour, for a whole day and night, and then he drove for another day. He ended up spending the next night in Nebraska."

Jill closed her eyes and played possum to avoid the rest of my story and I enjoyed the quiet for a change. I had delivered a load of old horses to the sale in Billings, and agreed to bring this girl back to meet up with her boyfriend, Silent Smith. It had never been explained to me why doing a woman a "favor" included subjecting myself to her verbal abuse. When I agreed to give her a ride from Billings, I didn't have any idea she could be so talkative. Certainly, the boyfriend I was delivering her to was no such chatterbox, but I was beginning to understand that a little better as we went along.

Jill reached over and fiddled with the radio for about the hundredth time, and for the hundredth time, all she found was static.

"You failed to mention the fact that you don't have radio in Wyoming," she crossed her arms. "What do you listen to?"

"I don't know," I grinned. "I suppose we just like it quiet once in awhile."

The hiss of the radio faded into the buzz of snow tires on the blacktop, and day faded into night in the middle of nowhere. Ahead of us, the scenery didn't change much. A white line divided the highway and the highway divided the desert.

Gophers tugged insistently at their splattered friends and relations, more interested in the meal than saving the carcass. Magpies waited for the last instant to jump from the roadkills, then hovered on the airflow above the pickup and settled back to their feasts. Jackrabbits bolted from the barrow pit and challenged the truck, then caught their breath on the other side of the highway and waited for the next car to pass. Life and death courted each other on Highway 26, but neither side seemed to gain much of an advantage.

"What's the deal with the rabbits?" Jill asked, and she stared out the window as a mottled jack faded into the tall grass.

"What do you mean?" I looked at her.

"What do they do? Where do they live? Why are there so many of them?" she asked, and she closed her eyes when one of them didn't quite make it to the other side.

"They live everywhere, and they chase cars for a living," I said. "There's so many of them because they're rabbits. When they aren't chasing cars, they multiply."

"Why are they here?" she asked.

"They can't afford an airline ticket," I said, and Jill rolled her eyes.

"Why do they call them 'jackrabbits?'" she wondered.

"The males have antlers," I explained. "They call the males jackalopes.'"

"I haven't seen any rabbits with antlers," she glared at me.

"They only grow the antlers in the summer," I told her, "like a deer."

"How big are their antlers?" she crossed her legs.

"Depends on the size of the rabbit," I shrugged, and she stared out the window at the prairie. She didn't believe me, but she wasn't quite sure that I was lying either.

She was kind of a pretty girl, just sitting there in the last light of day with her mouth shut. I couldn't begin to pronounce her last name, something French, with lots of e's and apostrophes, like one of the new breeds of cattle that people were getting all lathered up about. Her hair was long and straight, pulled into a thick braid over her shoulder, and whenever she talked, she twisted the braid tighter and tighter. As much as she talked, I figured that braid to be as tight as a galvanized nail.

She was born and bred to a different life than me, a childhood filled with swimming pools, debutante balls, and more than a little bit of money. I think she came from Chicago or Cleveland, or maybe it was Atlanta. It was some big town where there's debutantes and no jackrabbits.

Jill caught me staring at her, so I focused my attention back on the center line while she reached over and fiddled around with the radio again.

"Fifteen-twenty," I said.

"Fifteen-twenty, what?" she looked up, her blue eyes sparkling in the glow of the dash lights.

"It's KOMA," I grinned, and turned the dial to the familiar nighttime voice from Oklahoma City. The sound was crystal clear.

"Why didn't you tell me that sooner?" she pouted.

"Couldn't get it sooner," I shrugged. "You have to wait until it's dark."

"It's country and western," she sneered.

I looked at my watch.

"Another half hour and KSTP will power up," I advised. "That's rock and roll out of St. Paul. The Albuquerque Dukes will be playing triple-A baseball in an hour. That's 770, KKOB."

"The country will be fine," she decided, and she stared out into the night.

"It sure gets dark out here, doesn't it?" she whispered.

"Yep," I agreed. "Sun goes down, it gets dark. Happens every day."

"Not where I grew up," she sighed and stared at the stars.

I rolled the window down and let the fresh spring air float into the cab of the pickup. I could smell the frost coming out of the ground, and I knew that there was green grass shooting out of the soft earth.

"How far is the next town?" she asked.

"Not too far," I said. "Twenty miles or so."

"I need to go to the restroom," she said.

I pulled my foot off the gas and let the pickup and trailer coast to a stop beside the highway.

"What are you doing?" she asked.

"You said you had to pee," I shrugged. "So, pee."

"I don't have to go that bad," she groaned, and she fiddled with the radio dial until she found a rock and roll station.

I pulled onto the empty highway and got the truck and trailer up to speed again, and ten minutes later, a single neon beer sign flashed a welcome. The yellow yard light tossed shadows from the single gas pump, and I coasted into the yard and got out. Jill looked around in dismay.

"What is this?" she whined.

"This," I shoved the nozzle into the tank, "is the next town."

An old gray dog stood up on the wooden porch, then wagged his tail and waddled across the dirt driveway. Behind the dog, a trio of sunburned faces stared out from beneath the beer sign and eyeballed the truck and trailer.

"Where is the bathroom?" Jill stared at the old dog.

"I think the women's is the one on the left," I pointed, and her eye followed my finger.

"There's a bathroom in that shed?" she gasped.

"That shed is the bathroom," I smiled.

"Good God," she sighed, and she curled up in a ball next to the door of the pickup.

The screen door opened and a stocky woman marched out.

"Hey Big Time!" I yelled. "I see your gas is still twenty cents higher than it is anywhere else in the world!"

The stocky woman stopped and looked me over.

"You little rat!" she barked as she waddled over, pulled the nozzle out of the tank, and then hung it back on the pump.

"You forgot to wash my windows," I said.

249

"Pipe down!" she took a swat at my head, and then she threw her big arms around me and squeezed me until I thought I might run out of air.

"I ain't seen you in awhile," she grinned.

"You'd think if a guy drove all the way out here to buy your watered down, overpriced gas, the least you would do is buy him a beer," I suggested.

"Well, belly up to the bar," she laughed and I followed her inside the gas station, store, bar, cafe, and house.

While she rang up the gas, she reached into the cooler and tossed me a beer, and I twisted the cap and drank it down.

"What are you doing out here?" she asked.

"I hauled some horses to Billings," I said. "Now I'm headed home."

The big woman slipped a pocket knife out of her pants and carved at a sliver in her thumb. She squinted at the sliver. I wasn't sure if it was a squint to see if she had managed to get the sliver, or a squint because it hurt to carve up her thumb with a pocket knife.

I looked out at the pickup. The big dog was standing up on the passenger side of the truck, his black nose pressed against the window. Jill had slid over behind the steering wheel, and her eyes were wide. I paid for the gas and scratched the dog behind the ears, then pulled back onto Highway 26.

"Who is that woman?" Jill asked.

"She runs that little place," I explained. "She's great."

"Does she have a name?" Jill hissed.

"Big Time," I grinned.

"Her parents named her 'Big Time?'" Jill sneered.

"Beats me. Everybody I know calls her Big Time. I don't know her parents."

I stared in the mirror. The yellow light faded into the dark night, and the trailer followed the pickup diligently across the blacktop. Only the sound of the tires on the highway broke the stillness of the night, and I turned the radio over to the Albuquerque Dukes. They were winning, six to three.

Jill slouched in her seat and stared at me. She didn't look very happy. We were halfway from Billings and halfway from Friendly Creek, and I guess there isn't a whole lot in between if you came from the debutante ball in Chicago.

The single blue light of Hiland beckoned when we came over the hill, and Jill sat up and stared back when we passed the little town and headed west toward another. She whipped her long braid from one side of her head to the other, then twisted it in her fingers.

"A wide spot in the road," she snorted. "Blink and you'd miss it."

"So, don't blink," I stared in the mirror, "or you'll miss it."

"Who cares?" she yawned, and she pulled her legs up under herself and stared at the white line on the highway.

"Whoever left the light on cares," I smiled, and the headlights led us across the desert, to a place where Jill de l'Etoile finally stepped out of the pickup and peed by the road.

The wind was still cold enough to remind me that it wasn't really Spring, but the snow was beginning to shrink away, and the ground was muddy, even after the sun went down. There were new calves all over the Keller Place, and when I turned for home, the meadow was totally quiet. I stopped at the crossing and watched the tiny heads butt hard against their mother's flanks, then turned my horse on a good trot and headed home.

It was dark when I rode through the gate, but the light was on in the barn. I reined up and squinted into the darkness. Usually, it was my forgetfulness that left the thing burning, but I'd been late leaving this morning, and there had been no need for the light. As the bay bowed his neck and tried to hurry, I held him close and he sidestepped down the road. I stepped out of the saddle and stretched my legs, then led the bay inside.

The only evidence that he was there was the smell of cigarette smoke, and I stripped my saddle and bridle, then left them on the board floor and poured a gallon of oats in the bunk. The bay stepped around me, and I walked to the back corner of the barn.

Joe was sitting on a bale of straw, his legs pulled up to his chest. A pile of cigarette butts littered the floor in front of him. It looked like he'd been there awhile.

"Victor's dead," he said.

It was very final, as if he had found a cow that couldn't calve. Victor hadn't "passed away" or "gone." Victor was dead.

"How did..."

"Heart attack," Joe sighed, and he lit another cigarette. "He went out to check heifers and never came back."

I sat down on the floor and stared at the rafters.

"Just yesterday," Joe shook his head, "the old son-of-a-bitch was bragging on his Angus cows, how they never need to be checked....."

The bay horse wandered around the empty stalls, his heavy feet clattering on the cold planks of the floor, and one of the border collie pups wandered around the corner and climbed up on the bale of straw next to Joe. The boss dropped an arm absently and his hand scratched the black and white dog behind the ears. The pup sighed heavily and laid its head down on Joe's knee, and a pair of renegade cats wandered over and rubbed their sides against the straw. Their purring was the only sound in the dark barn. A little black mouse with gigantic ears darted across the floor, but the cats and dogs were too busy with Joe to notice.

"One day, you're sitting in the bar, giving each other hell, and the next day, you can't hardly sit in the bar," Joe blinked. "I never figured I'd see this day."

I guess none of us did.

"Are you coming to dinner?" Maggie asked from the open door.

"We're on our way," Joe whispered, and he stood up and followed her to the house.

I put my saddle in the tack room and shut off the light.

Victor's casket was a simple, polished oak box, and it sat in front of a hole in the ground on top of the hill south of the valley. Four strips of too-green astroturf surrounded the hole, and a row of gray marble markers noted previous generations of Wilsz existence.

People slowly filed from their cars to the gravesite, the women dabbing shamelessly at their eyes, men staring across the valley, careful not to look at one another, for fear they too might burst into tears.

In front of the hole in the ground, Joe, Red, Shorty McGregor, Woody Schmoe, Davey Boyd, and Boby Baker sat shoulder to shoulder on lawn chairs. Their suits were too tight, and their cowboy faces were as brown as dirt. With their thin hair combed back where their hats should have been, the milky white foreheads stood out like halos, sort of. All six looked straight ahead, hands on their knees, fingers digging into the strange fabric of the suit pants.

On the other side of the grave, empty chairs stood at attention like sentinels, waiting for the family.

The undertaker pulled his car up next to the plot, then stepped out and walked to the empty chairs, turned around and waited for the family to come and be seated. Jimmy came first, seated his mother and grandmother, then sat down between them. The oldest girl, the Justice of the Peace, sobbed on her husband's arm, then sat down next to her mother.

Then *she* walked across the cold ground and sat in the last chair.

"Oh no!" I whispered, and at least four women turned to shush me.

I looked at my boots, and when I looked up, she was staring straight back at me. I stared at the casket, but it couldn't hold my eyes, and I looked over at her again.

She was still looking at me.

Her name was Victoria, after her father, but I had known her as "Tory" since the first day we met, when I was eight and she was six and she rode her horse around a willow bush and caught me taking a leak.

She was a freckle-faced girl in pigtails then, and she let me finish my business before she asked me who I was. She was sitting up on a big roan mare that her daddy gave her for her sixth birthday, and I suppose she was pretty then, but I wasn't paying much attention to that.

She'd told me her name was "Vicky," but I didn't think too much of that, so I called her "Tory," and she smiled and slid down the big roan's front leg.

"By your death, you took away the sting of death," the preacher read from his book. "Grant to us your servants so to follow in faith where you have led the way, that we may at length fall asleep peacefully in you and wake up in your likeness."

The preacher paused for effect, and the wind ruffled the pages on his book.

"For your tender mercies sake, amen."

"Amen," we all said, and the preacher closed his book and held it in front of his waist, his head bowed.

"Just a minute," a voice called out, and everyone looked up. It was Joe.

"I'm sorry, Father," he smiled, and his blue eyes burned a hole through the preacher.

"Victor deserves more than a regulation funeral," Joe said. "He deserves more. He wasn't some line in a prayer book. He was a big part of this valley. He helped build the schools, and he helped pay for the roads. He did like the rest of us . . . he believed in this place. He mighta fought us while he was here, but he defended us when he wasn't here. He did a lot of good things."

Joe let a handful of rocks and dirt fall out of his hand, rocks rattling against the wooden box, dirt blowing away through his fingers.

"We've all made a lot of mistakes, Lord," he said, "but, just this one time, forget all of those and listen to me."

Joe's gray hair blew over his head in the wind, and then he turned and looked at the valley below.

"Take care of this cranky old man," he grinned. "He was a tough old bugger, but he was fair . . . and Lord, he was our friend."

If the Lord wasn't listening, the rest of us darn sure were.

There was a cooler full of beer on the front porch of the Wilsz house. Jimmy was standing next to the door. I shook his hand and told him how sorry I was, but I was trying to see through the crowd, hoping that Tory was there.

All the way from the cemetery I had been thinking about the hot summer days when I would saddle my old horse, Buster, and ride down the creek with a fishing pole, knowing full well that I would find her at the Blue Hole, waiting for me to show up. She could wrestle and she could fish, and she could ride as well as any boy I knew. She could catch frogs and spot porcupines in willow bushes, and she could run as fast as I could.

I guess Tory was my first best friend, the first person I could tell about my dreams and anxieties without worrying that they would show up the next day on the playground. It never once occurred to me that my best friend should be a boy, and it never occurred to her that her best friend should be a girl. I guess "best friends" just happened without a lot of planning and worrying.

Most of the Hoosegow gang, the pallbearers, were standing out on the back porch. Bobby had closed the bar and offered to tend bar at the house, and Fingers was cutting up a ham in the kitchen. A gang of old ladies was sitting around the dining room table, picking at the food on their plates with arthritic fingers, clucking about how hard it would be on Faye without Victor around to tell her what to do.

Tory wasn't in the house.

"Helluva deal, huh?" Red shook his head when he walked by. I nodded.

"Oh, there you are!" Faye cried as she gave me a hug. "Have you seen Victoria?"

"I saw her up at the cemetery," I tried to smile. "Do you know where she is?"

"She may be down at the stables," Faye suggested.

It always amused me the way Faye referred to their barn as "stables," while the rest of us were content to have a barn. I walked out the back door and headed toward the place where horses were saddled, whatever it was called, while Faye was spirited away by some of the old ladies who were worried that she wouldn't have someone around to tell her what to do.

I didn't even look in the barn. I knew where she was.

She was sitting in the tall grass on the other side of the Blue Hole, and she was prettier than I ever remembered. Her dark hair fell over her shoulders in thick, shiny curls, and her brown eyes were soft and warm, just like they always were. The freckles were gone, except for a belligerent bunch that wouldn't leave her nose, and she was sitting with her legs crossed, just like she was the last time I rode over to the creek.

I walked around a big red and gray willow and looked across the frozen Blue Hole, then sat on the bank in the yellow grass, just staring at her.

"How long have you been here?" I asked.

"All of my life," she smiled.

"Sorry about your dad," I said, and I gathered a fistful of tall grass. It broke off in my hand, and I stripped the seeds off the stalks and tossed them onto the ice.

"Why do you do that?" she asked, and I looked up.

"Do what?" I wondered.

"Rip the heads off those plants," she giggled. "You've done that ever since I can remember."

I dropped the stalks of grass and tried to smile.

"How've you been?" I asked.

"Are you gonna sit over there, or are you coming over here?" she asked, and I walked across the ice and put my hands on her shoulders, and then she was standing up and her hair was in my face and we were both sobbing.

I held her tight, but she cried harder. I let go and looked in her eyes, and then I needed to hold her again. Finally, I looked up and wiped my eyes, and she laughed.

"Am I the only one who ever saw you cry like that?" she asked.

"You're the only one who ever made me cry like that," I ran my finger over her cheek. Her soft skin seemed too perfect for my cracked finger to touch, but I did it anyway.

"You're taller," she whispered.

"You've been gone a long time," I said.

"Remember when we tried to catch the fish through the ice?" she smiled, and her fingers wrapped around mine. "You had it all figured out."

"You made too much noise," I laughed.

"I was trying to kiss you," she said.

That surprised the hell out of me. At the time, every guy in five counties was determined to kiss Tory Wilsz, but they weren't making much headway. Girls weren't too interested in me, and they all hated Tory for needing a bra. I could remember laying in the yellow grass and advising Tory which boys were alright to kiss and which ones weren't. Most of the time, I hated the boys for being boys, and part of the time, I hated Tory for being a girl, but when we were at the Blue Hole, it never seemed to matter.

We'd spent a lot of time at the Blue Hole the summer when boys started paying attention to Tory. We'd read the same books and we had talked about what they meant, and we both hated math, so we never asked any questions that required adding, subtracting or multiplying.

Mostly, we'd just talked a lot and laid next to each other in the soft grass and tried to solve the problems of the world.

"I wish you hadn't left," I sighed as I sat back down on the bank of the creek.

She rested her head against my chest, and we sat there. Just sat there, that's all. I don't know what was on Tory's mind, maybe her dad, but all I could think about was the girl who had gone away to some fancy school in the east, to a place where her parents figured she would get a fine education and meet a better brand of people than those who lived on Friendly Creek. I didn't understand it then, and I'm not sure Tory did either, but she only came home at Christmas after that, and I hadn't been to the Blue Hole since.

There was so much emotion in me I didn't know which way to turn.

"I hear you're leaving," she whispered against my chest, and I took a deep breath. I felt a hot tear roll off of her cheek and across the back of my hand, and I gathered her in my arms and kissed her softly. Her long fingers reached across my temples and tugged at my hair, and I looked at my hand against hers, then rolled over on my back and stared at the blue sky.

"I haven't said I was leaving," I sighed, "but, everybody seems to have it in their heads that I am. I'm not sure where they got that idea."

"It's in your eyes," she said, and she rolled over and put her head against my heart. "You need to go."

"I needed you," I said. "I needed you so many times, and you were gone."

"I needed you too," she whispered. Her hands reached under my arms. "As much as I'll miss you, you need to see something else. It's your turn to go."

She was trying to cheer me up, just like she always had.

"Maybe someday I'll come back," I thought out loud.

"It will still be here," she smiled, and she raised her head enough to kiss me.

She smiled, and her soft, dark hair fell over my eyes, and I held her close.

"I love you," she whispered, and I closed my eyes and felt the ache building in my throat.

"This isn't fair," I fought the tears, then lost. "I thought you would never come back, and now, I can't stay. I'm afraid if I leave, I'll never come back again....."

I buried my face in the dark hair at the back of her neck and cried.

"You need to go," she said, and she stood up.

Her legs were as long as a filly's, and she carried herself with an incredible air. Some strange transition had occurred between the little girl I had always known and the woman I was seeing for the first time.

"The only people who lose sight of what they have are the ones who never leave," she said. She lifted her head to let her lips brush mine, and we fell back into the tall grass next to the Blue Hole and loved each other more than anything in the whole world.

And for one long afternoon on a cold day, we forgot about leaving and coming home and just sat by the creek and didn't think about anything but each other and ourselves. It was a terribly selfish time, and on that cold white afternoon, I felt life begin again, just like it had the first time she rode around that willow bush.

He was sitting on the only curb in town, gray hairs curled between the twisted fingers of his old broken hands. A cauliflower ear bloomed under his left thumb, and his crooked nose stuck out like an axe in a chopping block. His broad back was bent, and his elbows seemed unstable on his knees, yet he sat as still as a monument. Only the faded red fire hydrant in a vacant lot down the street seemed steadier.

Inside the Hoosegow, a local band was playing a cotton-eyed Joe to patrons more interested in drinking than dancing. I pushed my way through the crowd and grabbed a beer, then wandered over to a table by the window and watched the sun drop lower in the sky.

Old Hootch was still sitting on the curb.

Up at the bar, a gang of cowboys had a barrel racer named Connie Carson talked up onto the bar, where she crossed her legs and tossed a mane of golden hair, then threw back a shot of tequila, licked the back of her hand and bit down hard on a lime.

"Yeee! Haw!" the cowboys cheered, and they lined up four deep to buy her another shot and ask her to dance to the off key version of "Kiss an Angel Good Morning."

By the time the bar closed down, Connie Carson would be the only one to leave with her rodeo check in her pocket, and despite her warm reception to all of the cowboys, the check was the only thing that would wind up in her jeans.

Joe Barnes and Carl Loper had Lee Willoughby cornered back by the men's bathroom, and I could tell from the expression on their faces and the jabbing of their index fingers they were heavy into brainwashing the banker about the major differences between money on Friendly Creek and money at the federal reserve. Twice, the banker tried to escape, but he was still fairly green, so he stood there politely taking in all the free advice. His third try at escape was to have his date come over, look longingly at him, then ask if he was going to dance.

Most places it would have worked. In the Hoosegow, it was worse than failure. Joe danced with Lee's date, and Loper never missed a beat in his lecture on economics.

Red, Shorty, Davey, and Fingers were oblivious to the celebration. They were busy playing pan. They had the forest ranger and the game warden convinced that they were getting the hang of the game, but every time the barmaid came by, the ranger and the warden bought more change.

They were lucky to see a barmaid at all, but she had to buy change back from Red on a regular basis, so she brought drinks when she needed money.

I finished my beer and walked back up to the bar, and laughed along with the others when Lynn Bourn rode her gray gelding through the back door, past the bathrooms, reined up at the bar to order a "shooter and a beer," then rode the horse out through the front door. Nobody was quite sure why, but every time there was a hint of a celebration, Lynn rode her horse through the bar, and every year, the reactions were pretty much the same. The locals paid little attention and the first-timers howled with glee that their views of Wyoming had become reality.

Bobby Baker saw me coming and held up one finger, then raised his eyebrows when I held up two. He tossed two cans over the jam of cowboy hats and waved my money away.

"On me," he pointed at himself.

I took the beers and walked outside, then moved down the street to where the old man sat with his chin in his hands.

"I bought you a beer," I said, and I sat down beside him.

"If I wanted a beer, I guess I would walk in the bar and buy one," he advised, but he took the can I offered and pulled the ring with a gnarled finger.

"So, how are you doin'?" I asked.

"Great," he sighed. "Or at least I was until this curb got so crowded all of a sudden."

"Well," I stood up. "You're drinkin' beer and you're talking, so I guess you really are more alive than a fire hydrant."

"Sit down," he waved, and I sat down.

All of the seats on the only curb in town were taken.

"My name is . . ."

"Parker William Barnes," he finished the sentence. "Hell, I remember the day you were born."

"You do?" I frowned.

"Sure," he smiled. "it was the end of April. It'd rained for three straight days, and then the sun came out and there was a big old rainbow over there by the river."

I followed the bend in his finger and squinted into the hazy sundown.

"So, what's your name?" I wondered.

"I guess they call me 'Hootch,'"

"I know what they *call* you," I sighed. "What's your name?"

"Right to the point," he laughed, and the lines around his eyes folded and creased. "You're all Barnes."

"Whatever that is," I shrugged.

"It ain't bad," he scolded, and he stood up and walked into the Hoosegow and came back with a six pack and a bag of ice.

"Reservation cooler," he said, and he shoved the cans into the ice, except for a pair that he opened.

"I owe you a beer," he smiled and held out his old brown hand. His grip was firm and warm, and his eyes were bright and clear.

"Name is Barney," he said. "I go back a long ways with your family. I guess I worked for every one of your relatives one time or another, but I gave that up and went off to work on the rigs, then fixed fence for the forest circus for awhile, sold cars over in Vernal . . . a little of everything."

"What do you do now?" I asked.

"I'm on the county," he chuckled. "I'm just sittin' back, starving to death on the social security Uncle Sam makes you pay."

I let the empty can drop to the gravel beneath my feet and fished a fresh beer out of the bag.

"So why do they call you Hootch?" I wondered.

"Habit," he guessed. "One man says something and the next one repeats it. What the hell? It's just a name."

"You didn't answer the question," I said.

"You are all Barnes, aren't you?" he laughed.

"You don't have to answer me if you don't want to," I said.

"I picked up that name in 1924," he said, and his eyes drifted back to another time.

"Yessir," he smiled. "There was a time when I was the best damn whiskey runner west of the Green River. All of the Italians and the Polacks in Kemmerer and Diamondville were makin' whiskey to beat hell, but the feds came in and wiped 'em out, and there was so many deputies and ladies of the temperance union crawlin' over the hills that you couldn't find a jackrabbit to save your life."

"But," his eyes sparkled, "I could get white lightnin', sour mash, scotch, even blended whiskeys."

"How did you do it?" I laughed.

"Bought it from the Mormons over in Logan," he chuckled. "All them federal agents and church ladies were so busy giving the wops and the polacks hell, I just licensed my old Ford in Utah and claimed I was a visiting elder."

"And it worked?" I grinned.

"Wore out four cars in eight years," he laughed.

"Hootch," I shook my head and laughed.

"Why aren't you in there?" he jabbed his thumb toward the bar. "There oughta be lots of tight jeans and curls wanderin' around tonight."

"There are," I agreed, "but, they're already outnumbered five to one by hotshot cowboys."

"So?" he looked at me.

"In case you haven't noticed, I'm no hotshot cowboy."

"The way I hear it, you're one of the best hands in the country," Hootch tossed a handful of pebbles across the road.

The band in the Hoosegow cranked up again, and Hootch looked over his shoulder at the lights in the windows.

"I suppose that Connie Carson girl is sittin' up on the bar slammin' tequila hookers," he laughed and dug out another beer.

"It's in her blood," he went on. "Her Grandma did that, and her mama did it and her daughters'll do it. I chased her Grandma for years."

265

"I'm too poor to chase Connie Carson for years," I thought out loud. "All I ever got chasing her was an empty wallet and a hangover."

"Who's Red fleecing at pan?" Hootch asked, and I laughed.

"The forest ranger and the game warden, mainly," I told him, "but, they think they're catching on."

"Like Fingers Filiatreau?" Hootch laughed out loud. "Hell, he's been gonna beat old Red since they was both kids, and he's still sittin' there losing, every time they get a game up."

"You figure Red cheats?" I asked.

"Nah," Hootch scoffed. "Red knows when to play a hand and when to get in and when to sit it out. He's a patient bugger, that Red."

"The rest of them boys would be better off buying Connie Carson drinks," he suggested. "She can't drink as long as Red can win, and they might get a kiss from Connie."

"Connie Carson's kisses are about as passionate as being gummed by a salamander," I said, "and I can get gummed by a salamander for nothing."

"She ain't your type of girl anyhow," Hootch smiled. "Your type of girl ain't gonna show up tonight because her daddy would hear of it."

"You sure know an awful lot for an old boy who sits on the curb and watches the sun go down for a living," I kidded.

"You're trying to figure out how to leave this place," Hootch said, and his gray eyes burned a hole in mine.

"Either that," I took a deep breath, "or how to stay."

I stared out into the descending darkness and felt so much uncertainty and so much loyalty that it seemed my body might explode into fragments and litter the eroded street with human gravel.

"What makes you so sure I'm leaving?" I stared into the dusk.

"It's all the same," he smiled, and he pushed some pebbles

around with the end of a stick. "When a kid your age is sitting out here with an old coot like me on a night like this, he's looking for something he ain't found."

"Maybe you're right," I admitted.

"Maybe?" he squinted. "The only question now is whether you've got the guts to go out and see what the hell it is you think is out there, or whether you're going to sit here and hope that Connie Carson and everything else in this valley changes. Well, this valley ain't gonna change enough in your lifetime to answer your questions, so if you're gonna get 'em answered, you're the one who's gonna have to answer 'em."

"Why do you sit out here every night?" I changed the subject.

"Lawrence Welk," he said.

"What?"

"I *hate* Lawrence Welk," he smiled. "Every night at seven, my wife sits down, puts her feet up on a stool and stares at that dang Norwegian and his bubbles for an hour."

"A one an' a two an' a..." Hootch stood up and pantomimed Lawrence Welk for me and the fire hydrant.

"After forty years of being in love with the same woman, I just decided that it was better for both of us if I just left the trailer."

"How long did it take you to leave?" I smiled.

"Twenty years," he sat down. "Can you believe I watched that show for twenty years and hated my wife *and* Lawrence Welk before I figured out that I could walk outside and watch the sun set instead?"

"But, everybody says you're an old drunk!" I objected.

"Everybody calls me Hootch," he shook his head. "It's just the fools who never ask questions that call me an old drunk."

"Fools like me?" I asked.

"Yep," he looked at me. "You were one of them fools."

I took a pull on my beer and looked up at the stars, and then I felt his hand on my elbow.

"Where do you figure you'll go?" he asked.

"Go?"

"When you leave."

I'm not so sure I'm leaving," I objected.

"Oh yeah," he nodded. "You're leaving. It's in your eyes, your voice. It's in your head. You *have* to leave."

"What makes you so sure?" I threw a pebble across the road.

"You've been driving that road past here for ten years," he looked into my eyes, "You never stopped until tonight . . . And that ain't bad . . . you're the only kid that's come out here and asked my name in twenty years."

"Maybe the others were watching Lawrence Welk," I teased.

"No," he was serious. "The others are all in the bar tryin' to get in Connie Carson's pants."

"Can't be done," I laughed.

"At least not now," he nodded. "But, she'll change too. One day, she'll wake up and find out that her tight jeans won't make it over her thighs, or she'll see a wrinkle on her forehead, and then she'll walk into that bar and find somebody who remembers what she was like tonight, and she'll do it fast, because she'll be scared that she won't be able to do it two days later."

"Maybe I'd better stick around," I smiled.

"She ain't gonna pick *you*," he stood up and tossed a pebble in the direction of the fire hydrant, "because you'll be gone."

"Oh yeah," I remembered when his big arm fell across my shoulder. "You're giving me until sundown to get out of town."

"Don't leave at sundown," he grinned. "That's the best time of day on Friendly Creek."

Don't go looking for Friendly Creek or Buzzard Butte on a globe or an atlas, 'cause they aren't there.

They are, in reality, nothing more than wide spots in the road, little towns where most of the census is taken in the sagebrush, and there are thousands of towns just like them scattered around the world. Some of them don't even rate a zip code, but that's alright. In a little town, it's pretty easy to find what you're looking for if you just ask around.

There's a lot of heritage and pride in towns like those, from dirt streets named honorably for founding fathers to the plaque in the park to honor the boys who defended the nation and never made it home again. Almost anybody you meet can tell you the history of the valley, and they'll be happy to take the time. Of course, some of them might throw in a tall tale, but don't discount the stories you hear. Usually the ones that seem least likely are the only ones that are true.

There is an inspiring sense of family that permeates these towns, and it comes from the openness and warmth of the people. Babies and old timers are something special, and they're often found together. In the little town of Fleming, Colorado, where 388 people get their mail, one of their children is deaf, and there is a sign at the edge of town to remind you. Keep your eyes open when you pass through Fleming, and take your foot off the gas.

You can feel the spirit in towns like Friendly Creek, a sense of humor, and a zest for conflict that dissolves into compassion when understanding is needed most. It is love in its purest sense, fire in the belly and a willingness to fight one another when both are strong, and yet, the depth to console each other in times of need. There may be gossip on the streets, but there's loyalty on the corners.

Every day, cars blast through these little towns, and people don't even look up from their road maps. About the only time places like Friendly Creek take on any importance are those times when travelers are short of gas, broke down or snowed in. Then, the little towns seem to take the blame for the problem.

"I was broke down once in Eagle, Colorado," someone told me. There was something wrong with my car, and I called every mechanic in the book. Took me two hours to find one, and he was in some other little podunk town. Took him two hours to fix the car. I hate Eagle, Colorado."

I was broke down in Eagle once myself.

I asked the lady at the motel where to get my truck fixed, and she called the garage over in Gypsum. I don't remember how long it took, because the deputy sheriff in Eagle is married to a cousin of Shorty McGregor's daughter. He'd been up to Friendly Creek for a family reunion and met almost everybody, so we sat in his car and shot the breeze until my truck was done. All I remember is that it cost me twenty bucks. And, it was the clutch, not the town that was the problem.

271

I kinda like Eagle, Colorado.

Big talk around the garage was the high school basketball team. There aren't any opera houses or professional sports in these tiny towns, but *everybody* follows the high school teams, and the school plays always sell out.

In Kemmerer, Wyoming, the high school boys haven't won a basketball game in sixty odd tries. What the heck? Somebody has to lose, but there's no reason the losers shouldn't hear a cheer when their shot goes through the hoop. Winning doesn't seem so important as long as the gym is full, and in Kemmerer, the gym is always full.

I guess above all, if I learned anything when I left Friendly Creek, it was the importance of those simple values that are still alive in little towns where a single blue bulb lights the only street.

If there are truly necessities to life, they are common sense and honesty. Like they say on Friendly Creek, if a man can keep track of those two things, the rest of his life will usually fall into place.

Also available from Laffing Cow Press

Send Fresh Horses
by Bob Budd
illustrations by Jerry Palen

ISBN 0-943255-00-7	hardback	**$12.95**
ISBN 0-943255-01-5	paperback	**$8.95**

STAMPEDE Books by Jerry Palen

Don't Write a Book About It, Flo!

ISBN 0-943255-30-9	paperback	**$4.95**

What's Cooking, Flo?

ISBN 0-943255-31-7	paperback	**$6.95**

Stampede, The First Really Big Book

ISBN 0-941803-00-7	paperback	**$5.00**

For a Complete Catalogue of all
Laffing Cow Press Books, call or write:

P.O. Box 7802
The Woodlands, TX 77387
713/363-3577

MasterCard and VISA accepted